NICA

SPECTACULAR AND UNSPOILED

In its fifth year of peace, Nicaragua is being rediscovered for
- The world-class Montelimar beach resort
- Colonial Granada, where time stood still
- Masaya, center of tradition and artisans
- Pacific sunsets
- Untouched rain forest
- The world's most spectacular volcano park
- Its old-time ways, its warm-hearted people
- The absence of mass tourism

FROM PAUL GLASSMAN, AUTHOR OF THE MOST ACCLAIMED BOOKS ON CENTRAL AMERICA

"Filled with useful information . . . thoroughly explores the territory and subject." *(Booklist)*

"Don't leave home without it." *(International Travel News)*

"If you have to choose one guidebook, Paul Glassman's contains a wealth of practical information with a sharp eye and a sense of humor." *(Travel and Leisure)*

THE AUTHOR

Paul Glassman, series editor for Travel Line, also wrote the highly acclaimed Passport Press line of guides to Central America.

ACKNOWLEDGMENTS

Sincere thanks to Andy Alpers of L. Martinez Associates and Mario Duarte Zamora of the Ministerio de Turismo of Nicaragua. Perhaps this book would have been written without their assistance; but it surely would not have been written yet. They hesitated not at all to answer every question patiently, and to provide what they could.

Thanks as well to many, many Nicaraguans who shared their knowledge of their land. They are building a better future for themselves; it's for us not to stand in their way.

Any omissions are the responsibility of the author, and not of these most gracious persons.

NICARAGUA GUIDE

SPECTACULAR AND UNSPOILED

BY PAUL GLASSMAN

TRAVEL LINE
CHAMPLAIN, NEW YORK

Copyright © 1996 by Paul Glassman

All rights reserved. The reproduction of any part of this book without the author's written permission is strictly prohibited. This book is sold under the condition that it will not be adapted in any way for publication or electronic transmission without the written permission of the copyright holder.

Derechos reservados. Está prohibida la reproducción parcial o total sin previa autorización del autor. Este libro se vende bajo la condición de que no será adaptado para publicación o para transmisión en cualquiera forma.

ISBN 0-930016-22-X
Library of Congress Catalog Number 95-68397

Published and distributed by:
Travel Line
Box 1346
Champlain, New York 12919
e-mail: 74471.1774@compuserve.com
Cover photos courtesy of L. Martinez Associates and Ministerio de Turismo of Nicaragua.

Readers' comments, suggestions and updates are greatly appreciated. Please write to Paul Glassman, in care of Travel Line Press, Box 1346, Champlain, NY 12919.

This is a work of description, carefully verified as of publication date, but it is in no way a substitute for normal caution and preparation on the part of the traveller. Prices, facilities, schedules and services are subject to change. No responsibility is accepted for conditions different from those described.

PRINTED IN CANADA

CONTENTS

1. NICARAGUA: THE LAND PASSED BY — 9

2. LAND AND CREATURES — 15
Bigger Than Its Borders — 15
Nicaragua by Region — 17
A Continent of Natural Treasures — 20

3. TYRANTS, TURBULENCE, TRAGEDY: NICARAGUAN HISTORY — 29
Long Before the Spaniards — 30
New Masters — 32
Colonial Geopolitics — 34
Filibusteros — 36
The Invention of Guerrilla Warfare — 39
The Sandinista Departure — 41
Right Face — 43

4. NICARAGUANS — 45
Nightmares in Nicaraguan Legends — 45
Knowing Nicaraguans — 46
Society of Classes — 47
Arts: Dance, Ceramics, Writers — 48
More Nicaraguans — 51

5. PLANNING YOUR TRIP — 55
First Things First — 55
Climate and Weather — 57
Managing Your Money — 61
Visas and Tourist Cards — 65
What to Take — 67
Information Sources — 69
The Nicaraguan Calendar — 72

6. ON YOUR WAY — 75
Getting There — 75
Getting Around — 80

7. WHAT CAN YOU DO IN NICARAGUA? — 89
Activities for Visitors — 89
   Cruising, Fishing, Shopping and More
More Practical Information — 96
   Costs, Food, Health, Phones

8. MANAGUA — 109
Managua Old and New — 109
On Your Way to Managua — 112
Finding Your Way — 115
Hotels — 119
Restaurants — 130
Bars and Clubs — 139
Gaming — 141
Morning in Managua: Seeing the City — 143
   Downtown, Museums, Cathedral — 142
   Huellas de Acahualinca — 146
   Heart of Commerce: The Markets and Shopping — 147
   The Outskirts: Lakes and Springs — 150
Our Patron Saint, and Other Parties — 152
Art Scene — 153
Managua Minutiae — 154
   Banks, Transport, Embassies, Entertainment, Etc.
Recollections of the Third World Vanguard — 157
Leaving Managua — 165
   Air Service, Car Rental, Etc.
Trips from Managua — 167

9. HEARTLAND OF NICARAGUA — 171
Masaya Volcano National Park — 173
Masaya — 179
Granada — 182
Along Lake Nicaragua Shores — 191

Asese and the Lake Islands	193
The White Towns	196
Jinotepe	196
Hertylandia	198
Diriamba	199
San Marcos	200
Masatepe	201
Nandasmo, Niquinohomo, Catarina	202
San Juan de Oriente	203
Down to the Sea: Pacific Beaches	204
Pochomil	206
Montelimar: Nicaragua First-Class	207
La Boquita, Chacocente	211

10. LEON AND THE NORTHWEST — 213

Nagarote	214
Puerto Momotombo and Old León	214
Momotombo Volcano	218
La Paz Centro	219
León	220
Poneloya and the Coast	227
Chinandega	229
Gulf of Fonseca	229
El Realejo and Corinto	230

11. THE SOUTHEAST — 231

Rivas	232
San Jorge	234
Ometepe	235
San Juan del Sur	237
Peñas Blancas and Costa Rica	240

12. HIGHLAND NICARAGUA — 241

Hacienda San Jacinto, Moyuá	242
Matagalpa	243
Jinotega	247
San Isidro, Estelí	248

13. THE ROAD TOWARD THE CARIBBEAN 253
Boaco, Juigalpa and Chontales 254
El Rama 255
San Carlos 256
Solentiname Islands 257

14. THE OTHER NICARAGUA: CARIBBEAN LOWLANDS 259
The San Juan River 261
El Castillo 263
San Juan del Norte 266
Bluefields 266
The Corn Islands 270
Puerto Cabezas 272

15. SPEAKING NICA: SPANISH IN NICARAGUA 275

INDEX 282

MAPS
Nicaragua 16
Where is Nicaragua? 28
Managua 116
Heartland of Nicaragua 172
Masaya Volcano National Park 176
Granada 184
León 222

1
NICARAGUA: THE LAND PASSED BY

What if mass, modern tourism forgot about a country? What would it be like?

It would greet a visitor as someone out of the ordinary. Local people would express curiosity, answer questions patiently and lead newcomers to where they are going by the hand, if necessary. A visitor wouldn't be taken for granted.

The country might not have as many hotels as some others, but those that existed would be mostly small, intimate hostelries, or off-beat regional resorts that have developed without the uniformization of the international vacation trade. They'd be long on character and charm, rather than "amenities." That older fellow sitting in the wicker chair in the lobby, under the potted palm, reading the newspaper, with his granddaughter in his lap, might well be the owner.

There would be few dining establishments prepared to handle hordes with pre-tested menus of "international" cuisine. Meals would be cooked to order in small and interesting restaurants, where one sat down with the locals.

Packaged tours to such a country might be a bit hard to find. They might not even exist. But, once in the country, you'd find small travel shops eager to customize a plan to suit the interests of exactly one person.

A traveller might find himself getting around by bus or in a rented car; he might hie himself by steamer or hydrofoil to the far side of a great inland lake; or navigate on a temperamental boat of African Queen heritage, down a lazy tropical river, its bank lined by royal sentinel trees trailing vines into the water, his passage marked by the bark of howler monkeys, or the silent flight of troops of scarlet macaws through the canopy.

Some whims of the traveller might go unfulfilled. But practically anything the traveller might do would be fulfilling.

Such a place would be a lot like Nicaragua.

How many countries have been almost totally bypassed for the last ten, fifteen, twenty years by the day-to-day changes that have affected so much of the world, by techno-growth and the worldwide triumph of the market and the drive for efficiency? What would one such country be like?

Faxes and computer networks would be just be starting to make an appearance. People might exchange news and the time of day by knocking on each other's doors and stopping to chat as they met in the street. They might sit in cafés and read the paper, or perch on a chair on the sidewalk in front of the house, as an honorable and valid way to pass the time of day once the corn has been gathered and all the really necessary things have been done.

People would get around and tend to their tasks with such means as were available. Some of the cars on the streets would also be ancient Chevrolets and Ladas, nurtured into old age in exile, far from their native soil. But in city and in countryside, the most common modes of transporting people and goods would be horses and oxcarts; and outside of the capital, one might saunter down the middle of a street or run bases in a pickup baseball game with no more chance of interfering with traffic than in a park. Life would unroll at no more hurried a pace than that of personal locomotion.

As it does in Nicaragua.

What if time stood still in a Latin American country with a rich heritage? What would it be like?

The Land Passed By

Cobbled streets would echo still to the rolling of stagecoach wheels and the clop-clop of horseshoes, backdropped by tile-roofed, thick-walled houses concealing mysteries behind their walls; as in Granada.

Churches many centuries old, their intricate Churrigueresque façades intact despite earthquakes and bygone civil strife, would hold treasures of silver and carved wood and fine paintings; as in León.

The nation's greatest poet would be honored not only in books and universities, but with statues and museums, and a tomb in the greatest Cathedral of the land, and a city named in his honor; as is Rubén Darío.

Pageants and dance-ceremonies speaking of the mysteries of ancient gods and of the One of today, of warriors arriving from across the ocean, and of memories of a world destroyed, would be performed not for a paying audience, but as the deepest form of communal expression; as they are in small towns all over the heartland of Nicaragua.

Ancient crafts, from pottery to jewelry-making to sisal work, would thrive, because pride and tradition rule.

What if the tropical jungle remained largely untouched?

The giants of the forest would survive to replenish the air; and among them would flourish thousands of plant species dependent one upon another, drawing nourishment at every level from ground to canopy. And among them would live thousands of families of insects and birds and creatures from rainbow-bright frogs to panthers, in deadly competition, but ultimately in harmony.

The mysterious secret herbs of the rain forest could be harvested to create medicines; and revealed to the visitor. As in Nicaragua.

What if a people awoke to peace?

It would appreciate every moment, every daily activity, every acquaintance made, every friendship sealed, without the threat of sudden disruption, sudden ruination, of a call to arms against those from outside, and against brother and sister.

And if a visitor happened into Nicaragua today, what would she find?

The Great Lakes of Central America, Xolotlán and Cocibolca (lakes Managua and Nicaragua), and lesser lakes from puddles to remnants of cataclysms, filled with fish, and even sharks, watched over by sentinel volcanoes and with volcanoes erupting in their midsts, dashed with islands home to fishermen and colonies of painters.

Colonial Granada and Colonial León, once-rival cities that stopped in their tracks a century ago.

Pacific beaches hundreds of yards wide stretching unbroken and largely unpeopled up the coast; and more beaches wrapped in secret coves, stretching down the coast; all with sun for up to ten months a year, and only a resort or two to test the possibilities.

A fortress of stone erected to keep pirates at bay, where the young Horatio Nelson surrendered ignominiously to the Spaniards.

The White Towns, where the Central America of tradition lives on, in tile-roofed, whitewashed, humble dwellings; in subsistence plots of corn and beans, and the enchanted dwarf forest of shiny-leafed coffee; in leatherwork and fine woodwork and embroidery and jewelry-making and fiber crafts.

Managua, a city rebuilding from strife and disaster; and oddly, the most modern of capitals, organized in functional clusters, with broad vistas to volcanoes, pristine waters nearby, a distinct way of life, access to every point of interest, and what all cities covet, clean air.

Cattle and cowboys, on grasslands stretching to the horizon, broken by giant guanacaste trees, and haciendas of adobe with peeling plaster.

Cool highlands of pine and oak ridges, broken by rivers rushing over granite boulders; stands of enchanted cloud forest bedecked with ferns and bromeliads.

Hot springs bubbling from the living earth below.

A second country, apart, where the lingua franca is English, and the beat is reggae.

The most remote of the isles of the Caribbean.

National parks that cover a sixth of the country's land, from mangroves to turtle-nesting beaches to dripping rain forest to mountain peaks to the most easily visited active volcanic cones anywhere.

The adventure of going where so many others have not yet gone.

WHY YOU NEED NICARAGUA

Did you want to get away to a beach resort with all the amenities, and an inclusive price for room and gourmet-class meals and sports?

Or did you require a remote village, where the sand is shared with fishermen repairing their nets, and the catch of the day is offered from a stand of rough boards?

Are you looking for an ecotourism experience without the cachet of high tour prices? Birding under the major flyway from North America to the tropics? Plant hunting in the rain forest? Watching the nesting of sea turtles from a non-threatening blind? And all of it within easy reach of the international airport? Or taking rooms in a jungle refuge, along a remote river where intrigues or world import have been played out in every century, but only the howler monkeys bicker today?

Is it shopping you're after, for crafts available nowhere else? Or a lesson in making pots as they were made before the time of Columbus?

Maybe it's cutting into a steak in a country restaurant overlooking the waves on Lake Nicaragua, while watching a puff of cloud wrap around the peak of the volcano Mombacho. Or a cruise on the lake, with stops at an island tropical buffet, and a siesta in a hammock slung between palms. Or a trip across a continent in a single day—most of it by jungle riverboat.

Or maybe it's the last outpost of un-touristy prices and inexpensive booze.

Or fishing for tarpon in one ocean, and billfish in the other, while staying in the same hotel.

Or is it that you are moved by a people you can take to your heart?

Maybe you'll ponder all the possibilities while you take a week at a beach where the sun shines 300 days a year, and leaf through the pages of this book.

WHY NICARAGUA NEEDS YOU

Sometimes we worry about the negative effects of tourism, the heavy-handed impact of too many visitors, the clump of too many boots on the delicate floor of the rain forest, the out-of-place demands that we make in the home of others.

But sometimes we can do something positive, without particularly trying.

In Nicaragua, simply by visiting for your own pleasure, adventure, enrichment, and personal enlightenment, you can also do a good turn.

Nicaragua is in the process of moving beyond its bouts with dictatorship, natural disaster, and civil strife. Resources are needed to repair roads, update communications, build housing, and feed the kids.

As a visitor, you are part of the solution. You create jobs for hotel workers and guides, you create income for the owners of small hotels and restaurants. You help to keep the wheels of commerce turning. And you do it without polluting.

You come to appreciate the treasures of Nicaragua: colonial churches, heritage cities, the works of artisans and craftsmen. Your visit is part of the impulse to keep those monuments preserved; your purchase keeps a craftsman at work.

You come to learn about the bewildering treasures of the tropical forests, to adventure down a remote river bordered by sentinel giant trees; and you impart value to the forest just as it is, rather than cut down for lumber, and to create pasture.

You keep the doors open—and just remember, not much good happens when we turn our backs on a country.

And when you go home, you'll probably spread the word that Nicaragua is a proud, self-confident country, at peace with itself, and with all who come.

But this is not an appeal to charity. It's an appeal to your self interest.

2
LAND AND CREATURES

BIGGER THAN ITS BORDERS

Nicaragua is just a shade smaller than Michigan or Georgia, and slightly larger than Greece.

Yet Nicaragua is transcontinental, Nicaragua is densely inhabited, and at the same time, Nicaragua is virtually untouched by the presence of humans. Nicaragua is flat and volcanic, steamy and cooled by refreshing breezes, low-lying and mountainous.

A Being can pack a fair amount into a small place.

WHERE?

Nicaragua lies smack in the middle of Central America, bordered by the Pacific and the Caribbean, by Honduras to the north and Costa Rica to the south. In a region of mini-states, Nicaragua qualifies as a giant, extending over 130,000 square kilometers (51,000 square miles).

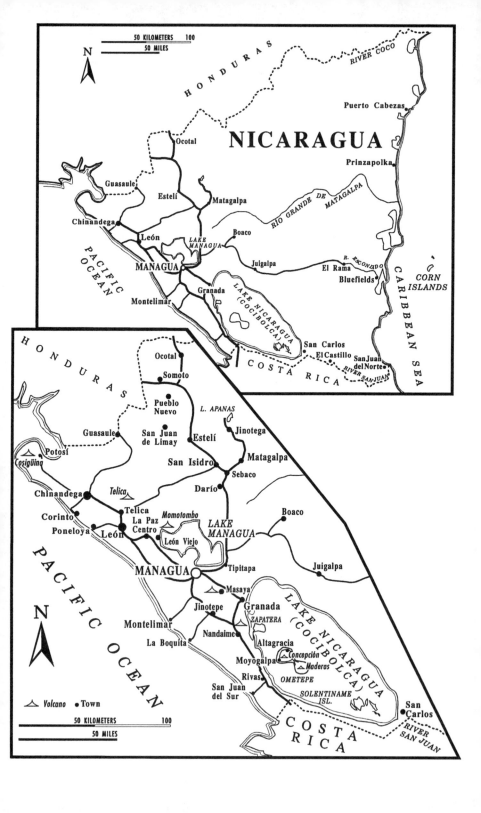

Land and Creatures

WHO'S THERE?

About four million people live in Nicaragua. That makes it the least with the most—the smallest population of any country in Central America except Belize, with the largest territory. We'll get back to the people in a few pages.

NICARAGUA BY REGION

FOR SHORT

Nicaragua's face is varied, ranging from cool to near desert to a couple of great lakes (10,000 square kilometers of Nicaragua are water) and many lesser ones to jungles still unpenetrated; not to mention extraordinarily wide beaches, volcanoes both smoking and sleeping, grasslands, cool plateaus, and cloud forest.

But as a matter of shorthand, and partly for historical reasons, we usually speak of three zones: the Pacific coastal plain; the central highlands; and the Caribbean lowlands.

PACIFIC PLAIN

The rich, rolling Pacific Plain (Llanuras del Pacífico) extends in a strip from the Gulf of Fonseca (where Nicaragua meets Honduras and El Salvador) to Costa Rica in the southeast. Dividing the plain into two thin strips just 30 kilometers inland is the Cordillera de los Marabios, the chain of 25 volcanic cones that is the most noted and imposing and inevitable feature of the landscape for every visitor. Also here are shallow Lake Managua, which Nicaraguans know as Xolotlán; and the great lake of Central America, placid Lake Nicaragua, or Cocibolca, across which the volcano chain marches as fuming and dormant islands.

Much of the plain is, and has been since time immemorial, tropical savannah, natural grassland that flourishes in the rainy season, and dries into standing fodder once the rains stop. Over the centuries, additional flat lands, once home to seasonally dry tropical forest, have been converted into an artificial sort of savannah, planted with grasses to nourish grazing animals; though occasional giant silk-cotton and guanacaste trees remain to provide shade.

SNAPSHOT

Coordinates	11 to 15 degrees north latitude, 83 to 88 degrees west latitude (or from 79 degrees 30 minutes, starting from the Corn Islands in the Caribbean).
Area	130,000 square kilometers (50,000 square miles)
Lakes	10,000 square kilometers
Altitude	Nicaragua is the lowest-lying of Central American countries, at an average height of 71 meters (233 feet).
Population	4,400,000; growth rate, 3.8%; density, 36 per square mile; 63.3 % urban.
Urban population	55 percent
Youth	50 percent of Nicaraguans are younger than 15.
Density	31 per square kilometer / 79 per square mile
Altitude	71 meters (on average)
Temperature	27.5 degrees Centigrade (81.5° F) average
Religion	Largely Roman Catholic, not state supported
National flower	Sacuanjoche (plumeria rubra, a yellow frangipani)
National tree	Madrone (Calycophyllum, or strawberry tree)
National bird	Guardabarranco (Eumotota superciliosa)

But the "plains," as Nicaraguans think of them, include vast swaths that are no plains at all. Between Managua and the Pacific is the rolling heartland of Nicaragua, hilly country reaching several hundred meters above sea level, once a leafy tropical forest, and now largely planted in a dwarf forest of shiny-leafed coffee trees.

In many respects, the coastal plains *are* Nicaragua. Most of the

Land and Creatures

population lives here. In fact, more than a quarter of Nicaraguans live right in or near the capital, Managua, and most Nicaraguans are within an hour's drive of the capital, between the cities of León and Granada. The hilly country of the heartland, its volcanoes and rains and heat and clay, has shaped those who people its white-walled villages; and out of this land has sprung the national character of Nicaraguans.

HIGHLANDS AND MOUNTAINS

Directly north of Xolotlán and Cocibolca (lakes Managua and Nicaragua) is the mountainous zone. "Mountains," in the Nicaraguan context, means not great, bare, craggy peaks, but furry and firry rolling humps and spines, in a triangle-shaped area roughly inset from the sea borders of this triangular-shaped country. In between the high spots are upland valleys, cool plains, and the major rivers that drain toward Nicaragua's great lakes or the Caribbean.

The extreme heights here are strictly junior—as great as 2107 meters (6912 feet) at Mogotón Peak in the piney Dipilto y Jalapa range on the border of Honduras, where torrents of water flow over granite boulders and occasionally eject gold nuggets.

Just to the south, shouldering the Estelí river, are the coffee altitudes, highlands of no more than 3000 feet, broken by streams that tumble over falls toward the warmer country. Coffee, indeed, is what is grown under shading banana and fig and avocado trees in much of the zone, within reach of the Pan American Highway that leads onward into Honduras.

Where the land is not tamed by farmers—and it is still sparsely settled along the higher ridges running to the northeast from Jinotega and Matagalpa—broadleaf cloud forest bedecked with moss and ferns and orchids flourishes in the moist air, along with stands of pines, inhabited by flocks of bellbirds, toucans, and linnets, and the occasional resplendent quetzal.

CARIBBEAN LOWLANDS

The eastern fringe of Nicaragua is the Land Apart, a long table that tilts slightly seaward from the eastern foothills of the central highlands and the rolling, steaming pastured lands of Chontales beyond Lake Nicaragua; separated by history, topography, and even ethnicity from the rest of the country.

Nicaragua Guide

In the north of this Caribbean nation are pine forests; to the south is dense rain forest, cut by deep rivers that are the only highways. Of all the countries of Central America, Nicaragua is the one that has kept most of its native forest, fully 31 percent of its total area; and most of that tree cover is in the Caribbean lowlands.

Think of heat and humidity and regular downpours, and you'll feel the Caribbean region of Nicaragua. Think of anteaters, tapirs, white-tailed deer and howler monkeys, and toucans and parrots and macaws and wild turkeys, and you can almost hear and see the active and largely undisturbed wildlife of the lowland rain forest.

Think of pirates and slaves, and you'll get a picture of the ethnic make-up. This is Nicaragua's Miskito Coast, inhabited not by descendants of Spaniards and indigenous American related to the Aztec and Maya, but by Afro-Caribbean peoples, for whom English is the lingua franca, and to whom Managua is almost a foreign capital.

In recent years the lowlands have been recognized as what it has long been in fact, the Región Autónoma del Atlántico Norte and Región Autónoma del Atlántico Sur (Atlantic-North and Atlantic-South Autonomous Zones).

Caribbean Nicaragua doesn't come to an end at the sea and Bluefields, the major town (and little more than an airstrip and scattered houses). Out to sea, the nation also includes the Corn Islands (Islas del Maíz in Spanish but more usually, Corn Island), an outpost of coral reef and beaches and even 200-meter peaks, and ebullient Afro-Caribbean culture that ended up as part of Central America when the borders were settled after independence.

A CONTINENT OF NATURAL TREASURES

Start cataloging the natural treasures of Nicaragua, and there's no telling when you'll stop. There are hundreds of species of orchids, more bird species—over 700—than in all of Europe, and butterflies galore. The plant count was last over 8000 (a thousand or so of which are orchids), with more types found just in the valley of the River Maíz than in all of Canada. Add a couple of hundred each of mammals and fresh-water fish, and 300 reptiles and amphibians. And anybody who starts counting insects manages to come across a few that haven't been described before.

These are just rough figures, of course. Nicaragua hasn't seen the extensive cataloging that has gone on in some other tropical countries.

PLANT VARIETY

Where *do* they all come from? Abundant rainfall and the lack of a killing cold season contribute to this intense evolution and competition, along with, in some cases, poor soils, which encourage plants to specialize according to the specific conditions in each patch of earth. According to the microclimate, they'll live in symbiosis, or attack each other for the nourishment not found in the ground, send out roots into decaying trees, funnel rain water with their leaves, or catch the moisture in the air.

Then, too, Nicaragua's position on the land bridge between the continents jacks up the animal count. The raccoon is found in Nicaragua, along with its tropical cousin, the coatimundi. Squirrels familiar and squirrels miniature and exotic share the forests. Air space is taken by elusive, long-tailed quetzals; dozens of parrot kin; and familiar orioles and jays down for the winter or taking a break on their way to points farther south.

WHAT'S TYPICAL, AND WHAT'S UNUSUAL?

Broadly speaking, here's what you'll find in, on, and over the earth in the various habitats of Nicaragua:

Tropical savannahs are the rolling, grassy expanses that cover the part of Nicaragua most seen by visitors, between the chain of volcanoes and the Pacific. In the dry season, they have the aspect of the great plains of the American wild west, and some of the animal species are similar to the denizens of that area: foxes, coyotes, rabbits, vultures, hawks and owls. Permanent waterholes attract quail, osprey, turtledoves, swallows and pigeons. All are of a size that can hide out in the limited cover of the grasses, or burrow into the ground.

Highland and cloud forest cover the hilly parts of Nicaragua, largely up toward the north, on the way to the long border with Honduras, and in island-patches on the uncultivated peaks of volcanoes along the Pacific edge.

NICARAGUA BY WATER CONTENT

LAKES

The Great Lakes of Central America are all in Nicaragua. Lake Cocibolca (Nicaragua, 8264 square kilometers) and Lake Xolotlán (Managua, 1000 square kilometers) are depressions formed as the earth's tectonic plates slipped, clashed and slid below. But there are many, many other spots and expanses of water in a country that is so notably dry and sunny for much of the year. Some are found in the Pacific area, easily accessible to Nicaragua's major towns, which were founded in locations to take advantage of a steady supply of water and fish; some consist of the craters of volcanoes, once smoking and rumbling, now placid with runoff from the surrounding farmed slopes.

Lakes Apoyeque, Xiloá, Asososca and Tiscapa are volcanic lakes near or right inside the city limits of Managua, while Masaya and Apoyo, in the heartland of Nicaragua southeast of the capital, lie in volcanic basins. Lakes of imprisoned water lie in the craters of the volcano Cosigüina, jutting into the Gulf of Fonseca, and Maderas, on Ometepe island.s

RIVERS

Nicaragua has three watersheds: the Pacific, the Caribbean, and the lake watershed, which gathers the waters of westward-flowing rivers and diverts them to lakes Managua and Nicaragua, and eventually, the Caribbean.

Cloud forest occurs on misted lands over 1000 meters in altitude. Above lands farmed for coffee or tobacco, are stands of mixed oak, walnut, Spanish cedar and, less frequently, mahogany, bedecked with ferns and Spanish moss and orchids, and tangled with vines, often in a semipermanent mist that nourishes plants that never touch the ground. Emerald toucanets, linnets, hummingbirds and bellbirds and chachalacas thrive on the wild fruits, along with the elusive resplendent quetzal.

Land and Creatures

The Pacific rivers are short, rocky, and either dry or trickling in the Nicaraguan summer. Even in rainy periods, the volcanic soil easily absorbs precipitation, and the western rivers rarely flood. Longer rivers flow from the central highlands toward the south and west. In prehistoric times, these descended to the Pacific, but as the bottoms of lakes Managua and Nicaragua-to-be sank below the level of the surrounding plains, the waters of the rivers Viejo, Mayales, Viejo, San Antonio and others were captured, and diverted toward the San Juan flowing out to the southeast, and emptying into the Caribbean. The San Juan was the route of pirates to the center of Central America in colonial times, and part of a transit route across the continent in the last century.

Along with the San Juan, several great rivers drain the Caribbean lowlands, and at the same time, serve as highways for the movement of people and goods. The River Coco (or Segovia, or Wangki), longest in Central America, runs 780 kilometers, mostly along the border with Honduras, from gold-bearing highlands down through dense jungle, to banks along which the vegetation has been peeled back by Miskito Indian inhabitants. The Grande de Matagalpa, second longest in Nicaragua with a course of 450 kilometers, runs from the central highlands. The shorter Wawa, Kakalaya, and Kuwrinwus culminate in lagoons separated by sandy bars from the sea beyond. The Escondido, in one of the rainiest parts of the country, also has the most assured flow, and so serves as a reliable riverine highway between Bluefields on the coast and the end of the highway at El Rama.

Pine forest covers great expanses of northern Nicaragua; and unlike other tropical forests, with their great variety, pine forests are often pine and pine alone. In some parts of the lowlands, where the soil is sandy, along the Coco and Wawa rivers, Caribbean pines flourish on the flatlands, and are harvested for timber.

Nicaragua marks the limit of pines on this side of the equator; a specifically Nicaraguan variety, Segovian pine, grows on high mountain slopes,

NICARAGUA BY ALTITUDE

LOWLANDS

The lowlands on the Pacific and Caribbean sides of Nicaragua include most of the country. Fully 70 percent of Nicaragua lies below 850 meters in elevation.

TEMPERATE ZONE

The northern highlands and the volcanic slopes parallel to the Pacific include Nicaragua's temperate areas—25 percent of the country's surface—between 850 and 1500 meters in altitude.

"COLD COUNTRY"

Anything above 1500 meters is considered cold country in Nicaragua. This covers just 5 percent of Nicaragua's land area. Frost can occur, but rarely does.

---

sometimes alone, sometimes mixed with oak. On the highest slopes, above 1500 meters, the *pinabete*, or tropical fir, can be found.

Lowland rain forest covers much of the eastern half of Nicaragua—it once took up over half the country's territory, but with deforestation, it now makes up as little as a third of Nicaragua's area. In shallow, nutrient-poor, rain-leached soil, a treasure house of botanica flourishes, Its species passing on to each other the basic elements of life in cycles of predation, decay, and symbiosis, at every level from ground to virtually unbroken canopy. Dozens of species of tree flourish on any randomly chosen acre, bedecked with orchids, ferns, and vines. In a similar spot in the temperate zones, in rich soil, a couple of greedy species in climax forest would eventually have crowded out all others; but in the rain forest, it's dog-eat-dog at all times, and the lowliest plant can come out the winner, pressing its roots into the decaying trunk of a once-mighty forest giant.

Land and Creatures

Among the many, many tree species in the eastern lowlands are ceiba (silk cotton), guanacaste (earpod, or tubroose), mahogany, Spanish cedar, and almond. Orchids in the rain forest along the San Juan River include the Góngora uniclor, unique to Nicaragua and neighboring Costa Rica.

Typical lowland forest animals include peccaries, tapirs, white-tailed deer, jaguars, and snakes (including the poisonous bushmaster and fer-delance, among others) along with iguanas and brightly colored lizards and frogs. Strictly by number, forest mammals that live in the trees predominate: monkeys (especially howlers but also white-faced and spider), coatis, raccoons, and sloths. Parrots and their relatives, macaws and toucans (emerald toucanet and collared aricari among them), coexist with hawks and crested and harpy eagles and hummingbirds and motmots and guardabarrancos. Along the San Juan River, cormorants, anhingas, herons, muscovy ducks and northern jacanas can all be sighted without difficulty, along with the strange "lizard turtle." The numerous insect species that mimic vegetation to escape their predators are still being classified.

Seasonally dry tropical forest—trees that drop their leaves to conserve water and energy in the annual drought—still survives in clusters along the Pacific slopes of Nicaragua, though it has largely been wiped out in more densely populated lands to the north. Most notable are the frangipani tree, which blooms with the yellow national flower, the sacuanjoche (sa-kwan-HO-cheh); and the madrone, the national tree. Also characteristic are brasilwood, divi-divi, the gourd, or calabash tree, and bull-horn acacia; pochote, olive, laurel, guaicam, rosewood and blackwood, used in fine woodcrafts, and the oak and canafistula, or drumstick tree.

Typical fauna in the dry forest includes raccoons and their tropical cousins, coatimundis, peccaries, monkeys, weasels, and deer and skunks and squirrels. Typical birds are woodpeckers, jays, mockingbirds, and the guardabarranco, the national bird. Migrating birds include white-tailed dove. Reptiles include snakes, and lizards.

Marine environments in Nicaragua include mangroves, the tentacle-trunked trees fingering their roots into salt-washed waters in the lee of islets and in river estuaries. Mangroves serve as nurseries for crab and deep-sea fish. Turtles nest regularly on beaches on both coasts: the Ridley and leatherback on the Pacific, and the endangered hawksbill and green on the Caribbean. Turtle eggs are said to have aphrodisiac powers, and are much in demand, as are turtle meat and shell, despite conservation measures.

VOLCANOES

Volcanoes *are* Nicaragua. Volcanoes are in the national coat of arms, on the flag, and more notably, at least 90 percent of Nicaraguans look up and see a volcano or two or three at some time during the day.

Twenty-five—count 'em, twenty-five—volcanoes march in a line that meanders only slightly, down the Pacific side of Nicaragua, crossing fertile plains and seasonal deserts, erupting from great basins and popping out of lakes as unexpected islands.

Or maybe there are more than 25. A volcano is clearly a volcano. Unless it's a single mountain rising into a double cone branching into multiple craters, with lesser former cones collapsed upon themselves far in the valley below. Not to mention the volcanoes that are doubtless to be, or those too minor to figure in the count of grown-up cones.

Whatever the cataclysms that gave them birth, most of Nicaragua's volcanoes are sleeping giants (dormant), and a few are definitively ghosts (extinct). But wherever you go in the heartland of Nicaragua, you will be within sight of some evidence of the periodically irascible innards of the earth, whether steaming, fuming, or belching fire and ash and lava and boulders, or the very fertility and porosity of the ash that periodically spreads over the land

The immediate effect of an eruption, of course, is to burn crops, or bury them in ash and lava and boulders. But in the long run, weathered volcanic soil is rich in organic matter and minerals, and wonderfully porous in a way that retains and metes out water to crops, and allows excess moisture to percolate down to the water table.

And the volcanoes have played a role as civilization builders. Before the Spaniards arrived with iron, obsidian, or volcanic glass, was used to make tools, and volcanic pigments were used to color pottery.

Here's the lineup of the major volcanic mountains of Nicaragua.

Cosigüina   807 meters
Jutting out into the Gulf of Fonseca, blew its top in 1835 in the greatest eruption in the hemisphere in recorded history, heard as far away as Quito. A placid lake now occupies the crater.

El Chonco   1100 meters

San Cristóbal   1750 meters
Reigning Nicaraguan volcano in terms of height, last erupted in the seventeenth century, in time to guide a pirate raid on the port of El Realejo, followed by a surprise attack on León. Has been fuming once again since 1971.

Casita   1500 meters

Telica   1038 meters
Directly north of the city of León, multi-cratered Telica has several craters, the deepest of which regularly erupts, if only modestly.

Cerro Negro   450 meters
Born in a field northwest of Old León only in the last century, and semi-active ever since, intermittently shooting out dust and ash.

Las Pilas   1000 meters

El Hoyo   1075 meters
Multi-humped Cerro del Hoyo last blew in 1954, and still fumes from a fissure in its crater.

Momotombo   1360 meters
Perched at the western end of Lake Managua and eternally fuming, so reliably that electricity is generated using steam heated in the volcano's entrails.

Masaya   635 meters
Nicaragua's showcase volcano is a short drive from Managua, its fuming cones and craters accessible by paved highway.

Mombacho   1363 meters
The extinct lord of the city of Granada, alongside Lake Nicaragua, crowned with cloud forest.

Concepción   1610 meters

Maderas   1326 meters
The twin volcanoes of Concepción and Maderas *are* Ometepe island near the south rim of Lake Nicaragua. Concepción is occasionally active, Maderas is extinct.

Manatee, or sea cows, are found in Caribbean lagoons, munching on leaves. Offshore, around the Corn Islands and the Miskito and Pearl Cays, are reefs of coral frequented by schools of Technicolor fish. Off San Juan del Sur, swordfish, sailfish and marlin are caught by sportsmen.

Lakes form a larger part of Nicaragua's surface than of any other country in the region. Lake Nicaragua is noted for the bull shark, and also holds swordfish and shad.

Lowland rivers hold crocodiles, caimans, and otters. In the San Juan River, fish species include sardines; guapote, a bass-like species; snook; the famous bull shark that, uniquely, commutes between the Caribbean and Lake Nicaragua; and huge tarpon, the holy grail of many sport fishermen.

3
TYRANTS, TURBULENCE, TRAGEDY: NICARAGUAN HISTORY

Some nations have a history out of all proportion to their size, and that is the case of Nicaragua.

Here is a country with only four million people today, not even as extensive as Florida. Yet Nicaragua was a key theater of battle between the British Navy and Imperial Spain, in a struggle that decided the fate of large parts of the hemisphere.

Nicaragua was a major link between the Atlantic and Pacific oceans at the time of the California Gold Rush, important enough to attract American adventurer-conquerors; and stands once again to become a key bridge in world trade.

Modern guerrilla warfare was invented in Nicaragua by a dissident general and politician, Augusto César Sandino.

Nicaragua was ruled by one of the longest-lived family dynasties in Latin America; and it was one of the last battle grounds of the late cold war. The effects of that struggle are still being felt today.

LAND OF NICARAO

According to one version, it was Nicarao, an indigenous ruler at the time of the Spanish conquest, who lent his name to the Spanish province that was to include his domains.

"Nicarao" is a Nahuatl name, Nahuatl being the language of the Aztecs, which was also spoken along the shores of the great Central American lakes. The language evidences ancient ties with the lands to the north, in the same way that English in the Caribbean betrays British influence. Those who lived around the lakes were known as the Nicaraguas, or Niquiranos., or Nicarao

But some say that chief Nicarao took his name from his people, who in turn took their name—or were called by others—in accordance with their geographical situation: Nicaragua can also be a contraction of Nic-atl-nahuac, "next to the water," a derivation that is apropos in other Central American place names as well, and indicates that the Nicaragua were following the orders dictated by a prophecy: When Teotihuacán fell, the ancestors of the Nicarao left the land of Mexico and migrated southward; their priests foresaw an end to their wanderings only when they discovered a lake with a double-peaked mountain at its center. When they reached Cocibolca—today's Lake Nicaragua—with the volcanic cones of Ometepe rising from its waters, they knew that the prophecy had been fulfilled, and that they had reached their new home.

Not to mention that Nicaragua was also a land of civilization and the arts, a continental crossroads, when Europe was awakening from the dark ages.

LONG BEFORE THE SPANIARDS

The human species has a venerable history in Nicaragua. Masses of bones of megatheres, an extinct animal, have been found at El Bosque, in the department of Estelí. This suggests that hunters arrived in the highlands of Nicaragua something like 30,000 years ago, perhaps pushed on from more northerly latitudes by advancing glaciers. The ancestors of these hunters might have been the first migrants from Asia across the Bering Strait; or they might have been Polynesians who had crossed the Pacific on rafts.

The pedigrees will perhaps never be traced; and whether those first hunters stayed or moved on is somewhat of a mystery. But we do know that people were present in Nicaragua at least on and off since that time. Ancient arrowheads and basalt tools, predating any identifiable culture, are still discovered throughout Nicaragua. The Huellas de Acahualinca, fossilized footprints in modern-day Managua, indicate that hunters lived alongside the lake 10,000 years ago.

The successors to the first inhabitants eventually settled down, in part, from the hunting life. Root crops were cultivated. Civilizations developed on the isthmus based on the cultivation of corn, beans and squash by large, well-organized groups agriculture, or their successors. Pottery came to replace gourds in domestic use, and then, more delicately decorated, came into ceremonial and religious use.

Whatever became of any specific group, it is clear that Nicaragua was part of a Central American land bridge; that migrants, refugees, traders and conquerors moved from north to south and south to north, and especially through the sash of land between the Great Lakes of Central America and the Pacific. Several ways of life and language spread in their wake.

By the time the Americas became known to the Europeans, today's Nicaragua was a cosmopolitan mis-amalgam of peoples with roots in and links to central Mexico, the lands of the Maya, the mainland of South America, and the islands of the Caribbean. They spoke different languages, created pottery in different styles, and lived lives sometimes as unrelated as those of peoples thousands of miles apart.

Those on the Caribbean side lived in small groups. They burned and cleared the rain forest for agriculture, and moved on when they had exhausted the thin soil. The ancestors of the Sumos and Ramas probably arrived from South America or the Antilles, or were conquered by exotic tribes who imposed the practices of distant regions.

Farther west, the peoples of Nicaragua were more settled, on richer soil that supported repeated, bountiful crops of corn, and with it, all the structure of the settled communities of administrators, priests and warriors that the Spanish invaders eventually discovered.

Along the eastern shores of Lake Nicaragua, and in the highlands, lived a people called the Chontales, or Matagalpas, in places that now bear the names Somoto and Limay and Oluma.

The Chontales are variously thought to speak a language related to Chibcha, of South America; or to be a remnant offshoot of the ancient Maya and one of their successor nations, the Lenca. It is perfectly possible that they were related to both.

In the northwest, near today's city of León, lived the Maribios, or Subtiavas.

But the dominant groups were the Nicaraos, who lived between the lakes and the Pacific; and the related Chorotegas, who lived in the adjacent lands to the south.

The Chorotegas originally occupied virtually all of the plain between the great lakes and the Pacific. They were either descended from peoples of Mexico, or acculturated by them.

Loosely confederated and ruled by a council, they included tribes such as the Dirianes, in what is now the heartland of Nicaragua around Masaya; and the Nagrandanos, in the plains to the west.

The Nicaraos, ruled by a single chief, or *cacique*, spoke a Nahuatl language related to that of central Mexico, and had probably migrated from the north when the Olmec began to dominate their homeland in the eighth century. By this time, Mayan rule in northern Central America was in decline, and the arrival of the migrants hastened their demise.

With their tight organization, honed in years of wanderings, the Nicaraos soon dominated the Chorotegas.

Like the Maya, the Nicaraos used cocoa beans as a unit of value and means of exchange. And just as the Chinese enforced a monopoly on silk cultivation, the Nicaraos based their power partly on a monopoly of the cultivation of cacao. They developed a characteristic style of pottery, with brick-red and black designs, which is still made in Nicaragua today. Their statues carved in volcanic rock, found on Zapatera and Ometepe islands, show gods in the guise of animals, indicating a commonality of spirit with other beings.

NEW MASTERS

Christopher Columbus was grateful to see what was to become Nicaraguan territory. The year was 1502, the occasion was the fourth voyage of discovery and subjugation by the Admiral of the Ocean Sea. Caribbean storms looked about to blow apart the venture and the participants; but Columbus ordered his ships onward along the coast, and when they rounded

History

the cape at the easternmost point of the isthmus, the waters calmed, as if anointed from on high. The cape was named, appropriately, Gracias a Dios, "thanks to God"; the land that welcomed was to become Nicaragua.

Alas, no native account survives of any contact with the Admiral during this expedition, nor is one to be sought. The inhabitants of the rain-forest side of the continent were a scattered lot, living by hunting, and gathering fruits and nuts from the forest, and moving on when local resources had been run through.

Nor were later Spanish attempts to conquer the isthmus from the Caribbean side to meet with any success. If the weapons of the scattered local people were ineffectual against the muskets of the Spaniards, the invaders had no remedies for heat and yellow fever, diarrhea, endless rain, mud, and mosquitos.

On the far side of the continent, however, a different tale would unfold. Here, the land was of a more familiar and solid substance, and the well-settled indigenous nations made for easier pickings. Gil González Dávila (or "de Avila") became the first European to explore the Pacific side of Nicaragua. In 1522, he was received in peace by chief Nicarao, near the present-day city of Rivas. But attempts to move beyond the lakes were resisted by chief Diriangén, and the Spanish retreated to their base in Panama, leaving a thousand dead to battle casualties, hunger, and disease.

A new probe by the Spaniards was more determined. In 1524, Francisco Hernández de Córdoba arrived not in peace, but to conquer. Working on the model that had succeeded in Mexico and Guatemala, the Spaniards exploited existing enmities between settled peoples. First one group was conquered, while the neighboring nations, with a history of subjection and tribute at the hands of the leading group, looked on with satisfaction, and even aided the Spaniards in their task; until it was their turn, as well, to fall into enslavement.

The subjection of Nicaragua occurred brutally, and in short order. By 1524, two major settlements had been founded, Granada, on the shores of Lake Cocibolca, and León, at the western end of Xolotlán (Lake Managua). Indian populations were removed to new villages, built in peninsular style, with a plaza and neatly laid-out streets. Each settlement had its church and civil administration, both key elements in re-creating the ways of Spain in the New World. The population was put to work in whatever way the Spaniards saw fit: continuing with their agricultural labors, but for new masters; constructing and decorating churches and palaces in the Spanish towns; searching for gold in the mountains of Nueva Segovia on the borders of Honduras; as bearers in treks through dense forest and jungle to find the outlet of Lake Cocibolca. Between venereal disease, smallpox, and abuse, the Indians suffered a holocaust from which their numbers did not recover for hundreds of years.

When the Spanish rulers were not occupied fully with subjugating and enslaving the native population, they fought among themselves to enhance their personal fiefdoms, sometimes on the fringes even of the tenuous legality that provided a pretext for their rapine. The maximum perpetrator of the Conquest of Nicaragua, Francisco Hernández de Córdoba, was himself convicted of rebellion, and his head was chopped off in the main square of León.

The Spaniards, indomitable in their engagement with the native peoples, were powerless in their engagement with the greater forces of the earth. In 1610, the earth, never at peace in this zone, rumbled in one of its periodic outbursts of anger, shook the substantial stone and brick buildings of León erected for the Spaniards by their slaves, and left the capital of the province shattered.

But never mind. Buildings were expendable, and so were the Indians who built them. A new site was chosen, and León was re-erected, on its present site, grander than before.

The Nicaragua that emerged from the lands of Nicarao developed new social classes to replace the old system. At the top were a few hundred native-born Spaniards, followed by Spaniards born in the new world. Mixed-blood offspring had their place as artisans and merchants, while the pure descendants of those who had always lived in the land were at the bottom. As populations were shifted about, to work the fields or dig in the mines of the Spaniards, the old indigenous divisions began to weaken, and the culture of the natives gradually fused with, but never totally gave way to, that of the Spaniards.

COLONIAL GEOPOLITICS

The colony was ruled as part of the Captaincy-General of Guatemala, and might have lived in benign neglect by mother Spain. Nicaragua's mines were not as productive as those elsewhere in the New World, while its agricultural output—indigo and cochineal and cacao—was not crucial.

But one crucial geopolitical factor was evident both to the Spanish and to their enemies: the River San Juan, running from Lake Nicaragua to the Caribbean, provided a route for ships almost all the way across the continent. Whoever controlled the river could unify the Spanish realms, or cut them in two.

And so, throughout the colonial period, the security of Nicaragua was always in play.

The exposure of the Caribbean coast—claimed by Spain but never settled—to English pirates and naval fleets based in the Caribbean, made Spain's authority over the river a tenuous one. Pirates ascended the San Juan time and again, and even reached Lake Nicaragua, to sack and burn the city of Granada. Henry Morgan himself was repelled in 1672 at the Castillo de la Concepción fortress.

When piracy was suppressed with the cooperation of the English crown, the Royal Navy became the threat. In the world war that accompanied the American revolution, an English force, under Captain Horatio Nelson, captured the Castillo, and held it for several months. Nelson lost an eye in the battle, and went on to greater glory at Trafalgar.

While control of the river was reclaimed, Spain never secured the Caribbean access. British strong points were set up all along the coast of Honduras and Nicaragua, and trading posts brought British goods to the Miskitos and Sumus and Ramas. England established a protectorate over the peoples living from Belize southward, and slaves and ex-slaves from the Caribbean islands came to populate villages and the Corn Islands offshore. Armed by the British, the coastal settlers kept the Spanish at Bay, even after the British had officially surrendered their claims at the end of the American Revolutionary War.

INDEPENDENCE . . . AND LITTLE CHANGE

Nicaraguan independence from Spain was an event that happened elsewhere. The separation of Central America was declared in Guatemala on September 15, 1821, by prominent *criollos*, or creoles, Spaniards born in the colonies who lacked the privileges of those born in Spain. Support came from merchants, who, legally at least, could only trade with the mother country. Opposition came from the privileged Church, while most of the inhabitants had no say in the matter. No notable changes came about, save the abolition of slavery.

The independent isthmus was soon absorbed into the newly minted Mexican empire of Agustín Iturbide; but in 1823, the United Provinces of

Central America asserted their independence once again. They also asserted the factionalism that has been the political heritage of the region. Liberals, the proponents of independence, battled Conservatives, the heirs of Spanish rule. The political split tore the union apart, and in 1838, Nicaragua became totally independent of its neighbors.

Independence from the Central American federation meant, in effect, independence to continue the bickering on a playing field somewhat reduced in size, and Nicaragua, with two major settlements and neither in a dominant position, was notably suited to a continuing feud of families. León, reconstructed in a new western location after the 1609 earthquake, a center of learning with its university, became the stronghold of the Liberals, the party of economic openness. Granada, on Lake Nicaragua, was ruled by Conservatives, the coterie of ecclesiasts and landowners who succeeded to the aspirations of the Spanish ruling class. With neither town able to dominate the other, the administration of the nation finally settled, as a compromise, in the town of Managua, about halfway between the two, in 1852.

FILIBUSTEROS

It was the eternal feuding, combined with Nicaragua's strategic position athwart a water route nearly navigable all the way from Caribbean to Pacific, that provided the setting for the most curious, ignominious, comic, and ultimately disastrous episode in nineteenth-century Nicaragua.

Isolated in colonial times by the mercantilist policies of mother Spain, which permitted the colonies to trade only with the ports of the metropolis, Nicaragua was a babe at independence, open suddenly to the commerce of the world, but unknowing of its ways. English merchants, mostly, moved in to provide manufactured wares.

Then gold brought Nicaragua on the world scene, gold discovered not in Central America, but in California. The rush from American east to American west took place overland, and by ship around stormy Cape Horn, and even, in part, across Nicaragua, where Commodore Cornelius Vanderbilt, of American ferry and railroad fame, had begun a service of steamboats up the San Juan River from the Caribbean port of Greytown, and over Lake Nicaragua and almost to the shores of the Pacific. In so doing, Vanderbilt brought Nicaragua and its feuds to the attention of the Americans who passed through on their way to the gold fields.

One who learned of the situation was William Walker, native of Tennessee, occasional California newspaper editor, doctor of medicine, and, most notably, filibusterer, a breed of privateer and soldier of fortune of the terrestial rather than maritime persuasion, who found it irresistible to intervene in the affairs of other nations for the good of higher causes, such as slavery, and, only incidentally, on behalf of himself. On one such expedition, Walker established a republic in Baja California; and his defeat and withdrawal served only as enticement to repair his fame when he heard of the warring white tribes of Nicaragua whom he might play off one against the other, just as the Spanish had done centuries before with the Indians.

Escaping from San Francisco on a rickety ship, Walker arrived in Nicaragua in June of 1855 at the head of a band of 56 men, invited, with the inducements made by a good salesman, by the Liberal faction. In short order, Walker conducted himself in the manner of a tragic hero, rising rapidly, but in the end succumbing to a fate foretold in his own character. Without any authority, he concluded a peace treaty with the Conservative enemy, established headquarters in Granada, appointed himself commander in chief, and promptly set about creating enemies. In the whirlwind of his reign, he had opponents arrested and executed, held an election of sorts that resulted in his ascendancy to the presidency, and re-instituted slavery as an inducement to support from the American South; all of which provoked not only the unity of the Liberals and Conservatives of Nicaragua, but of the former partners of Nicaragua in the Central American Confederation. Costa Rica and Nicaraguan exiles and Hondurans invaded and skirmished and fought pitched battles with Walker's men at Rivas and Santa Rosa.

Most stupidly, Walker confiscated the properties of Commodore Vanderbilt's Transit Company, and turned them over to his cronies. What honor and revindication could not achieve on the battlefield for the enemies of Walker, capitalism offended indeed could. And the agents of Vanderbilt, acting in concert with the British Navy, organized the forces of Costa Rica and Nicaraguan exiles while blockading the San Juan River supply route. In the end, Walker abandoned and set afire the city of Granada, and retreated to the safety of a U.S. warship early in 1857. He attempted unsuccessfully to return to Nicaragua, and when his attention later turned to the Bay Islands of Honduras, he ended up before a firing squad in Trujillo.

In victory, Nicaragua was nevertheless reduced. Under the treaty that ended hostilities, Costa Rica pushed its border right to the San Juan River, and the crucial transit route was complicated by the jurisdictions of two sovereignties. Vanderbilt, examining the balance sheets, chose to accept a payment from competitors *not* to resume the service. Nicaragua's brief international stardom faded.

Exhausted Nicaragua was ruled by coalitions for several decades, but mostly was dominated by Conservatives, as the country opened to world trade with the planting of coffee on a large scale, and the establishment of cattle ranches, both of which displaced either subsistence farming or the old-time world of self-sustaining haciendas. Railways were built to connect the major towns between the lakes and the Pacific, and to take produce to port. For some, this was progress. For others, it was of no particular benefit, but was mandated by the way things were done in the world all around.

The most notable figure in the nineteenth century, after Walker, was General José Santos Zelaya, a liberal who took power by force of arms in 1893. Zelaya established sovereignty over the Caribbean side of Nicaragua, which Britain had technically ceded years before, in 1894, though the enmity between Mosquitia and the Hispanic center of Nicaragua continued unabated into the twentieth century. The general imposed a constitution that guaranteed individual rights, freedom of religion, and private property, and outlawed the death penalty. But Santos in effect ruled in the best Latin tradition of *personalismo*, attracting support not for what he stood for, but for what he was as an individual.

Santos went into exile in 1909, after the United States connived in a Conservative coup, and foreign capital began to dominate parts of the economy. U.S. Marines made their appearance for the first time in 1912, technically as embassy guards, but mainly to evidence U.S. interest in stability. In 1916, the Bryan-Chamorro treaty gave the United States rights to build a canal across the country, as well as a lease on the Corn Islands; the treaty remained in force until 1971.

A conservative coup by General Emiliano Chamorro in 1925 led to renewed factional fighting, and the Marines returned. The United States recognized Conservative Adolfo Díaz as president.

When a liberal general, José María Moncada, rebelled in 1927, the United States intervened to broker a peace settlement. The United States supervised the 1928 elections, which were won by Moncada.

History

THE INVENTION OF GUERRILLA WARFARE

It was the American involvement at this time that was to shake Nicaragua, and to some extent all Latin America, for years and years to come. One Liberal general, Augusto César Sandino, refused to sign the 1927 Pact of Espino Negro. As *General de Hombres Libres*—General of Free Men—he led his troops off to the remote mountains along the border of Honduras to continue his fight, this time not only against the Conservatives, but also their new coalition partners, and against the U.S. Marines who had been brought in to prop up the government.

Sandino fought for more than seven years against the Americans and their Nicaraguan partners, and in parts of the country, was the de facto head of government. His was the first *guerra de guerrillas*, a "war of little wars," in which an outgunned force used mobility and knowledge of the terrain, as well as the support of the local populace, and its ability to choose when and where to fight, to nullify an army far superior in weapons.

The Americans, seeing no victory, created a new military, the National Guard, to exert control and order, under Anastasio Somoza García, and this first of his dynasty used treachery where arms had failed. Sandino came down from the mountains in 1933, after the Marines were withdrawn under Franklin D. Roosevelt's Good Neighbor policy. On his way to negotiations, Sandino was murdered on Somoza's orders.

Directly and indirectly, the Somozas went on to run Nicaragua along the lines of a private company for the next fifty years. Anastasio Somoza García obliged the elected president, Juan Bautista Sacasa, to resign in 1935, and was himself elected president in 1936. Thereafter, he either ruled directly, or gave instructions to the current president as commander of the National Guard.

The first Somoza was assassinated in 1956; his sons, Luis Somoza Debayle and Anastasio Somoza Debayle, followed in turn, amassing family fortunes in everything from beer distributorships to automobile franchises to chicken restaurants. Steadily, the last Somoza became ever greedier, altering the constitution to extend his power. Even aid destined for the relief of victims and the reconstruction of Managua after the 1972 earthquake ended up in Anastasio Somoza's pockets. Opponents were warned if they were lucky, or exiled, or simply murdered.

Opposition to Somoza went underground. The Frente Sandinista de Liberación Nacional—FSLN, or Sandinista National Liberation

GOVERNMENT AND ADMINISTRATION

Nicaragua is a unitary (non-federal) country, with all powers concentrated in the central government. The capital is Managua.

Nicaragua is divided into 16 *departamentos* ("departments," or provinces), in two zones, and one "special zone."

Pacific zone: Nueva Segovia, Madriz, Estelí, León, Chinandega, Managua, Masaya, Granada, Carazo, Rivas, Boaco, Chontales, Matagalpa, Jinotega.

Atlantic Zone: Atlantic North Autonomous Region, Atlantic South Autonomous Region, and Río San Juan special zone.

The constitution of Nicaragua has been through adjustments, revisions and amendments since the overthrow of Anastasio Somoza in 1978. Currently, there are legislative, executive and judicial branches, as in the United States, plus an electoral branch.

The legislature consists of 90 deputies elected for six-year terms, each with an elected alternate, ready to step in, much in the way of an alternate juror.

The president, as chief of state, appoints cabinet ministers at his or her discretion. The current presdent is Violeta Barrios viuda (widow) de Chamorro, elected in 1990 for a six-year term.

The court system culminates in a supreme court, the judges of which are selected by the legislature from nominees of the president.

The **supreme electoral council** operates independently of other government branches to organize and ensure the fairness of elections.

Front—was organized in 1961. As Somoza's deeds became more outrageous, even the middle class and the wealthy began to oppose the government. The Sandinistas became more daring, and kidnaped officials. The final straw was the assassination of newspaper editor Pedro Joaquín Chamorro in early 1978. The Sandinistas responded with a daring raid on the National Palace. Fighting broke out throughout the country, but was inconclusive. With renewed fighting in June 1979, the outcome was clear. On July 19, a Sandinista-led coalition took power after Anastasio Somoza had fled the country.

History

THE SANDINISTA DEPARTURE

The Sandinistas began their administration as first among equals in a coalition that included middle-class supporters and businessmen who had seen only ruination in the personal corporation that Somoza had made of Nicaragua. But with time, they hewed more closely to the doctrine and dreams that had been expounded during their period of clandestinity: "to forge a Nicaragua without exploitation, without repression, without stepping backward; a free, progressive and independent country."

The Sandinista program called for expropriation of the plantations and businesses of the Somozas and their allies, either professed or objective; land redistribution; establishment of a new army; and strict state control of the economy. Nonalignment and a free press were guaranteed. The Sandinistas tried to halt migration to cities by creating opportunities in the countryside.

Not surprisingly, the partisans of Somoza had largely fled the country as the Sandinista triumph neared; but with the imposition of state economic controls, middle-class supporters left the coalition. Even some "stars" of the Sandinista revolt, including Edén Pastora, the Comandante Zero who had once led a daring commando raid on Somoza's legislature, joined the "Contra" forces that were beginning to harass the new government from bases in Costa Rica and Honduras.

The United States, after initial accommodation under President Jimmy Carter, turned under Ronald Reagan to a policy of isolating and undermining the Sandinistas. Exports of strategic goods from arms to tractors were cut off; and weapons and training were supplied, directly and indirectly, to the Contras.

But the Sandinistas forged on, undeterred. Aid came from Cuba and the Soviet Union. Medical care improved for many, and a drive was launched against illiteracy. Many workers had a hand in managing their places of work and their farms for the first time. In the 1984 elections, the Sandinistas received overwhelming approval.

But the burdens of reconstruction after the 1972 earthquake and the war against Somoza, the continuing struggle against the Contras, and isolation from the region all meant hardship for most Nicaraguans. As the U.S. blockade tightened, prices soared by the day, and transportation broke down. Though they were told that they now controlled their destinies, many Nicaraguans were no better off than they had been under Somoza.

ECONOMY

Agriculture is the main activity of Nicaraguans, and as many as 60 percent of the people make their living from the land. Much of the land is taken up by the "basic grains," crops grown for local consumption: corn, beans, rice and sorghum.

The major agricultural exports are coffee, cotton, cane sugar, bananas, meat, tobacco, cottonseed, rice, corn, beans and sorghum.

Growth industries, moving up this scale, include fish farming, especially shrimp culture, and tourism.

WHAT DO THEY EARN?

Minimum wage, by law, is about $100 per month in Nicaragua. Casual laborers—those who pick coffee at harvest time, for example—might make $2 per day, or they might make less.

How do people make do on this small amount, when prices for basic commodities are not correspondingly low? In many cases they can't, and move on to the United States if they can, or to Costa Rica at least to pick coffee, or even to Guatemala and El Salvador, where there is more commercial activity. Or, they count on family members abroad to send something home.

Those who actually earn their livings in Nicaragua might have a family farming plot away from where they perform their wage labor. One taxi driver I know in Managua, for example, tends corn on the side near León, and he's by no means atypical.

TIME ON THEIR HANDS

Even with these low wages, there's still not enough for people to do, or to make it worth their while to do it; so one of the scenes of street life everywhere in Nicaragua is people sitting on the steps and porches of their houses, passing the time of day. In part, it's tradition; in part, it's gracious; and in part, it's inescapable.

EDUCATION

Primary education is free and compulsory for all Nicaraguans, though facilities are not available in some areas. Instruction is in Spanish, except in the autonomous Atlantic regions, where native languages are used.

And notably, the *style* of the revolutionary government was a departure from the *personalismo* that had gone before. In Latin America in general, and in Nicaragua in particular, governments have often coalesced around the personality of the head of state, without regard to, and often in open contradiction of, stated doctrine. Name and family and tradition count for everything in Nicaragua, where Chamorros, Lacayos, Sacasas and Mayorgas crop up in every era of the nation's annals. Cuba had its revolution, but it also had the *persona* of Fidel Castro. But the heroes of the Nicaraguan revolution, from Augusto César Sandino to Carlos Fonseca Amador, were dead. The head of government, Daniel Ortega, bore the mark of unpardonable lack of color and personal authority.

RIGHT FACE

Elections were held again in 1990, under the pressure of collapsing east-bloc support, continuing economic and military harassment, and dollar intervention on behalf of the opposition; and the Sandinistas were defeated. Violeta Chamorro, publisher and widow of Pedro Joaquín Chamorro, took office as president, at the head of UNO, the center-right opposition coalition that included everyone from ex-Sandinistas to former supporters of Somoza.

And though interference in the campaign from foreigners had been open and acknowledged, President Daniel Ortega accepted the "popular verdict" and stepped aside. Sandinistas remained in key positions, to prevent revenge against their partisans—most notably, Humberto Ortega stayed on as head of the armed forces.

Though numerous achievements of the Sandinistas—increased literacy, improved public health services, a sense of control of ordinary people over their destiny—remained in place, other aspects of the Triunfo began to be

Nicaragua Guide

unwound. The army was reduced in size. Businesses taken from alleged anti-social elements (former Somoza supporters) were returned to their previous owners. Attempts were made to sort out land ownership.

Promised U.S. aid to post-Sandinista Nicaragua was largely delayed, as old claims remained pending. And the burden of reconstruction has fallen to a government that receives little outside help from other countries, or from ideological supporters.

And yet, the outlook is brighter in Nicaragua than it has been in years. Those who resorted to force of arms have been exhausted, and disputes are once again being settled by debate and vote. Such strife as there is, is generally of the verbal sort. The threat of going off to war or being blown apart by terrorist bombs has been lifted from the shoulders of young and old.

More importantly, Nicaragua is catching up to missed opportunities. Its coffee can once again be widely marketed, its needs supplied by manufacturers all over the world.

Among the bright spots is tourism, which has raced ahead in neighboring countries. Visitors have already become one of the main sources of foreign exchange, and the tourism business will no doubt boom, as word gets out about Nicaragua's volcanoes and beaches and climate and rain forest and living colonial heritage, and the grace and resilience of its people.

4
NICARAGUANS

NIGHTMARES IN NICARAGUAN LEGENDS

Dictatorship . . . earthquakes . . . boycotts . . . civil war . . . foreign intervention . . . For all that they've been through in recent years, Nicaraguans are a remarkably sedate, cheerful, dignified people.

But then, they've always lived through difficult times, which run as an undercurrent through their folklore. On the walls of a reception area in one governmental building, woodcuts depict legends of the people: skeletons prowling at night in search of human prey; two wolves accompanying wanderers, one black, seeking victims, one white, protecting against the other; La Mocuana, a hirsute harpy seeking out children to steal; Las Seguas, beings with phenomenal female bodies and the heads of horses and wolves, who leave men in a state of permanently reduced capacity.

No wonder, then, that waking up to reality, any reality, can be a cheering experience.

KNOWING NICARAGUANS

AN OPEN PEOPLE

What are some of the things you notice about Nicaraguans?

They are more open than most Latin Americans about themselves, their lives, their problems, their aspirations, about sexuality, the dark side and the light side. If a Nicaraguan mentions sexual practices, prostitution, lovers' hotels and such, it most likely is not part of a come-on, but genuinely inquiring conversation. Advertisements for hotels of a certain sort explicitly trumpet the availability of condoms. Billboards speak frankly of family breakdown in the aftermath of the recent disruptions. *Mi papá se fue de la casa* ("My father left home") cry two sad eyes on one large public-service ad currently seen in Managua.

AN ANCIENT PEOPLE

Who are these warm, open people? Quite simply, they are largely the descendants of the indigenous nations that inhabited the land at the time of the Conquest, combined with the Spanish and later migrants from Europe and other areas. But the Spaniards who took Nicaragua were never very many—as few as 500 at the beginning, according to some.

So the Nicaraguans of today are largely what they have always been, a nation of indigenous people. And, despite 500 years of Hispanic cultural domination, they remain determined by their experience as Indians and as a conquered people, distant cousins of the peoples of present-day Mexico who share some of the same past. To understand the Nicaraguan people, look to the past, and to the past in the present.

A HISPANIC PEOPLE

Along with the indigenous heritage, a lot of what is initially striking about Nicaraguans comes straight from Iberia and the Latin heritage. The starting point, and main cultural bond with other nations, is the Spanish language.

Then there is the Church. In common with other Latin Americans, Nicaraguans are overwhelmingly Catholic, though they've kept and blended elements of their spiritual life from before the Conquest. Traditionally, education has meant advancing in the Church hierarchy, if not in law or the arts or literature, and technical education and administrative skills have not been as highly regarded as they are in some other countries.

SOCIETY OF CLASSES

Nicaraguan society is a society of classes. What the Spanish found when they conquered Nicaragua was a stratified civilization. Elites of priests and nobles ruled over laborers and slaves, and collected tribute from neighboring nations that they had subjugated.

This was not a system that the Spanish wanted totally to disrupt, and they didn't. In place after place in the Americas, the Iberian conquerors destroyed only the ruling classes, and substituted themselves at the top of the social pyramid. Only where there were no sedentary, developed cultures did the Spanish fail to establish their authority permanently—as on the Caribbean side of Nicaragua.

And so, throughout most of its history, concepts such as social mobility have been foreign to Nicaragua. Those who were agricultural laborers were descended from agricultural laborers and expected their children to be agricultural laborers. And those who had money and power intermarried and held on to what they had.

There have been exceptions, of course, as some humble persons have climbed the pyramids. But look at the phone book in Nicaragua, and you'll see that a certain number of business names have the non-Hispanic ring of outsiders who did not feel bound by the rules of the local game.

Aside from immigration, recent times have put a dent in the system. Many Nicaraguans who went abroad as economic refugees achieved a status that they couldn't find at home, and are not about to assume limitations when they return. And the Sandinista experience put a damper on the old ways from the very beginning. While past revolts and even the movement of Sandino himself in the thirties were led by established, dissident generals, the latter-day Sandinistas attempted to take their power for the first time from the broad mass of citizens, and to give even the poorest workers a sense of control over their destinies. Whether they succeeded in fact, they instilled ideals that will not easily be shoved back into the bottle.

PERSONHOOD

Remember that Nicaraguans were ruled by *caciques*, powerful chieftains, before the Spaniards arrived, and you'll understand the political tradition, *personalismo*, that has been a bane, blessing and fixture of so many Latin nations. We think of Perón in Argentina and Vargas in Brazil and so many others who attracted political support that had as much to do with how a leader strutted his stuff and looked after his supporters as what he believed in or how he disposed of legislators.

Nicaragua has had its leaders in the same tradition, starting with the Liberal and Conservative politicians of León and Granada who drew support as much for where they came from as for what they stood for. José Santos Zelaya was in this tradition, as was Sandino to his supporters. And even the Somozas, with their politics of greed, fit the mold of less-than-ideological leaders.

FAMILIES

What's life without a family? In Nicaragua, not much. More than likely, your family and family connections will determine where and whether you work, what your political associations are, and who you marry. If you come from somewhere else and work in Managua, there's a good chance you'll go home to your family every weekend, rather than to the beach or the bars. And likewise, if you've left the country for one reason or another, trips back to the family, at whatever expense, will be part of your new life.

Of course, we're talking about old-style families here, where a man's man rules. Businesses are likewise family affairs, ruled from above, where it's up to the boss to look after the well-being of workers, or not look after them. And even the entire country can be seen as a big family, if a divided one at times, where the president of the day is a father figure (or, more lately, a mother figure) as well.

ARTS

The native peoples of Nicaragua lost a good deal of themselves when they were conquered by the Spaniards. Their independence, as far as that concept meant anything to the privileged classes, was crushed. Their languages slowly withered, as they were forced to communicate in Spanish with their new masters. Their clothing was altered, to suit the concepts of modesty of the Church.

But the conquerors also became patrons of the arts, by employing or enslaving natives to sculpt the façades of their new temples and carve the altarpieces and paint the decorations inside and produce the utilitarian ware to furnish them. Native artistic talents and traditions survived the Conquest, and enrich the lives of Nicaraguans to this day.

CELEBRATIONS AND DANCE: ANCIENT WAYS IN THE PRESENT

Folkloric dance as a performance art is much, much stronger and more respected in Nicaragua than elsewhere in Central America. In Guatemala, traditional dances are confined to town fiestas; in El Salvador, they have been suppressed, along with many other traces of Indian heritage; in Costa Rica, any pre-Columbian heritage is denied; in Honduras, the separate traditions of Indian groups blended early in the colonial period.

But in Nicaragua, not only are traditional dances that are rooted in pre-Hispanic customs dusted off and trotted out at town fiestas, they are preserved and practiced and encouraged in folkloric dance groups, and taught to kids as after-school activities, along with aerobics and ballet.

Why is this? Partly, poverty, isolation, the separation of the broad mass of people from the currents of the outside world have kept local ways strong.

And also, for all the strife of recent Nicaraguan history, the broad class below the richest claims a fairly homogeneous Mestizo culture, without the deprecation of the ways of one group by another group that in its insecure way attempts to exert its superiority, as the small-town Ladinos of Guatemala do over the Indian population.

Certainly, the dances of Nicaragua bear a family resemblance to some of the traditional dances in Mexico and Guatemala. The Palo Volador, or "flying pole," is the same as in Guatemala and Mexico: a performer is strapped to a rope wound around a pole, and unwinds, swinging ever farther into thin air, to the accompaniment not of melody, but of staccato rhythms pounded on percussion instruments.

Common elements in Las Inditas ("the little Indian women"), El Toro Huaco, La Gigantona, and other traditional dances include pink masks with grotesque facial features that parody the large-nosed conquerors; feathered hats; costumes decorated with piping and spangles; and a story line, played out in gesture, that depicts the clumsy but overwhelming and inevitable triumph of the Spaniards or of some element of nature. Sometimes, the dances are playful, as La Gigantona, in which a giant woman is paired with a midget.

And almost always, the dances are performed before or after the solemn processions of the saints that are honored in the particular celebration of each town. Other essential elements of any celebrations are drinking, and music played on the marimba, an instrument that looks like a xylophone, with sounding boxes made of macawood.

One unique work stands apart from the traditional spectacles: the Güegüense ("gweh-GWEN-seh"), which, unlike more traditional performances, contains spoken social commentary on the state of the natives, in the manner of classic Spanish drama, along with dance and elaborate costumes. El Güegüense first appeared in Spanish and native languages in the 1600s, and though its structure suggests European authorship, it was immediately accepted by natives as a true reflection of their situation.

EARTHENWARE

The ceramic tradition of Nicaraguans has been unbroken since the first pots replaced gourds thousands of years ago. While the Spaniards sought to erase the "heathen" ways of the Indians, earthenware was seen as utilitarian, and continued to be made, even if ceremonial urns for burial of chieftains and the like disappeared. And today, in an age of cheap plastic substitutes, locally made earthenware, often produced in shapes and with decorations virtually identical to those of pre-Columbian pieces, continues to find a market among Nicaraguans, and not just as souvenirs for visitors.

Other artistic traditions either continue from the early times, or have been adapted by able hands. Silverwork, wood carving, embroidery, leather, hammocks and macramé and sisal decorations, basketry, sculpting in stone—all find a place in the homes of many Nicaraguans who don't have any idea of what a "collector" is.

WRITER AS HERO

The Spanish imposed a new language on a literate and artistic people; Nicaraguans mastered it and made it their own. León, the university center, though never a large city, took its studies of the Iberian world and its delvings into ecclesiastical matters as seriously as did Salamanca in mother Spain; and, amid the haciendas of indigo and subsistence plots of a remote colony and unheralded independent republic, created masters of the language.

The best-known of these, to anyone who has ever spoken Spanish in the last century, is Rubén Darío. Reared in León, he went on to work as an editor in Chile and El Salvador and Guatemala, and to publish books of verse. His landmark volume, *Azul* ("Blue"), considered among the first modernist works in Spanish, took the language beyond romantic description and into the mind of poet and reader. Darío was no isolated exile, despite all his travels; he returned to León for long periods, and served as a diplomat representing Nicaragua.

Darío's image, with trademark scowl, is to be seen on statues in Managua and León and in small towns; but he is by no means a unique poet-as-activist or activist-as-artist. It was an accomplished poet, Rigoberto López Pérez, who assassinated the first president Somoza, in León, in 1957. And poets, painters and novelists have doubled as ministers of government in the recent years of Sandinista administration, most notably Ernesto Cardenal, who was also a moving force in establishing a colony of artists in the Solentiname islands of Lake Nicaragua.

MORE NICARAGUANS

At least 90 percent of Nicaraguans trace their roots to the ancient peoples of the land and the late-arriving Europeans. But for hundreds of years, what is now Nicaragua has been shared with what outsiders might call minorities, but which are mini-nations who have largely developed on their own and run their own affairs, occasionally in conflict with and sometimes with the cooperation of the government in Managua.

Blacks have been part of Nicaraguan society almost since the earliest days of the colony. The Spanish, just as the English, enslaved Africans to work on plantations when and where the native population had been oppressed and reduced; but Nicaragua was never a significant exporter, and the first African slaves probably mixed in with the general population.

But later arrivals to the Caribbean area maintained a separate identity. In fact, they were associated in no way with the Spanish culture of the Pacific slope, but with the English pirates, buccaneers and traders, who preyed on Spanish shipping, looted the forests of valuable trees, and attempted to establish plantations in the British protectorate that encompassed much of Caribbean Central America.

Some of the blacks who came to Bluefields and the Corn Islands were escaped slaves; others were artisans and loggers in the employ of the British. Still others landed on the Caribbean shores when slavery was abolished in the British West Indies, and unemployed blacks sailed west to seek land to till and bases from which to fish. And American logging companies that worked the forests of the Caribbean slopes toward the end of the nineteenth century and into the twentieth century, often found it easier to recruit English-speaking blacks in the Islands than to bring over laborers from the more settled part of Nicaragua.

Indians, or indigenous Nicaraguans, are everywhere and nowhere in the more heavily populated Pacific and highland regions of Nicaragua. Most Nicaraguans are of indigenous descent, even if separate ethnic identities are a thing of the past.

The ancient languages of Nicaragua are no longer intact, though they sprinkle everyday speech. *Nacatamales, tiste,* and other items of food and drink have yielded no ground at all to the influences of the last 500 years. And the heartland of Nicaragua still speaks of the Mexica-Nahuatl heritage: Momotombo, Masaya, Nindirí, and Diriamba are Chorotega names, while Managua, Tiscapa, Tipitapa and Jalapa are pure Nahuatl. If these have a strange ring to the foreign visitor, they are no less exotic to a roaming Central American, for they speak not of the Maya heritage known to the north, or of the Spanish influence implanted in Costa Rica, but of the wandering Mexica and Nahuas from distant lands, who in the regions between the great lakes of Central America and the sea established their new home. And ancient ceremonial dances that are disappearing in Mexico, such as the *palo volador*, survive at fiestas in central Nicaragua today.

On the vast eastern plain of Nicaragua, indigenous heritage is more than folklore and memory; it is a separate way of life for the Miskito, Sumu and Rama peoples.

Miskitos (who call themselves Táwaira) inhabit villages along the lagoons and larger rivers of coastal Nicaragua. **Sumos** live in small communities upriver. They have a common origin in the pre-Columbian peoples of the area, who survived by fishing and hunting, and planting cassava in forest clearings, which they abandoned when the earth was exhausted. Their languages are related to those spoken in parts of South America. Despite their cultural ties, the Miskitos are racially distinct: their ancestors include blacks who migrated to the coast of Nicaragua and Honduras, or who escaped to these shores from slavery under the British.

For the Miskitos, the colonial power was not the Spaniards, who never found wealth enough to exploit along the Caribbean shore, nor a way to subjugate peoples without sedentary ways; but the British, who occasionally farmed in coastal enclaves, or sent woodcutters into the forests, and found markets among the natives for manufactured goods. The British established a protectorate over much of the coastal region and armed the Miskitos as well. Tensions between the Miskitos and Managua persisted after the British pulled out of the Miskito coast in 1858, and after Nicaraguan sovereignty was exerted in 1895. When Contras raided from Honduras, the Sandinista government attempted to resettle the Miskitos into defensible villages, alienating many. In the end, the Miskitos were granted autonomy in their local affairs.

Miskitos and Sumos still practice roving cultivation, and are fishermen par excellence. In a roadless world, they rely on water transportation to take their products to market and find supplies, using dugouts (*cayucas*) and flat-bottomed boats (*pipantes*). Many of the place names in the region are taken from their own languages: Kukalaya, Krawala, Raitpura from Miskito; Paiwas, Pancasá, Kilambé from Sumu. But the English influence is present in names like Monkey Point, El Bluff, and Pigeon Cay, and in the Methodist faith professed by so many who came under the influence of missionaries.

Ramas, another ethnic group, related to the Chibcha of northern South America, once roamed over large portions of eastern Nicaragua. Today, they remain as a separate group only on Rama Cay, an island in the Bay of Bluefields.

Garífunas, or **Caribs**, are, along with the Ramas, probably the smallest ethnic group in Nicaragua. They trace their heritage both to escaped African slaves, and to an Amerindian people with which the escapees intermarried on the island of St. Vincent. After a rebellion against the British in 1795, they were dispersed to islands off the coast of Central America. Caribs are found today scattered along the Caribbean coast, and on the Corn Islands, as well as in Honduras, Guatemala and Belize. Though largely indistinguishable from blacks of West Indian descent by appearance, they speak their own language of Arawak origin with African enrichment, and often have Hispanic names.

Whites, while generally not considered a separate ethnic group, are a presence that is evident, but often not discussed in the social mosaic of Nicaragua. As in Mexico, with which Nicaragua has so many ancient ties and similarities, the lighter one's skin, the higher one is likely to be on the social scale. Marrying a lighter-skinned person is thought to reflect an improvement in one's status.

The shading of social classes has gone on since colonial times, when the Spanish conquerors were at the top of the social pyramid. Concubinage was—and to some degree continues to be—common. National hero Augusto César Sandino himself was the product of what is euphemistically called an "informal union," which is not held against anyone, as it is in so many northern countries. But formal, legalized marriage, with the inheritance of property, and of social contacts, and ultimately of power, has been pretty much kept within a limited circle. European immigrants, relatively few in number, have had entrée to the upper ranks of society and commerce. For the broad class of Nicaraguans, it's been a tougher go; but the Sandinista heritage, the disruptions of staid ways by the late conflicts; and the general opening to new commerce and ideas in an era of mass communication, are all breaking down older barriers.

"Gringos," anyone with a North American or European background, are another presence in Nicaragua. The age when foreigners not only ran the local operations of foreign companies but also staffed them, is long gone; and the last American Marines departed in 1933. But the "international community" remains a visible fixture, at least in Managua. Those American and French and British and Dutch faces, with accents to match, belong to consultants and volunteers on aid and cooperation missions, to diplomats, and to transient executives looking after the operations of the local paint factory and the like. Come back next year, and the faces might be largely different ones; but the foreign community as a whole occupies the same apartments and uses the same stores and animates a fair sector of metropolitan commerce.

5
PLANNING YOUR TRIP

- What can you do in Nicaragua? When's the best time to go?
- What kind of documentation do you need?
- How should you carry money?
- Can you use credit cards?
- What are the buses like?
- Can you get to places of interest and back to the capital in a single day?
- Can you pick up a tour to the most interesting places?
- What do you have to bring?

Travel is full of nitty-gritty decisions on the way to even starting your trip, and this section will help you to make them.

FIRST THINGS FIRST . . .

THE TRAVEL SCENE

Tourism is not yet a big business in Nicaragua, so there isn't much of a chance that you will find a travel agent in the United States or Canada who knows the country and can easily handle all your arrangements. You'll have to take most of the responsibility for planning onto your own shoulders.

So keep in mind that . . .

- Nicaraguans are family oriented, and the limited beach facilities and resorts are likely to be *full* at Christmas and Easter with mama, papa, grandfather, grandmother, uncle, aunt, multiple children, and several domestic employees.

- If you're planning to travel at a holiday period, make ironclad reservations, either directly with a hotel, or through one of the Managua travel agencies listed elsewhere in this book. **Call** a travel agency (see page 168—many have personnel who can speak English) or call or **fax** a hotel. Use a hotel's toll-free number in the few cases where this service is available. Letters will generally not do you much good.

- At other times, it helps to book at least the first night's lodging in advance.

- If you're planning to drive around Nicaragua, reserve through a toll-free number to get the best rates, and to make sure a car will be available.

- Hotels are not abundant, but neither are tourists, at this time, so during most of the year, there's no need—no need at all—to worry about crossing every "t" and dotting every "i" before you go. A small dose of the unexpected and a bit of spontaneity are part of the fun of travel.

If you want to be absolutely sure of having a bed for the night, call ahead before you start out in the morning.

- The rainy season is not a problem. It *never* rains all day (well, hardly ever), and the lush greenery of the growing season is the main attraction of the tropics for many. Look ahead for more details.

- Don't overload your luggage, but take the essentials. You might not be able to find them in Nicaragua. You'll find a checklist in this chapter.

More tips? This book is just full of them!

Planning

NOT AS RAINY AS YOU THINK!
CLIMATE AND WEATHER IN NICARAGUA

Other Central American countries have eternal springtime. Most of Nicaragua has eternal summer. Not that there's no difference from month to month, or variation in hours of daylight, or ebb and flow of the rains, or cool uplands. Not that it's always sweltering and rainy and steamy—in fact, it's anything but.

But in almost all parts of Nicaragua that you are likely to visit, you can count on warm weather. Days can be sunny and warm, but the steady breezes during the dry season can make them, for the most part, comfortable; and it's quite possible to feel a bit chilled in March when the wind blows off Lake Nicaragua or the Pacific, even if the temperature is well into the seventies. "Cool" in Nicaragua implies a breeze, the dry times between November and March, the hours of darkness when the earth gives up its accumulated heat.

REASSURING PREDICTABILITY

There *is* changing weather in Nicaragua. But the visitor should be aware that it comes about in different ways from weather in the temperate zones. Rainfall varies from season to season and from one zone to another. Temperatures are cooler or warmer, depending on altitude. It's not like going to New York and wondering if you'll get a string of rainy days or sunshine, an Indian summer or early snow. Pick a date and season, and you'll pretty well know exactly what the weather is. That's one of the nice parts of travel to Nicaragua.

Of course, there's some variation from day to day in any season, and the effects of winter in the northern hemisphere can be felt. When a cold wave—a *Norte*—sweeps south from the Arctic, temperatures can drop all the way down into the sixties Fahrenheit (under 20 Centigrade) in Managua.

But on the average, around Managua, average high temperature is about 28 degrees Centigrade (82 Fahrenheit), with either dry air (November through March) or consistent humidity.

"WINTER" AND "SUMMER" RAINY VS. DRY

As far as most visitors are concerned, let's hear it for the dry season! From November through May along the Pacific slope, hardly any rain falls. Humidity is low, beaches have guaranteed sun, it's cold back home, and who could ask for anything more? The dry season—what the Nicaraguans call *verano*, or summer, is premier travel time.

As for the rainy season, or *invierno* ("winter") . . . Don't believe the fairy tale that it rains only for an hour every day, at the same time of day, and only in sprinkles. Sometimes the rain comes down hard! But in general, **Managua and Pacific Nicaragua are far less rainy than most of Central America**. On most days, the rain moves in from the coast and blows onward, and everybody can soon get go about their business outdoors again. And on the plus side, tropical foliage is never as rich as it is in the rainy times—which is why the period is also called the **green season**.

DIFFERENT ZONES, DIFFERENT CLIMATES

While latitude determines climate in the temperate zones, altitude, exposure to the coasts, and prevailing winds count for everything in the tropics. Nicaragua has three zones. Choose your preferences (cool, sunny and dry, green and exuberant), and you can decide when and exactly where you want to go.

PACIFIC CLIMATE

On the Pacific slope of Nicaragua, from the Great Lakes of Central America across the plains and valleys to the sea, the dry season starts at the beginning of November. Temperatures drop slightly from their yearly averages, and winds are common, especially from the northwest. Visibility is greatest in December and January, when the air is driest. Nights are always clear.

Some of the hottest and most uncomfortable days are experienced at the end of April and into May, the so-called "sea season" (*temporada del mar*), or during October. The sun is steady and direct, the air is still, and humidity has returned or has not yet left. Finally, occasional violent squalls herald the rainy season.

Planning

Rains arrive in full force in mid-May, usually in the afternoons, and aside from the moments before a storm, the air is still—and sweltering, except where there is a steady breeze along the coast. Generally, any morning in the rainy season is clear. Afternoon brings a downpour, but sometimes the rain can last into the night. Lingering clouds hold in the day's warmth.

For several weeks in July and August, in *veranillo* ("little summer"), the rains can disappear altogether. Afterward, September and October bring the most intense rains, occasionally lasting for days on end, when a tropical storm is stalled along the coast. But by November, the rains wax intermittent, and soon end altogether.

"ATLANTIC" NICARAGUA

Moving toward the "Atlantic," or Caribbean, slope of Nicaragua, the rainy season gets longer and longer. Near the water, storms can blow in at any time of the year. While western Nicaragua is enjoying its dry season, the Caribbean region still sees scattered rain into January and February. The real dry season doesn't start until mid-February or the beginning of March. By the end of May, rains are regular once again. Storms intensify over the following months, with a break toward mid-September

Rainfall increases toward the south, and around Bluefields and San Juan del Norte, there's hardly any dry season at all. Unlike the predictable rains of the Pacific slope, storms make their presence felt without warning, wreak their havoc, and depart. And yes, it can rain all day over several days along the Caribbean, in the steady, dripping way known to denizens of the temperate zones. The ground is always moist just below the surface, and the air is sopping at any time of year. Temperatures are always near 30 degrees Centigrade (85 degrees Fahrenheit and higher). And rainfall can reach 6000 millimeters (250 inches) in a year, versus 700 millimeters (30 inches) in some of the driest parts of the land.

THE "HIGH" COUNTRY

In the coffee altitudes toward the north and "top" of Nicaragua, temperatures throughout the year are generally a pleasant 22 degrees Centigrade (about 72 Fahrenheit).

The pattern of rain is similar to that along the Pacific slope. But conditions vary in every valley; mountain ridges either block or hold in the clouds. As a result, precipitation varies widely.

59

TEMPERATURES IN MANAGUA

January	26°C	79° F	July	26°C	79°F
February	27°	81°	August	27°	81°
March	27°	81°	September	27°	81°
April	29°	84°	October	27°	81°
May	28°	82°	November	27°	81°
June	27°	81°	December	27°	81°

WHEN IT RAINS

January	1 mm	July	75 mm
February	4	August	137
March	-	September	157
April	-	October	66
May	181	November	38
June	151	December	1

HUMIDITY (RELATIVE, AS %)

January	74	July	82
February	71	August	80
March	63	September	82
April	61	October	80
May	70	November	76
June	82	December	71

Planning

MANAGING YOUR MONEY

Nicaraguans bank **Córdobas,** named for one of the Spanish conquerors and the city (Cordova in English) whence he came. But colloquially, they pay in **pesos.** Don't let it confuse you. When Nicaraguans talk of pesos, they mean their own money, not dollars or Mexican currency.

CASH, CASH, CASH

There are some lightweight coins in circulation, representing 25 and 50 centavos of a córdoba, and smaller denominations. But mostly, prices are in even córdobas, and you'll pay from a wad of notes, worth from 1 to 100 córdobas.

HOW SHOULD YOU CARRY YOUR MONEY?

The wise traveller takes money in several forms, in order to get the best exchange rate in any particular circumstances, and to have an escape route if a particular hotel refuses a credit card or won't exchange travellers checks.

Here are the forms to consider, and where they're likely to be accepted:

- Take **U.S. dollars**, rather than Canadian dollars, sterling, or any other currency. *Only U.S. dollars*, in cash or travellers checks, *can be easily exchanged*. Dollars are widely accepted at hotels.

- Carry some dollars in **cash**, in small denominations, for initial and last-minute expenses. Consider using a money belt or some other secure device.

- Take most of your funds in **travellers checks** if you won't be using a credit card.

- Carry a **credit card**, or, better yet, two different credit cards (see below), preferably Visa and Master Card.

- There is usually no advantage in buying córdobas at airport exchange counters abroad (if you can find them), though you might consider buying some for initial small purchases.

CHANGING YOUR MONEY

The peso, or, uh, córdoba, currently trades at 14 cents in U.S. currency. And though at times in the recent past you could have come out ahead by

61

trading your dollars on the black market, there's hardly a difference at the moment between what's paid by banks, foreign exchange houses, and street money changers. This is subject to change, of course, though in general, the world is moving away from currency controls and black markets.

Here are your choices for changing cash or travellers checks:

Banks are located mainly in the center of cities. They're open weekdays from 8:30 a.m. to 12:30 p.m. and from 1:30 p.m. to 3:30 p.m.; on Saturdays from 8:30 to 11:30 a.m. Banks are subject to lineups and delays, but they're reassuring places in which to exchange a travellers check. *Not all banks will take a travellers check*, however.

Money exchange houses (casas de cambio) have longer hours than banks, and change dollars and travellers checks at comparable rates. They're generally located in the business areas of Managua. See listings in the Managua chapter. Or ask at the front desk of your hotel.

Hotels generally give only slightly less than what banks or exchange houses pay. Recently, when banks were paying 7.35 córdobas to the dollar, the Hotel Las Mercedes paid 7.3, and the Inter-Continental paid 7.2. That's not much of a spread, in return for major convenience.

Black market and **street changers** are not exactly illegal or unsavory these days. In fact, they're a public service. When banks are closed and exchange houses concealed by some undecipherable address, street money changers come to the rescue.

Where do you find black marketers? If you go where tourists go, in fact, if you go where commerce goes, you don't have to worry about finding them, they'll find you. Along the main streets, at public markets, at border crossings, a gent will come up and flash a wad of bills rolled over two fingers, green and American on one side, colorful and Nicaraguan on the other. In the other hand is a pocket calculator, and between the two hands, the money, the figuring, and a few mutually understood words, the exchange is accomplished in seconds, with no trail of paperwork, and no hassle.

If you don't need the services of a money changer who proffers his services, simply wag your finger. And if you do, make sure you count your money and then put it in a safe place before you take off.

THINKING IN DOLLARS

Don't be shy about asking "How much is that in dollars?" It might be offensive in some other countries, but it's exactly what most Nicaraguans do, following years of hyperinflation under the previous government. (The

Planning

córdoba in circulation at the moment replaces gadzillions of the old córdoba).

Taxi drivers, hotel owners, travel agencies and the like will usually quote you a rate in dollars, and it's not because you're a gringo or because they're trying to rip you off. That's just how values are accounted for when the local currency has a habit of slipping.

It's up to you to pay in dollars or córdobas, though there could be a slight advantage in the latter, when figures are rounded. For example, you flag down a taxi to take you from the airport to town, and agree to a fare of $5. You pay 35 córdobas at your destination, instead of 36.75.

In this book, all prices are in U.S. dollars.

USE CREDIT CARDS!

One of the unexpected conveniences of travel in Nicaragua is that **Visa** and **Master Card** are widely accepted, and not just in Managua. Modest beach hotels in San Juan del Sur, a family-run restaurant on Lake Cocibolca near Granada, a souvenir shop at the Augusto Sandino International Airport—all will take Visa or Master Card, as long as there's a working phone to get authorization. There are no surcharges on purchases (unlike cash advances), and approval is usually speedy.

If you have a Visa card *and* a Master Card, I recommend that you take both. Not because one or the other is more acceptable (a company called Credomatic represents both cards in Nicaragua), but because anti-fraud computer programs will sometimes not authorize charges away from home that don't fit your pattern of expenditures (despite all those television ads that maintain the contrary).

American Express is accepted at pricier hotels in Managua, but otherwise, will be of little use in Nicaragua.

CASH ADVANCES

If you're stuck for funds, most banks should be able to handle a cash advance on a Visa card or Master Card, but don't expect speedy service. It's not something that's requested every day.

If you have a problem in getting money at a bank, try Credomatic (the Visa and Master Card agency), Centro Comercial Camino de Oriente (Eastern highway shopping center), tel. 672511. *But be prepared to lose a substantial commission from the proceeds.*

MONEY FROM HOME

In case you're caught short, a cash advance from a bank on a credit card is the easiest way to go (see above). A bank at home can transfer money to a local bank, but make sure you find out exactly which bank it's going to! Local money-exchange shops handle transfers from the U.S., but to deal with a familiar name, try Western Union, opposite El Retiro Hospital, tel. 668126, fax 661812. Western Union has agencies in some branches of Banic (Banco Nicaragüense), as well as in León, Granada, Chinandega, Matagalpa, and Estelí.

ATM?

Sorry. Though there are automatic teller machines in Managua, they are not yet available for easy withdrawal of funds from your home account. This is subject to change, however. Call Visa at 1-800-336-8472 just before your trip to see if any Plus or Visa ATMs have been put into service.

SURPLUS PESOS

Getting rid of local currency before you depart is a fine art, especially in Nicaragua, where (at the moment, anyway) you can't buy dollars at the airport.

It's probably easiest to spend your last córdobas in town, and count on loose U.S. dollars to pay your taxi driver. Your departure tax *must* be paid in U.S. currency. Credit cards are accepted at airport shops.

If you've got a load of córdobas in your pocket, use them to pay your hotel bill, and charge the difference to your credit card. Nicaraguan currency won't do you much good abroad.

Planning

OVER THE BORDER
VISAS AND TOURIST CARDS

➔ Always re-check entry requirements shortly before you leave home. Changes can take place without warning. A Nicaraguan consulate (see page 69) or an airline that serves Nicaragua is usually a good source of information.

PASSPORT? YES!

Passports are required for travel to Nicaragua (with a very few exceptions). The passport must have six months of validity remaining.

VISA WORRIES? PROBABLY NOT

- **No visa or tourist card** is required of citizens of the United States, Argentina, Belgium, Denmark, Finland, Germany, Greece, Hungary, Ireland, Luxembourg, the Netherlands, Norway, Poland, Spain, Sweden, Switzerland, or the United Kingdom, among others.

- Citizens of most other countries, including Canada, require a **visa** or **tourist card**.

- A **tourist card** is easier to obtain than a visa. It can be issued by airlines and travel agencies, as well as by consulates.

A tourist card costs $5. It may be used for entry by **air**. It is valid one time only for 30 days, which cannot be extended. Children under 12 may be included on their parents' tourist cards.

- A **visa**, obtained from a Nicaraguan consulate, is required for **overland travel** to Nicaragua. The visa can be obtained in Honduras while on your way to Nicaragua, usually without delay.

- Citizens of China and Cuba and of some other countries must have their visas authorized in Managua. Citizens of these countries cannot use a tourist card.

OTHER REQUIREMENTS

* You could be required to show a return or onward ticket before being allowed to enter Nicaragua, or at least enough money to satisfy authorities that you can look after yourself.

HOW LONG CAN YOU STAY?

If you enter Nicaragua on a tourist card, you'll be allowed a stay of 30 days.

U.S. citizens entering without a visa are also allowed 30-day stays. Citizens of other countries not required to obtain a visa are granted 90-day stays.

OVER-STAYING

If you over-stay the period allowed on the entry permit in your passport, pay a visit to the Immigration Department (*Migración*), on the south side of Pista de la Municipalidad in Managua, near the southern highway. Or, inquire by phone, tel. 650014. Bus 118 for Lewites market passes nearby.

Generally, one's *permanencia* (permission to stay) may be renewed twice for periods of 30 days each. Processing fees are about $25.

PACKING CHECK LIST

I won't tell you what to wear, I'll just make suggestions.

FOR CLOTHES HOGS

Chill out! It's mostly warm in Nicaragua, and not even a sweater is needed, unless you're heading to the central highlands. Lightweight cotton and cotton blends are ideal.

Neat and *informal* are the key words. Only a businessman will need a tie and jacket from time to time, only a businesswoman will need a suit or formal dress on occasion; though most government employees wear an open-necked shirt. Just remember, though, that **shorts** are rarely worn in town.

Planning

DON'T OVERDO IT

Don't take too much. It's smart to travel light, especially if you'll be changing hotels often. You can always buy another tee-shirt locally. Just make sure you leave nothing out that's essential. Replacements for certain items might not be easily available. You can always leave some of your luggage at your hotel in Managua.

WHAT TO TAKE

Nothing here is *absolutely* necessary (except passport and money). But add whichever items you personally require.

- passport
- travellers checks
- tickets
- some U.S. cash in small-denomination bills, and
- a hidden place for money, such as a money belt.
- hat with brim.
- bathing suit
- shirts or blouses
- shorts
- comfortable walking shoes. Running shoes are adequate.
- socks, underclothes
- sandals or surf shoes.
- one long-sleeved top (for sun protection).
- a light sweater for travel in the central highlands.
- a raincoat or umbrella for travel at rainy times (not absolutely required—there are places to shelter until the rain passes).
- books or magazines in your own language (not easy to find English and other foreign books in Managua).
- candle and matches (useful during short power outages)
- sports equipment (for fishing, snorkeling, whatever)

- a small pack or mesh bag for day use (if they can see what's in it, they might not steal it).

Smaller personal items, including:
- pen, sunglasses, extra prescription glasses, mosquito repellent, sunscreen, medicines, travel alarm
- camera and film
- duty-free cigarettes and liquor

THE CUSTOMS RULES

All personal items for your own use while travelling can enter Nicaragua duty-free. (If you should have any disagreement with a customs officer over personal items, refer to *Artículo 10 del Título I del Código Aduanero Uniforme Centroamericano, "CAUCA"* (Article 10 of Title I, Uniform Central American Customs Code). That'll get 'em.

Personal items in your baggage include used clothing, jewelry, medicines and medical appliances, sports equipment, toys, still and movie cameras, up to six rolls of film for each, binoculars, typewriter, tape recorder, radio, books, and even musical instruments, one tent, and camping equipment, as long as the quantity is obviously not commercial.

Your personal allowance can include three liters of **liquor** or **wine**, 500 grams of **tobacco**, and two kilos of **candy**.

In *addition* to your baggage, you can bring in new items as gifts or for others, up to a *duty* (not merchandise value) of U.S. $100—which is a generous exemption. This exemption and the liquor allowance may be used once every six months, after an absence from Nicaragua for three days.

Samples for sales purposes may be entered if a list is prepared in triplicate with description, reference number and value of each item.

Specific items are prohibited from time to time for health or trade reasons. At this moment, coffee from Honduras, Land Rovers, certain processed oils from Guatemala, Costa Rican milk, and items made of kenaf and jute fibers from outside Central America are out of bounds. It's unlikely any such regulations will affect you.

Planning

WHERE TO FIND INFORMATION ABOUT NICARAGUA

Ministerio de Turismo (*Ministry of Tourism*)
Apartado 122
Managua, Nicaragua
Tel. (502-2)281337/281238
Fax (502-2)281187

U.S. representative
L. Martinez Associates
2216 Coral Way
Miami, FL 33145
Tel. 305-854-1544,
fax 305-854-4589

EMBASSIES AND CONSULATES

- Avenida Corrientes 2548, 4th floor, Office I, 1046 Buenos Aires, **Argentina**, tel. 951-3463, fax 952-7557.

- Buchfeldgasse 18/1/3, A1080 Vienna, **Austria**, tel. (00431) 7140552.

- 55, Av. de Wolvendael, 1180 Brussels, **Belgium**, tel. (00322)3745542.

- Praia de Botafogo 28, Apartado 602, Botafogo, 22550 Rio de Janeiro, **Brazil**, tel. 55-11-4-97, fax 55-19-7-87. Consulate.

- 130 Albert St., Ottawa, **Canada** K1S5G4, tel. 613-234-9361, fax 613-238-7666.

- El Bosque Norte 0140, Depto. 33, Santiago, **Chile**, tel. 23-12-0-34, fax 22-92-6-69.

- Carrera 4a No. 75-73, Bogotá, **Colombia**, tel. 61-68-2-16, fax 21-7-05-09.

- Avenida Central, Calles 25/27, San José, **Costa Rica**, tel. 233-8747, fax 233-9225. Consulate.

- Calle 20 No. 709, Miramar, Playa, Havana, **Cuba**, tel. 33-10-25.

- Profesor Emilio Aparicio No. 44, Ensanche Julieta, Santo Domingo, **Dominican Republic**, tel. (809) 567-1041, fax 563-2034.

- 71 Avenida Norte y Primera Calle Poniente No. 164, Colonia Escalón, San Salvador, **El Salvador**, tel. 246662, fax 241223.

- 8, rue de Sfax, 75016 Paris, **France**, tel. 45017791, fax 45009681.

Nicaragua Guide

• Konstantinstrasse 41, D5300 Bonn 2, **Germany**, tel. 362505, fax 354001.

• 10 Avenida 14-72, Zone 10, Guatemala City, **Guatemala**, tel. 680785, fax 357648.

• Colonia Tepeyac, Bloque M-1, Tegucigalpa, **Honduras**, tel. 324290, fax 311412.

• Via Brescia 16, 700198 Rome, **Italy**, tel. 8414693, fax 8841695.

• Payo de Rivera 120, Lomas de Chapultepec, C.P. 11000, México, D.F., **Mexico**, tel. 52-04421, fax 22-2772381.

• Zoutmanstraat 53-E, 2518 GM Den Haag, The **Netherlands**, tel. 363-0967, fax 363-0969.

• Avenida Federico Boyd y Calle 50, Corregimiento Bella Vista, Panama City, **Panama**, tel. 230981, fax 691847. Consulate.

• Avenida José Pardo 575, Miraflores, Lima 18, **Peru**, tel. 45-83-33, fax 41-02-60.

• Mosfilmovskaya 50, Korpus 1, Moscow, **Russia**, tel. 9382082, fax 9382064.

• María del Soc. Reyes Aragón, Parque Sierra 14, 20 A, 28400 Madrid, **Spain**, tel. 5555510, fax 5555737. Consulate.

• Sandhamnsgatan 40, 11528 Stockholm, **Sweden**, tel. 6671857, fax 6624160.

• 8 Gloucester Rd., London SW 4PP, **U.K.**, tel. (71) 584-4365, fax 823-8790

• Leyenda Patria 2880, Montevideo, **Uruguay**, tel. 70-43-66, fax 70-14-57.

• Prados del Este, Quinta Teocal, Calle Codazzy con Andalucía, Caracas, **Venezuela**, tel. 77-24-59, fax 97-99-1-67.

EMBASSY OF NICARAGUA IN THE UNITED STATES

• 1627 New Hampshire Av. NW, Washington, DC 20009, tel. 202-939-6570, fax 202-939-6542; tel. 939-6531 (consular section), fax 939-6532.

Planning

CONSULATES OF NICARAGUA IN THE UNITED STATES

- 6300 Hillcroft, **Houston**, TX 77081, tel. 713-272-9628, fax 713-272-7131.
- 2500 Wilshire Blvd., Suite N915, **Los Angeles**, CA 90057, tel. 213-252-1170, fax 213-252-1177.
- 8370 W. Flagler, suite 220, **Miami**, FL 33144, tel. 305-220-6900, fax 305-220-8794
- World Trade Center, Suite 1937, **New Orleans**, LA 70130, tel. 504-523-1507, fax 504-523-2359
- 820 Second Avenue, Suite 802, **New York**, NY 10017, tel. 212-983-1981, fax 212-983-2646
- 870 Market St., Suite 1050, **San Francisco**, CA 94102, tel. 415-765-6825, fax 765-765-6826

PUBLICATIONS

PERIODICALS

Guía Fácil, a bi-monthly newsstand publication selling for just over $1, covers events and entertainment in and near Managua, and also lists embassies, banks, and, importantly, baseball schedules.

MAPS

A detailed map of Central America which includes one of the better maps of Nicaragua is published by ITMB and is available from map and travel bookstores, or may be ordered from ITMB, P. O. Box 2290, Vancouver, B.C. V6B 3W5, Canada.

Within Nicaragua, the official mapping and geographical-studies agencies is INETER (Instituto Nicaragüense de Estudios Territoriales, located opposite the social security building (*frente oficinas de INSSBI*). To inquire about availability of maps, call 44739, fax 491890, or write to P.O. Box 2110, Managua.

A map showing major towns and highways in Nicaragua is available from the tourist office (Ministerio de Turismo) in Managua, a block west of the Hotel Inter-Continental.

THE NICARAGUAN CALENDAR

HOLIDAYS

Watch your calendar! Holidays occur at the most unexpected moments. Don't plan to buy a ticket home or go to a bank on any of these days:

January 1	New Year's Day
Moveable	Holy Thursday (Jueves Santo)
Moveable	Good Friday (Viernes Santo) (Many businesses close all Holy Week)
May 1	Labor Day (Día del Trabajo)
July 19	El Triunfo, triumph of the revolution of 1979.
September 14	Battle of San Jacinto (against William Walker)
September 15	Independence Day
September 24	Matagalpa, Virgen de la Merced (Our Lady of Mercy)
November 2	Day of the Dead (Día de los Fieles Difuntos)
October 12	Columbus Day (*Día de la Raza*)
December 8	Immaculate Conception
December 24, 25	Christmas Eve and Christmas
December 31	New Year's Eve

LOCAL CELEBRATIONS

Every town in Nicaragua has a saint to honor locally, if not two or three. More than some other countries in Latin America, Nicaragua has been faithful in preserving the syncretism of native spiritual tradition and acquired but deeply felt Christian passion that grew out of the Conquest.

It's a process that is still evolving. Parades of saints from churches to hill shrines where once pre-Conquest altars stood, dances that honor the spirits of animals and that mock the Spanish conquerors, beauty contests, games and dances are all part of the celebrations.

Planning

These are only *some* of the local celebrations, along with religious holidays which, while not official holidays, are widely celebrated. Dates are approximate.

January 6	Masaya, Day of the Three Kings (Día de los Reyes, or Epiphany)
January 15	Tipitapa, in honor of the Black Christ Esquipulas
January 18	El Sauce, for the Black Christ
January 20	Diriamba, Masaya, Acoyapa in honor of St. Sebastian.
February 2	Diriomo, Virgin of Candelaria
February 9	Juigalpa, Cinco Pinos, San Caralampio
February 9-10	La Concepción, Virgin of Monserrat
February	Sunday of Lazarus, Masaya.
March 19	Malacatoya, Solentiname, in honor of St. Joseph.
Palm Sunday	Masaya
Ash Wednesday	Masaya
April 3	Rivas
April 23-24	Wiwilí, Virgin of Fatima
April 24	San Marcos, Carazo, for St. Mark
April 29	Diriá, St. Peter, the Martyr
May 3	Masaya, Holy Cross
May 1-30	Bluefields (May Pole celebrations); Altagracia, Ometepe
May 13	El Corozo
May 15	Condega
May 17	Chinandega
May 24	Pío XII
June 13	La Concepción
June 24	San Juan de Limay; Granada; San Juan del Sur; Camoapa
July 25	Jinotepe; Boaco; Somoto; Managua

Nicaragua Guide

July 26	Niquinohomo, Masaya and Nandaime, Granada; Nindirí; Moyogalpa, Ometepe
June 29	Granada; Diriá
August 1	Managua for St. Dominic (Santo Domingo). Horse parades and religious processions.
August 15	Granada (horse parade); Chontales; also processions for Immaculate Conception in León, Chinandega; for the Assumption in Masaya, Juigalpa, Ocotal.
September 24	Matagalpa, León, Chinandega
September 30	Masaya and León
October 29	Pueblo Nuevo
November 17	Altagracia, Rivas
December 7	Immaculate Conception (celebrated in many towns) Images of the Virgin are carried from house to house, and offerings of food are made to the holy visitors.
December 12	León
December 25	Christmas everywhere, town celebrations in Masaya and Estelí
December 31	Catarina

And this is not to mention Doctors' Day, Translators' Day, Journalists' Day, and several other quite notable Days when the person you seek might not be available.

6
ON YOUR WAY

GETTING TO NICARAGUA

BY AIR

GATEWAYS

Managua is a direct, non-stop destination from Miami and Houston.

In addition, through routings (with stops en route) are available from Miami, Houston, Mexico City and San Salvador.

From the eastern part of the United States or Canada, or from major cities in the west, it's usually possible to reach Managua in a day.

FARES

American Airlines quotes a round-trip fare of about $725 to $900 between New York and Managua, and $575 between Miami and Managua.

These are at the *high end* of the fare spectrum. Off-brand Central American airlines, such as Taca, generally charge less, or have fewer restrictions at a given fare, from points that they serve directly.

Major airlines that have service to Managua, such as Continental and American, can more readily quote a *through fare*.

75

WHO FLIES TO MANAGUA?

American Airlines
800-433-7300
Miami non-stop
New York and major U.S. cities (via Miami)

Nica
800-831-6422
Miami non-stop

Lacsa Airlines
800-225-2272
Miami non-stop
San José, Costa Rica

Continental
800-525-0280
Houston

Taca
800-535-8780
New York, Miami, Houston via San Salvador

Mexicana
800-531-7921
New York, Denver, etc. via Mexico City

COPA
Panama

Iberia
800-772-4642
Madrid
Miami

Aeroflot
Moscow via Havana

Aviateca
800-327-9832
Miami (two stops)
San Francisco via Guatemala

VALUE ADDED

While fares aren't as competitive to Nicaragua as to some other countries, you can sometimes jiggle extra value out of what you pay.

• **Seat sales, advance purchase, weekend travel** and the like can bring down the price you'll have to pay. While regular fares tend to be somewhat higher on Continental and American Airlines, it pays to shop these brands for last-minute specials when they have unsold seats.

- **Stopovers** can give you an extra destination or two for the price of a ticket from here to there. From time to time, the Central American airlines—Taca, Lacsa and Aviateca—offer a flat rate pass that allows you to visit most of the countries in the region.

- **Children's fares** are half those of adults on international routes. If you're travelling with kids, going abroad might be cheaper than heading to a domestic destination.

- **Frequent flyer** points are available not only on major U.S. carriers, but through lower-priced Central American airlines as well, through Latin Pass. Latin Pass points are redeemable on USAir, and vice-versa.

- **Round-trip** tickets are generally cheaper to start with; but they also save discomfiting questions from immigration officials about when you intend to leave the country, and by what means; as well as unpleasant surprises in the way of taxes if you have to buy a ticket in Managua.

CHARTER FLIGHTS

Charters operate to Managua weekly during the northern winter from Montreal, Canada, and occasionally from European cities as well. These serve passengers booking a package vacation at Montelimar, Nicaragua's premier beach resort; but they sometimes have room for passengers on an air-only basis, and last-minute fares can be quite low.

Charter flights are *not* booked through the airline, but through a travel agency, often one specializing in package vacations. The travel agency has to contact the airline that operates the flight. Flights from Montreal are usually operated by Royal Airlines, tel. 514-739-7000.

DRIVING

Figure about two thousand miles, four or five borders (depending on your route) and a week as a minimum if you're driving from the southern tip of Texas to Nicaragua. Two weeks is more like it, if you stop anywhere on the way, as you should. That's a lot of travel, and a lot of paperwork, but if you've got the time, and can't do without your car, here are some considerations:

ROUTES:

At this time, the easiest route is along the Gulf of Mexico, then crossing the isthmus of Tehuantepec to follow the Pacific coast highway through southern Mexico, avoiding highland Chiapas.

El Salvador is probably a safe drive-through, but you can eliminate a couple of border crossings, at a price in driving distance, by swinging around through Honduras.

CAR CONCERNS.

It helps to have four-wheel drive and high clearance for travel on the sparse, rough roads of eastern Nicaragua. But for most travel, a sedan in good condition is adequate.

Preventive maintenance is crucial. Good tires and a couple of spares, clean fuel injectors, serviceable belts and hoses, will help make the trip worry-free.

Extras that you might not use for travel at home include a gasoline can, water can, two spare tires, spare belts and hoses, and basic tools.

DOCUMENTS AND BORDERS

You'll need your driver's license and vehicle registration. No international license is required either by Nicaragua or by the countries you'll transit from the States.

Most countries require **visas** for overland travel. Verify requirements before you get to the border!

Official border hours are usually from 8 a.m. to noon and 2 p.m. to 6 p.m. You can cross at other times, but you pay for the privilege.

ENTRY PERMITS

You can keep your own vehicle in Nicaragua for 30 days without incurring customs duties. After that, you have to obtain an extension from Customs in Managua (Dirección General de Aduanas, Km. 4½ Carretera Norte, tel. [2]493151); or leave the country.

MEXICO SPECIAL CONCERNS

Mexico imposes hefty transit fees on cars in transit to Central America. Declare your destination as Mexico only, and take at least five days to cross to Guatemala; or pay the fees.

Going

POINTS OF ENTRY

By Air Augusto César Sandino International Airport, Managua
By Land El Espino, Guasaule and Las Manos (Honduras)
Peñas Blancas (Costa Rica)
By Sea Corinto, Puerto Sandino and San Juan del Sur (Pacific)
El Bluff and Puerto Cabezas (Caribbean)

INSURANCE
Liability coverage is available in each country.

MAPS
See page 71.

BUS

- "First-class," Greyhound-type buses operate through Mexico to the border of Guatemala. The Cristóbal Colón line (southern terminal, Mexico City) offers through service to Guatemala City. Continuing service is available in stages from the terminal in each Central American capital.

- Cheaper "second-class" buses, sometimes with standing room only, offer cheaper, slower service from border to capital in each country.

- Count on a day per country of travel time from Mexico City southward, no matter how long or short the trip in kilometers.

- Visas are required for most countries en route, which could delay your travel.

GETTING AROUND

BY AIR

Several local airlines provide service in small planes from Augusto César Sandino International Airport to towns on the Caribbean coast, the Corn Islands, and even to San Carlos, on the far side of Lake Nicaragua, and to remote villages in Mosquitia. The fare all the way to Corn Island is about $60 one way.

The terminal for **domestic** service is at the western end of the main airport building (toward Managua).

La Costeña airlines, tel. 632142, serves San Carlos, Bluefields, Puerto Cabezas, and the Corn Islands, with several departures daily to the coast.

W+G Aero Servicios, serves Puerto Cabezas, Corn Island and Bluefields.

Tickets should be purchased three days in advance, if possible, either through a travel agency, or at the domestic airport terminal.

Recent schedules for some flights are given in the coverage of towns in this book.

BY BUS

Nicaragua's intercity buses are all of the old school-bus type. Some actually *are* old American school buses that have achieved public bus status, some were *born* as public-service buses in Central American factories, and some have had public service in Nicaragua thrust upon them after service in Costa Rica or Belize or what was the Soviet Union.

Whatever the pedigree, there are certain lasting verities about the public bus service in Nicaragua and the heroic units that ply the routes, among which are:

- Service is frequent. On most routes in the most densely populated area, from the Costa Rican border to Managua to León, buses run about every hour.

- Buses are crowded and uncomfortable. Bench seats have little padding, are spaced closely, passengers are packed three to a bench.

- Fares are low. Figure about two cents per kilometer of bus travel.

Going

- Buses are a daytime operation. With few exceptions, you can't count on travelling after sunset. Get an early start to your day.

- Buses are slow, not because the drivers take their time, but because they make many stops to let out and pick up passengers. But many places of interest are not far from Managua.

HOW TO TAKE A BUS

- Head for the bus terminal. Get there early, an hour before you intend to travel.

In Managua, bus terminals are located at major city markets. Specifics are given in the Managua chapter. *Exception*: Buses for Costa Rica have their own small terminals in Managua, and use larger buses than domestic companies.

In outlying towns, buses stop at a specific street corner, usually near a market.

- You can flag down a bus somewhere along its route, but don't count on finding a seat if you don't board at the terminal.

- Take limited luggage. Store what you can at your hotel in Managua. What you can't fit on a shelf inside the bus or under your seat, will be packed in the cargo rack on top, with baskets of fruit, and crates, and cardboard boxes full of merchandise, and the overflow of chickens from the passenger cabin. Which means that your goods will be out of view.

- Try to get a seat near the front of the bus, for less shaking. A seat on the aisle provides some extra leg room.

- Don't eat too heavily, and don't drink more than a minimal amount before you travel. There are no rest rooms on board, and no pit stops. Use the nearest toilet before you get aboard. (This is a *practical* guide.)

DRIVING

There's Pacific Nicaragua and highland Nicaragua and remote Eastern Nicaragua, and what you're driving, or should drive, depends on where you're going.

Pacific Nicaragua, the most heavily populated part of the country, can be tackled without safari-type preparation. Roads are two lanes wide, winding at times, but nothing different from what one might deal with from time to time in North America or Europe. The road between Managua and Masaya is often congested. Elsewhere, trucks will slow traffic on narrow main roads in stretches that are too winding for safe overtaking; but mostly, heavy traffic is not a problem.

Highland Nicaragua is more of a back-country experience. The region is far less densely settled than the Pacific plain. Gasoline stations are sparse, and many of the roads, aside from the northern branch of the Pan American Highway, are unpaved and rutted. Four-wheel drive is useful for any exploring.

Caribbean Nicaragua hardly has any roads, save the route to Rama, whence the ferry on the Escondido River departs for Bluefields; and a track over hill and through rain forest to Puerto Cabezas.

Here are some general indications and advice for driving in Nicaragua:

- **Road signs** are generally adequate in the towns of the Pacific plain. Directional signs near the main square indicate the route toward the next town in any direction. But routes are not marked with numbers, nor are some key intersections outside major towns.

Therefore, *ask for directions* at any intersection if you're not sure where you're going. A filling station is usually your best bet. People standing by the roadside may never have been far from home, and out of politeness, might give you an encouraging confirmation of whatever you suggest.

While you're at it, inquire about *road conditions*. Unpaved roads, especially, are subject to washouts and seasonal conditions.

- **Driving is cheap and expensive.** Gasoline costs about $2.50 per gallon, about double what it does in the States. But most rental vehicles are small, and distances are short in the Pacific plain.

- **Protected parking** and **car-watchers** are available wherever you might stop or park for the night. Use them! It's worth a small fee. And never leave anything valuable in your car.

- Your **local driving license** is valid for a temporary visit to Nicaragua.

Going

HAZARDS AND JOYS

What's the most picturesque aspect of driving in Nicaragua? Maybe its the mountains; or the curves always framing a new view, a new surprise; or the oxcarts laden with corn or straw or sugarcane, lumbering along in the right of way shared with motorists.

What's the most hazardous aspect of driving in Nicaragua? Maybe its the mountains; or the curves always framing a new view, a new surprise; or the oxcarts laden with corn or straw or sugarcane, lumbering along in the right of way shared with motorists.

Other items to look out for are:

- potholes
- a tree branch on the road, indicating a stalled vehicle ahead
- pedestrians in the streets everywhere in Managua selling useful trinkets, and celebrants anywhere else, who have had too much to drink
- nighttime driving: never, ever a good idea in an unfamiliar land.
- checkpoints. Stop at any police post, where your license and automobile papers are subject to inspection.
- narrow mountain roads. Yield to oncoming uphill traffic.

RENTAL VEHICLES

Rental vehicles are readily available in Managua. See page 167 for names and addresses of rental companies.

Rates vary from company to company and season to season, but here are some ball park rates:

- mini-car, such as Toyota Starlet, from $150 per week
- compact car, such as a Tercel, from $220 per week
- mid-size car, from $260 per week

Rentals by the day cost more, and usually carry a mileage charge.

Tax (15%) and **insurance** are additional. In some cases, insurance charges can be almost as high as the rental fee. Check with your credit-card company about basic coverage. Insurance that comes with credit cards usually does not provide liability coverage.

HOW FAR TO . . . ?
DISTANCES IN NICARAGUA

NORTHEAST FROM MANAGUA TO

Tipitapa	22 km	El Rama	293
Boaco	88	San Carlos	300
Juigalpa	139	Puerto Cabezas	557
Nueva Guinea	283		

NORTHWEST (PACIFIC) FROM MANAGUA TO

León	93	Chinandega	132
Chichigalpa	122	Corinto	152

EAST AND SOUTHEAST FROM MANAGUA TO

Masaya	29	Rivas	111
Granada	45	San Juan del Sur	141
Jinotepe	46	Peñas Blancas (Costa Rica)	147
Pochomil	62		

NORTH FROM MANAGUA TO

Sébaco	103	Jinotega	162
Matagalpa	130	Somoto	216
Estelí	148		

> Call major rental car companies to verify rates and reserve before you leave home. Sometimes seasonal specials are available that you won't be able to get on-the-spot.

HITCHING

Hitchhiking doesn't carry the cachet of youthful adventure in Nicaragua that it does in North America and Europe. Rather, it's a straightforward necessity for many Nicaraguans of humble circumstance.

In a country short of public transport, men and women of all ages put out their thumbs along the highways, rather than wait for a bus that has available seats (which can mean not travelling at all).

So if you hitch, you won't stand out like a sore thumb, but you should follow the rule of thumb, which is to offer payment when you're let out. The proper words are, "*¿Cuánto le debo?*" ("How much do I owe you?") You might get a polite demurral ("*nada*"—"nothing"), but it's equally polite to press *something* on the driver, perhaps the equivalent of a dollar or two between two large towns.

TAXIS

The road conditions are unfamiliar, the buses are crowded and uncomfortable, the tours don't go where you want to go when you want to go.

What's a traveller to do?

In Nicaragua, take a taxi.

Taking into account the daily rate of a car rental, insurance, tax, and fuel, you can probably save money by hiring a taxi. Consider an excursion from Managua to Masaya Volcano for two or three hours. Renting a car for the day would cost $40 at least, not to mention time spent making arrangements. You can probably walk out on the street, flag down a mini-taxi, and negotiate a price of about $25 or $30; or somewhat more if you use a taxi from the stand in front of your hotel.

You'll need a minimum amount of Spanish—the name of the place you're heading to, and a few numbers. And you can't expect your driver to be a complete guide, though any taxi driver is a fount of local wisdom.

In some cases, collective taxis are available for runs between major towns. Inquire in the area of bus stations. Otherwise, it's a charter trip ("*viaje expreso*"), but still at a reasonable price for a few people travelling together—figure a dollar per kilometer as the very top rate. You'll usually pay less.

Within Managua, taxis are plentiful, and usually inexpensive. See page 158.

TRAINS

Train service is no more in Nicaragua.

The trains stopped running just a couple of years ago, and are already sorely missed. They were the cheapest way to get from Managua to León and Granada, but the deficit was hopeless, and the neglected system beyond repair at any affordable price.

And now, a couple of years after the demise, the old track bed is visible from the main roads, but that is all. Rails have been pried up and sold, ties chopped and burned.

The railroad can never come back. But it's remembered with affection.

In a quite spontaneous manner, the station in Masatepe has been put into service as a crafts center, and no doubt, the beautiful buildings elsewhere on the line will be put to similar good use.

RETURNING HOME

Departure tax at Managua airport is $12, payable in U.S. currency.

CUSTOMS

U.S. citizens can bring home goods to a value of $400 without incurring duty. A quart of liquor and 200 cigarettes can be included in this amount. Duty is collected on the value of imports over $400. But many Nicaraguan goods, such as handicrafts, might qualify for exemption under the Caribbean Basin Trade Initiative. If you intend to return with a load of handicrafts, check with Customs before you go.

Canadian customs allows three tiers of exemption. Choose from a $50 one-day exemption; a $200 exemption for an absence of two days from Canada; or a $500 exemption that can be claimed only once per year. Duty-free goods can include 1.1 liters (40 imperial ounces) of liquor, and 200 cigarettes.

TOUCHY STUFF

It isn't difficult in Nicaragua to acquire goods made from turtle shell, black coral, alligator, and other protected species and substances. Even if protective legislation goes into place, enforcement is likely to be spotty.

This won't excuse you, however, if U.S. or Canadian customs finds items made of controlled substances in your luggage. So avoid the black coral, tortoiseshell, and rare skins. It's not the same as drug smuggling, but the goods could be confiscated, and you might even be delayed with a criminal charge. Who needs it?

Live animals, such as birds, can be exported only with the permission of the Ministry of Natural Resources (*Recursos Naturales*, MARENA). Technically, permission is also required for commercial export of anything made from wild animals.

7
WHAT CAN YOU DO IN NICARAGUA?

SOME ACTIVITIES FOR VISITORS

WATCH THE NATIONAL SPORT—BEISBOL!

The U.S. Marines who periodically "restored order" in Nicaragua left simmering resentments that still resonate in Nicaraguan politics, and one pastime that became incorporated into Nicaraguan life and character: baseball.

In almost every country of the world except the United States, the common athletic denominator is football (*fut, fútbol, soccer*). But in Nicaragua, it's *beis*.

In any alleyway, in the middle of any lightly trafficked street, on empty lots and on diamonds, kids and grown-ups are out and batting away with Louisville sluggers, home-made bats, and broomsticks. Stickball as I knew it may have been overwhelmed in the States by cable t.v., organized activities and nefarious pursuits, but it's thriving among Nicaraguans who see in baseball and its permutations not necessarily an escape from poverty into the *grandes ligas*, but pure pleasure.

The tallest structures in downtown Managua are the light towers at the baseball stadium.

And the greatest event in recent Nicaraguan life was not the the 1990 election or the visit of the Pope, but the world amateur baseball championship in Managua.

Yet the baseball name most associated with this land of volcanoes is not that of a Nicaraguan, but of Puerto Rican Roberto Clemente, star outfielder with the Pittsburgh Pirates.

Clemente had played in a championship series in Nicaragua in 1972, and was moved by the gentility of the people, and their warmth, good humor and generosity. He was particularly affected by a barefoot boy who gave him an iguana of his own, after one thrown onto the field during a game had given the Pirate slugger a fright.

A few weeks later, when news of the tragic Christmas earthquake of 1972 reached Puerto Rico, Clemente set out to raise funds, and collect food, medicines and blankets for the stricken people. Clemente chartered a plane and personally accompanied the relief shipment . . . and perished when the plane crashed in the Caribbean on its way to Nicaragua.

CRUISE TO A TROPIC ISLE

Nicaragua's little-known, idyllic, unspoiled, isolated, undeveloped, palm-shaded corner of the Caribbean is called the Corn Islands. The few—very few—vacationers who have heard of them usually fly from Managua. Or, the intrepid look for a working cargo-and-passenger boat in the port of Bluefields.

But you *can* cruise to Great Corn and Little Corn in style. In addition to regular visits by coastal vessels, the 80-passenger M/V Polaris calls at the islands several times each winter. Passengers go ashore, and snorkel at nearby reefs, as part of a cruise that includes the Bay Islands and Panama. For information, contact Special Expeditions, 720 Fifth Avenue, New York, NY 10019, tel. 800-762-0003 or 212-765-7740, fax 212-265-3770. Other vessels on Caribbean cruises make occasional—very occasional—visits as well. Check with a travel agency that specializes in cruises.

Activities

... OR ON A TROPICAL RIVER

The San Juan River flows out of Lake Nicaragua and runs 200 kilometers through virtually uninhabited lands and obscure but hugely significant chapters of history to the Caribbean.

This was an invasion route for pirates and the British navy in colonial times; the route by which many an American reached California during the gold rush days; and the scene of clandestine crossings from Costa Rica during the Contra war against the Sandinista administration of Nicaragua.

And yet, the San Juan remains a remote, unspoiled river passing through rain forest that is still largely undisturbed, holding plant species and insects that are still being discovered.

In the way of Nicaragua, formal, touristy boats have not yet gone into operation on the San Juan, with all their comforts and high prices. Yet the river is eminently cruiseable. All you have to do is get to San Carlos, the port village at the southeast corner of Lake Nicaragua, by air or bus (see page 256).

From there, you'll find long, flat-bottomed cargo boats that regularly head downriver to El Castillo, and even onward, to San Juan del Norte on the Caribbean. It's like hitching a ride on the bed of a pickup—you might get a seat on a bench, or you might have to sit on a sack of produce, but travel you will, and for a reasonable price. And in case a boat happens not to be headed your way, you can always engage a speedy outboard motorboat to take you downriver—which is equivalent to picking up a taxi.

Aside from monkeys howling in the trees along the river, and flocks of toucans on their way from here to there, and coatis scrambling through the brush, you might spy a shark headed the other way. The famous creatures haven't been seen lately, but don't jump in the water. You never know.

CATCH A FISH

Nicaragua has lakes and rivers, and the lakes and rivers are full of fish.

The Isletas (islets) of Lake Nicaragua, near Granada, support colonies of fishermen, and sport fishing for guapote, machaca and smaller species is said to be good from the Solentiname and Zapatera islands.

Pesky tarpon, considered by many the fightingest sport fish, can be found in the River San Juan. The tarpon season is generally from January through June. Other sporting species found near the mouth of the San Juan, and in lagoons northward along the coast, are snook (best January through June); its junior relative, called the calba; and machaca and guapote and mojarra, the latter resembling a bluegill; as well as mullet and jack crevalle.

For huge marlin, sailfish and swordfish, a few charter boats are available at San Juan del Sur, the port on Nicaragua's southern Pacific coast. Arrangements can also be made at Montelimar, the resort south of Managua. Peak season is usually from April through August. Also along this coast are schools of barracuda, yellowfin tuna, bonito, dorado (mahi-mahi), roosterfish, wahoo, rainbow runner, snappers, jacks, grouper, and corvina, or sea bass. Tuna are best caught in December and January, roosterfish from February through July, and snapper from May through August.

Charter fishing boats usually have all the gear you need for deep-sea angling. But if you want to try your hand at fishing for guapote, mojarra, or other smaller species, take along a lightweight rod and reel.

HUNT

Hunting *is permitted* in Nicaragua, but is strictly regulated, and conditions under which visitors may hunt are subject to change. Some animals, certain protected areas of the country, and specific weapons are off limits.

If you're thinking about hunting, contact a Nicaraguan consulate for the latest information. Arms may be imported only with the permission of the Ministry of Defense, and with the approval of the commander of the National Police, the Ministry of the Interior (*Gobernación*), and the Ministry of Civil Security. Up to 200 cartridges, a pistol, and hunting rifle can be brought in free of duty, if the necessary permits are obtained.

Off-limits to hunters are most cats (including jaguars), manatees, crocodiles, tapirs, sea turtles, monkeys and other tree mammals, and an assortment of birds that includes macaws, quetzals, wild turkeys and eagles.

Specifically *permitted* to be hunted, at this time, are white-tailed deer, peccary, agoutis and tepezcuintles, rabbits, armadillos, iguanas, doves, quail, and ducks.

GO TO SCHOOL

The University of Mobile (Alabama), a Baptist institution, has a Latin American Campus at San Marcos, Carazo, in the coffee country about 40 kilometers south of Managua. It's a small, modern institution that attracts students from throughout the isthmus who want to follow an accredited American program and live a U.S.-campus life . . . in English! The student

Activities

body also includes matriculants from the Alabama campus, and transient students. Spanish is not required as a prerequisite, or even in course work for most students.

Facilities include a computer lab, language lab, playing fields, chemistry and physics labs, library with over 120,000 books, and dormitories—all in all, comparable to the installations of a junior-sized college in the States. The school opened in 1993 on the renovated site of a teacher-training school.

Degree programs are offered in business, English, Latin American studies, computer science, environmental technology, and marketing, among others. An M.B.A. program is planned.

Tuition runs $3100 per semester, plus $1315 for room and board. For an application, contact University of Mobile, San Marcos, Carazo, Nicaragua, tel. (43)22314, fax (43)22336, in English. Students may enroll by the semester, and Spanish-as-a-second-language instruction can also be arranged.

SHOP!

In the great old Central American tradition, Nicaragua has towns that *specialize*, not anonymous, shopping-center suburbs. One town is a center of learning, another processes coffee, another services the cattle industry. One town makes pottery, another creates garments of homespun cotton, yet another is known for its woodworking or hammocks.

It would be ingenuous to think that a hand-made belt, an embroidered dress, a reproduction of a pre-Columbian ceramic could actually compete in the marketplace today with a locally made plastic product, or one imported from the sweatshops of the far east.

Nor are there sufficient tourists in Nicaragua to provide sustenance for the hundreds or even thousands of small-scale producers of handicrafts.

And yet, there they are.

So what are we to conclude? That Nicaraguans, despite their limited resources, have an appreciation and a preference for the products of their own tradition; that they will pay more than they absolutely have to, to buy what is authentically their own; that they are proud, and know who they are.

Oh, you'll see an occasional Guatemalan belt or weaving in the Masaya stands and the markets of Managua, but nowhere near the predominance of imports that passes for souvenirs in Costa Rica. Mostly, when you buy a handicraft in Nicaragua, you're buying, and supporting, authenticity. And the price is right.

What can you buy? In Managua, you can buy everything from all around the country. Elsewhere, you are likely to find the specialty of a town, and of the nearby villages.

In Masaya, clothing, leatherwork (belts, visors, sandals, purses), silver jewelry, woodware (including items made from fine hardwoods such as rosewood, lignum vitae, and amaranth), hemp (mats, macramé, hammocks), shoes, pre-Columbian ceramic reproductions, *cotonas* (native-style formal shirts) and embroidered shifts, and palm and palm- thatch items, including baskets

In San Juan de Oriente, reproductions and adaptations of red-hued pre-Columbian pottery . . . plates, pots, planters and more.

In Granada and the Pueblos Blancos ("White Villages"), embroidery, wicker furniture, shoes.

In León, formal shirts (*cotonas*), embroidered wall hangings.

In La Paz Centro, red pottery and incised cow-horn

In Diriamba, Güegüense dolls, and seashell creations

In Jinotega and Matagalpa, black pottery

In Estelí, leather furniture

In San Juan de Limay, Estelí department, carvings in white stone

And this is just a start.

Aside from market goods, some of the local tourist trinkets are above the standard that you'll usually find. How about tee shirts of unbleached cotton?

Then there are the everyday finds to be had in any Managua supermarket: hot pepper sauces; coffee; canned heart of palm (palmito) and other tropical delicacies.

And don't forget Nicaragua's world-beating rum, Flor de Caña, at the duty-free shop.

GAMBLE

Gaming is available, to a limited and tame degree, in casinos and clubs in Managua. The action is generally limited to a variation of blackjack, but some locales have craps and slots.

The most conveniently located casino is at Josephine's Elite Club, a block south of the Inter-Continental Hotel. Others are mentioned in the nightlife section of the Managua chapter.

Activities

VISIT THE NATIONAL PARKS

When it comes to intentions to protect its natural riches from over-utilization and destruction, Nicaragua—surprisingly—is among the leading nations of Latin America. According to recent figures, there are 71 protected areas of one sort or another, totalling 21,538 square kilometers, or 17 percent of the country's area.

Of course, regulating these areas effectively in a country scarce of resources is another matter. Woodcutting and hunting go on where they're not supposed to. Nor, in most cases, are there trails, camping areas, or visitors' centers. But a start has been made.

Take a look at a map of protected areas, and you'll see that they include samples of *all* of Nicaragua: Pacific beaches, virtually all of the volcanic peaks, dense lowland rain forest along the border of Costa Rica, mountain ridges above the Coco River, and spots of temperate forest in near Matagalpa.

Among the protected areas are these:

- **Masaya Volcano National Park** (Parque Nacional Volcán Masaya), the leading visitors' volcano in the region. See page 75 for a full description.

- **Zapatera Archipelago National Park** (Parque Nacional Archipiélago Zapatera) at Puerto Asese, near Granada, takes in Zapatera Island in Lake Nicaragua, where significant pre-Columbian carvings have been discovered (see page 195).

- **Chacocente Wildlife Refuge** (Refugio de Vida Silvestre Chacocente) along the Pacific, known for its howler monkeys and turtle nesting (see page 212).

- **Parque Nacional Agateyte**, which takes in San Cristóbal Volcano.

- **Río Manares Nature Reserve**.

- **Volcán Maderas** (volcano) **Biological Reserve**.

MORE PRACTICAL INFORMATION

Here's an assortment of practical information, tips, and useful observations for your trip to Nicaragua.

BUSINESS HOURS

There are no fixed rules, but stores in Managua generally open at 8:30 or 9 a.m. and stay open throughout the day. Some businesses take a break from 11:30 a.m. or noon to 1:30 or 2 p.m., but the midday rest is not as generalized as in other countries in the region. Many businesses are open on Saturday only in the morning.

Government offices vary in their working hours. Some open early and work through until early afternoon; others open from 8 a.m. to noon and again from 1 to 5 p.m. Government offices are officially closed on Saturday, though bureaucrats sometimes show up to polish off a work load.

Outside of Managua, where life follows more traditional patterns, it's not unusual to close up a shop for a couple of hours in the middle of the day.

COST OF LIVING

All things considered, Nicaragua's a fairly inexpensive place in which to travel. The services that visitors are likely to use generally cost less than in the States.

For specific prices, look at the chapters on Managua and other destinations. You'll see that mid-range hotel rooms cost from $40 to $60, and budget lodging can be found for under $10 per person. A luxury room will cost from $150 to $200 with tax.

As for food, sit-down meals run at least $10 per person in formal restaurants in Managua, less in basic places or in smaller towns.

In a general way . . .

WHAT COSTS MORE THAN IN THE STATES?

- Imported wine and spirits
- Manufactured products (cassette players, appliances, etc.)
- Cosmetics
- Automobile parts

Practical Details

- Gasoline
- Rents for housing in Managua when equipped to U.S. standards
- Good clothing
- Many processed and packaged foods

WHAT COSTS LESS THAN IN THE STATES?

- Fresh fruits and vegetables in season
- Beef
- Coffee and beverages
- Buses (about 2 cents per kilometer)
- Taxi rides
- Local airline flights
- Domestic liquor and beer
- Domestic labor
- Cigarettes
- Handicrafts

WHAT COSTS ABOUT THE SAME AS IN THE STATES?

- Automobile rental

ELECTRICITY

Nicaragua's electricity is 110 volts alternating current. Plugs are flat-pronged as in the U.S. and Canada, but sockets generally will not accept a grounding prong.

However . . . if you've brought along a hair dryer or computer, inquire about the voltage and frequency before you plug anything in.

Blackouts and **brownouts** are part of daily life in Managua—there's just not enough electricity to go around, so it's not unusual to lose the lights for a half hour or more at a time.

If you're sitting in a restaurant when the lights go out, conversation all around you will go on without missing a beat. The waiter will bring out candles and the ambience will improve immediately.

MENU SPANISH

Comida Típica (Nicaraguan Food)

Charraca	pork skin.
Chiles rellenos	stuffed peppers.
Fritangas	strips of fried vegetables
Gallo pinto	rice and beans with herbs and spices
Maduros	fried plantains
Mondongo	tripe soup.
Nacatamal	filled corn dumplings, steamed in banana leaves, similar to Mexican *tamales*.
Patacones	mashed plantain fritters
Pipas	young juice coconuts
Tajadas	deep-fried plantain chips
Tiste	beverage made from ground tortillas and cacao
Tortillas	classic corn flat-cakes; fold 'em, fill 'em, fry 'em, enjoy 'em.

Vigorón *yuca* (a root vegetable) with pork rind and greens, served in a banana leaf.

Meal times

Desayuno	breakfast
Almuerzo	lunch
Cena	dinner

continued

For most people and businesses, life does not depend on having totally reliable electricity. No pipes will freeze, no side of beef will thaw and spoil.

Most larger hotels have their own generators, which, if they don't supply power to the entire establishment, will keep the restaurant and front desk illuminated.

Practical Details

FOOD

What's Nicaraguan food like? You could well get the impression from a visit that Nicaraguans eat just the way Americans do; but you'd be wrong.

Nicaraguans have their own cuisine. But what they eat at home is not at all the same as what they eat in restaurants. Those who can afford to eat out enjoy a change of pace. So let's separate the two cuisines.

RESTAURANT FOOD

"International food," or "*comida internacional*," is how Nicaraguans describe restaurant food. It's a pretty meaningless term, but in the Nicaraguan context, it's a way of saying that you won't get Nicaraguan soul food.

What you *will* get is what Nicaraguans eat on special occasions, and what that usually means is steak—grilled steak (*bistec a la parrilla*), grilled sirloin (*lomo*), steak smothered with onions (*bistec encebollado*), steak with spices, the house steak, Châteaubriand, "filet miñón," and the like. It's not extra-special fancy or delicate, but it's something you can cut into and chew.

In case you like something different, there's grilled chicken, chicken with spices, house chicken, and the like; and the same goes for pork. When fish is available, the modes of preparation are once again rather standard: in garlic sauce, breaded, fried, or *a la veracruzana* (in a spicy tomato sauce).

Let me venture to say that for most visitors, this is fairly good news. What you'll find in restaurants is likely to be wholesome, uncomplicated, and nourishing.

Often, you'll get familiar dishes served in Nicaraguan style. Your side dish is likely to be rice, rather than potatoes. Garlic and onion will be present in the spices. And your vegetable might be peas or beets, but it could just as well be beans, fried plantain, *chayote*, or yucca.

COMIDA TÍPICA

Let me assure you that there *is* a real Nicaraguan cuisine. It has something in common with Mexican food, and a family resemblance to the cuisines of Honduras and Guatemala. But some of the food specialties are strictly local.

The first place to look for *comida típica* ("typical," or native-style food) is in somebody's home. But if you're not lucky enough to make friends

Nicaragua Guide

Staples

arroz	rice	(de naranja)	(orange)
atún	tuna	langosta	lobster
avena	oatmeal	leche	milk
bistec	beef	lomito	sirloin
café	coffee	mantequilla	butter
calamar	squid	mermelada	marmalade
camarón	shrimp	milanesa	breaded (veal
carne	meat		or beef)
cerveza	beer	naranja	orange
ceviche	marinated fish cocktail	omelete	omelet
		pan	bread
chorizo	sausage	papa	potato
chuleta (de cerdo)	(pork) chop	(frita, al horno, puré)	
churrasco	charcoal-broiled meat	(French-fried, baked, mashed)	
		pastel	cake
coco	coconut	pescado	fish
corvina	sea bass	piña	pineapple
dorado	dolphinfish (mahi-mahi)	plátanos	plantains
		pollo	chicken
ensalada	salad	pozol	corn soup
filete	filet	queso	cheese
frijol	bean	refresco	beverage
frito	fried	ron	rum
fruta	fruit	salsa picante	hot sauce
helado	ice cream	sopa	soup
huevos	eggs	té	tea
jamón	ham	tostadas	toast
jugo	juice	vino	wine

Practical Details

with a Nicaraguan, head for the markets. Otherwise, try a roadside stand, or one of the very few restaurants in Managua that proudly serve Central American food.

Here are some of the items you might find:

- *Nacatamal*. Elsewhere in Central America, *tamales* are a festive food, invariably made with turkey cooked in a spicy broth. But in Nicaragua, *nacatamales* (a more purely Nahuatl word, but the same idea) are an everyday celebration of what's available in the market. Usually included is some kind of meat, often pork, mixed with potatoes and a tomato-based sauce, all wrapped in corn dough and steamed in a banana leaf, which also serves as a disposable plate.

- *Tortillas*. The classic flat-cake of Mesoamerican cuisine, always made with ground, lime-treated corn. Tortillas are eaten as they are, or in myriad combinations, foldings, and fry-ups, with or without fillings.

- *Vigorón*, a name redolent of vitamins and strength, is yuca (a root vegetable eaten much as a potato) with pork rind and greens, served at many a roadside and market stand in a banana leaf.

- *Mondongo* is tripe soup.

- *Charraca* is the local word for chicharrón, or pork skin.

- *Fritangas* are strips of fried vegetables, usually sold at open-air stands. *Chiles rellenos* are stuffed peppers.

- *Gallo pinto* is rice and beans (literally "spotted rooster"), often spiced with garlic and fresh coriander. Delicious, and sometimes eaten at breakfast. Other vegetables are *yuca* (yucca), a starchy and somewhat fibrous root vegetable served in much the same way as potatoes; and *chayote* (variously known as vegetable pear or chocho in English), a green vine vegetable with cream-colored flesh and large, edible seeds, usually boiled but sometimes mashed.

- *Tiste* is a beverage made from ground tortillas (corn flat cakes) and cacao, served cool or at room temperature. It has something in common with Mexican *atol*.

- *Pipas* are young juice coconuts, sometimes sold at roadside stands. Other fruits you may come across are *zapote*, brown on the outside, with a delicious reddish flesh, mangos, *marañón* (cashew fruit), and many, many others. Plantains (cooking bananas) come in many forms:

as *tajadas* (deep-fried chips), *maduros* (fried, and served as a vegetable), or as *patacones* (mashed plantain fritters).

- *Salsa picante*—hot sauce—is a staple on most restaurant tables, usually in store-bought, prepared form.

FOREIGN FOOD

It's mainly in Managua that you'll find foreign cuisines. Italian is the most popular sort, both in formal restaurants, and in pizzerias, of which there is one in every shopping center.

As in the United States, really fine food is French food, and there are several quite credible restaurants with French main courses, as well as a couple of German establishments.

Outside of Managua, you'll find an occasional pizzeria or Chinese restaurant; and the fine dining at the Montelimar beach resort; otherwise, it's back to "international food."

SERVICE

Service is good in Nicaraguan restaurants, but it's much less intrusive than in North America. Your waiter will not keep rushing over and asking if everything is okay. When you want water, or another beer, or the bill, signal or ask for it, and you will get it. You'll never be rushed to the door.

TAX AND TIP

The standard 15 percent sales tax applies to restaurant bills, and 10 percent is often added as a service charge. It's not obligatory to pay the latter, but it's difficult not to; and you needn't leave anything in addition, unless service has been beyond the call of duty.

WINE AND BEER AND LIQUOR

Wines are *not* widely available in Nicaragua, though you can get a decent bottle of Chilean or California at a hotel or good restaurant in Managua.

Beer comes in limited variety in most of Nicaragua. Victoria is a full-strength beer, with a perfectly acceptable taste—nothing offbeat or individualistic about it. It costs less than a dollar in most restaurants. Toña is a low-alcohol beer.

Practical Details

That's all the choice you're likely to get, except at some of the higher-priced hotels and eating places in Managua, where you can find U.S. brands and other imported beers.

As for **liquor** . . . Flor de Caña, the local brand of **rum**, is excellent. It comes light, dark, young, aged, and everything in between, with tastes and textures ranging from aquavit-like to smooth and mellow. Bet you never knew there was so much range in rum!

Imported liquors are not available everywhere, so bring along a duty-free bottle of your favorite, if it's important to you.

Bottled sodas, with such familiar brand names as Pepsi and Coca-Cola, are available everywhere in Nicaragua.

HEALTH?

Check with a local tropical disease center, or call the Communicable Disease Hotline in Atlanta (404-332-4555), to see if there are any late advisories concerning Nicaragua.

In any case:

- Keep up to date on immunizations for tetanus, polio and the like.

- Arrange for immunization against typhoid or cholera *if recommended*, and against hepatitis if you plan extensive off-the-beaten-track travel. But the **best protection** is to eat foods that have been well cooked from plates that have been washed in hot water, and to drink bottled or hot beverages.

- Take along any medicines you use regularly.

- Take an extra set of prescription eyeglasses.

- Take anti-malarial medication, such as chloroquine, once a week if headed toward the Caribbean. Insect repellent, and screened sleeping quarters, are just as important. Since few visitors go to the Caribbean, this probably won't be a concern.

- Water in Managua and in most other towns is chlorinated, and is generally considered safe to drink. For reasons that are not well understood, travellers are sometimes susceptible to upset tummies when they change their source of drinking water. Just to be safe, you might want to stick to bottled drinks. In Managua, bottled drinking water is available at some supermarkets and gasoline stations. (Just as in the

103

United States, this is not an indication that the local water will kill you, at least not quickly.)

If you're off the beaten track and aren't sure about the tap water, a couple of drops of laundry bleach will kill most of what might harm you.

- The sun is powerful, and if you've just come from winter in the north, limit exposure.

- Before you check into a hotel, inspect the room for cleanliness and insects. Though a few crawlies are inevitable in the tropics—shake out your shoes in the morning to prevent unpleasant surprises.

POSTAL SERVICE

Telcor is the local PTT, or post office-telecommunications monopoly. In any town, ask for Telcor if you need to mail a letter, send a fax, or make a phone call.

As in most countries, the postal service is used to send letters and post cards, and only letters and post cards. Regulations regarding enclosure of items of any value can be abstruse, and security is not always guaranteed.

Courier services provide an alternative to the post office for urgent letters and packets. Among those operating between the U.S. and Managua are:

- C.P.S., Kilometer 13, Carretera Sur (Southern Highway), tel. 658101, fax 658102; in Miami, tel. 305-594-7675, fax 594-8597.

- DHL, one block north of Hotel Inter-Continental, tel. 284081.

- AirPak, tel. 668126, fax 661812, with branches in León and Granada.

- SkyNet, Plaza Bolonia 10, tel. 665793, fax 664629.

- Trans-Express, from Hotel Inter-Continental, one block west, 75 meters south, tel. 226352, fax 227588.

TAXES

Almost all goods and services in Nicaragua are subject to a value-added tax ("*I.G.V.—Impuesto general al valor*") of 15 percent.

This includes meals and hotel bills.

Practical Details

At the airport, the exit tax is currently twelve dollars, payable in U.S. currency.

TELEPHONES

Automatic, direct-dial service is available to most towns in Nicaragua.

CALLING NICARAGUA

From the United States or Canada, dial the international prefix, country code, and area code (*número de entrada*). For Managua, the numbers are 011-505-2.

For an operator-assisted call, dial 01-505, plus the area code and number; or dial 01 and wait for an international operator.

¿HABLA ESPAÑOL?

If you speak Spanish, you can talk directly to a local operator in Nicaragua. This service is mainly for collect calls. Dial:

1-800-223-NICA	from U.S.A. via AT&T
1-800-234-NICA	from U.S.A. via MCI
1-800-775-NICA	from U.S.A. via Sprint
1-800-463-0729	from Canada
179	from Costa Rica
197	from Guatemala
000-8019	from Brazil
990-90-505	from Spain

BEYOND THE REACH OF A TELEPHONE?

This is not uncommon in Nicaragua, where not everybody has a phone. Ask your international operator for a *messenger call* ("*citación*"). Give the name and address of the person you're trying to reach, and when you expect a return call. A messenger will go out at the other end to "cite" your party to the phone office. It works!

CALLING IN NICARAGUA

Each town has its own area code, or dialing prefix, referred to in Nicaragua as the *número de entrada*. Within Nicaragua, use the zero in the

TELEPHONE NUMBER ROULETTE

As the telecommunications system in Nicaragua modernizes, phone numbers metamorphize to allow for additional combinations and expanded capacity.

Some five-digit numbers have had a "6" added at the beginning. When there's a conflict in phone numbers listed for a hotel or restaurant in two different sources, the longer number is probably correct.

If you're not sure of the number, check with directory assistance. In Managua, dial 112. From outside Nicaragua, ask your operator to connect you with directory assistance in Managua. There is usually no charge for this service, and international operators speak English.

SERVICE NUMBERS IN NICARAGUA

Within Nicaragua:

110	Operator-assisted calls *within Nicaragua*.
112	Telephone number information (domestic)

For international calls:

114	Telephone number information (international)
116	Operator-assisted international calls (English spoken)

To speak to an operator in your home country, dial:

162	Spain Direct
164	AT&T USA Direct (outside Managua, dial 02-164)
166	MCI to U.S.A. (outside Managua, dial 02-166)
168	Canada Direct (outside Managua, dial 02-168)
171	Sprint to U.S.A. (outside Managua, dial 02-171; for service in Spanish, dial 161, or 02-161)
163	Brazil Direct
176	Guatemala Direct
179	Costa Rica Direct

prefix (02 for Managua, 052 for Masaya, etc.) when calling out of town. You don't need the zero when dialing from abroad.

CALLING FROM THE PHONE COMPANY OFFICE

For international calls, especially from outside Managua, it's usually easiest to go right to the Telcor (telephone company) office to place your call.

Telcor can also handle public fax transmissions.

DIAL DIRECT

From a private phone in Managua, dial 00-1 (for North America), followed by the area code and local number.

Or dial 116 to reach an English-speaking international operator.

Or use USA Direct or a similar service (see box).

CALLING FROM HOTELS

Before using a phone in your hotel, inquire about surcharges for international and local calls.

Local calls also cost as much as 50 cents, but not every hotel charges to use the phone.

PUBLIC PHONES

Many public phones in Managua, when you can find them (often in the lobby of hotels), work with magnetic cards, rather than coins. The cards can be purchased at post offices (Telcor, or PTT).

TIME

Nicaragua stays on Central Standard Time (Greenwich Mean Time less six hours) throughout the year.

Both American-style time indications and 24-hour clock time are in use. For example, you'll see both 5 p.m. and 17:00 horas (hours), and they mean the same thing (time for a drink).

TIPPING

In most situations, you don't have to worry about how much to tip.

In formal restaurants—the kind where you're presented with a written bill—a service charge of ten percent is usually added. It's not required by law, as in some countries, but most people pay it and add no more, except for truly exceptional service.

Taxi drivers negotiate a fixed fee, and no tip is expected.

Probably, the only places where you'll have to give any though to tipping are at a hotel or the airport. For a porter, 50 cents per bag is an adequate tip. If you've stayed a few days and are satisfied with a hotel's service, you can leave a few dollars in an envelope for the chambermaid.

WEIGHTS AND MEASURES

In general, the metric system is in use in Nicaragua: liters for liquids, kilometers for distance, etc.

But there are notable exceptions. Gasoline is sold by the U.S. gallon.

And informally, old Spanish measures are in use to indicate distance. "*Cien varas*" or "*100 varas*," 100 old Spanish yards, indicates a city block, though you'll usually hear "*100 metros*" (100 meters). In the countryside, you might come across an *arroba*, 25 pounds, or *libras*; or a *quintal*, 100 pounds.

8
MANAGUA

- *Metropolitan Area Population: 1,000,000;*

MANAGUA OLD AND NEW

Managua is as old as the 6000-year-old Footprints of Acahualinca, impressed in volcanic clay by some of the first lakeside inhabitants; as new as futuristic *centros comerciales* on the ring roads, and concrete office towers that serve the government and poke fun at the risks of life in an earthquake zone; as traditional as the everyday trade in fruits and products of the land that has gone on in the city's markets for hundreds of years; as tragic as the ruins that still recall the earthquake of more than twenty years ago; as unexpected as a delicate piece of earthenware crafted to pre-Columbian patterns, or the masterpiece of a theater named for a national hero who is neither soldier nor politician nor sportsman, but a poet who changed the use of the Spanish language; as inspiring as the educators and businessmen and tradespeople who have prevailed through dictatorship and disaster and political disaffection, and have put aside the past and their differences to build a future.

Managua was selected as capital of the republic only in 1852, when it was a moderately sized village situated on the wagon trail between

Granada and León, the feuding Conservative and Liberal strongholds. But it was populated thousands of years ago, as the fossilized footprints of Acahualinca attest. And the chronicles of the Spanish conquerors describe a vast marketplace, and settlement of 40,000 souls and gardens extending from the modern city up to Tipitapa. Of course, the Spaniards laid waste to all they found in order to erect a new subservient society from the ashes.

PRECARIOUS EXISTENCE

As a colonial town and as a young capital, Managua always lived a perilous existence. Floods occasioned by cloudbursts on the table of hills rising to the south washed out the town in 1730 and 1876. In 1931, an earthquake did severe damage.

The city that rebuilt each time was not one of the venerable centers of colonial architectural heritage, or of graceful old ways. But it was typically and energetically Central American, with stately, squat, cement-plastered buildings standing shoulder to shoulder along narrow streets, porches and balconies and generous cornices sheltering pedestrians from rain and sun, and commercial signs poking out above the snarled traffic and pedestrians.

Under the rule of fifty—severe earthquakes occur no more frequently than every fifty years in any one place—Managua should have enjoyed extended tranquility well into the eighties. But rules are broken, and tragically, this one was broken in Managua. The city was destroyed—shattered, sundered, wrecked and buried—in the great earthquake of December 22, 1972. At least 20,000 persons were killed in the capital and the surrounding area.

CITY WITHOUT A CENTER

The exceptions to the destruction, the buildings that survived the earthquake, can be counted on the fingers of a couple of hands, though a flavor of the lost city can be gleaned from photos that decorate some of Managua's restaurants (look in at Los Antojitos, or the Centro Cultural Managua). And the loss, the emptiness in the aftermath of the tragedy, still resonates in Managua today, even among those who were not born in 1972.

And yet, any description of Managua as a still-ruined city is a deception. Managua is very much alive and functioning in new and different ways from those that prevailed before what is still called *el desastre* (the Disaster). The center of the city was never re-erected, what with theft of relief funds, economic dislocation in the wake of the overthrow of the Somoza regime, and the diversion of resources to the war of Sandinistas against Contras. Instead, the rubble was carted off, and broad boulevards were laid out through newly created green space.

Commerce dispersed, from a single downtown to newly created shopping centers (*centros comerciales*) and office complexes and former residences on the outskirts. Industry regrouped in the flat lands between the old center and the airport. New suburbs grew, while "spontaneous settlements"—jerry-built by squatters, but better than slums, with basic services and a community life—appeared on unallocated lands.

It's a process that has gone on slowly in so many other Central and South American cities, where commerce and industry have removed from the old city, leaving the core to wither and decay. In Managua, what remains of the old center is vestigial, symbolic, and in many ways more attractive than central cities elsewhere in the region. With its mutually dependent functional clusters, Managua is the culmination of an urban trend, a city of the future, not unlike Los Angeles or Stockholm, but with chugging buses and collective taxis and pickup trucks serving as the lifeblood between its farthest reaches, rather than private automobiles or suburban trains.

CLEAN AIR

Managua spreads southward from its lake—and is still spreading—along a broad front onto a gentle wall of hills. Beyond are the volcanic peaks of Masaya and Mombacho to the southeast, while the cone of Momotombo pokes up to the northwest.

The capital has its share of polluting factories, blowing dust, and, worst of all, untuned buses belching black diesel smoke. Yet, compared to the highland capitals of Central America—Guatemala City, Tegucigalpa, San José—Managua is a breath of fresh air. The lake at its front step, the open, rolling land stretching to the Pacific, and a steady breeze assure clear skies and continuous air circulation, without the choking oppressiveness one often associates with Third World cities.

And though Managua is not a green city, at least toward its center, the stunning beauty of the land all around is ever present.

Nicaragua Guide

> ## WHERE THERE IS AN EXTENSION OF WATER
> ## XOLOTLÁN: MANAGUA THE LAKE
>
> Lake Managua covers about a thousand square kilometers directly north of the capital. Its surface is about 40 meters above sea level, though in periods of heavy rains, it rises, and its waters spill over into the Tipitapa River, and flow onward into Lake Nicaragua, to the east.
>
> "Managua" derives from the name of one of the major indigenous groups that inhabited the lakeside region at the time of the Conquest. And what they appear to have called their natural reservoir was Xolotlán ("ho-lot-LAN"), which translates as "where there is an extension of water," or, more prosaically, "lake."
>
> Encased along the rim of Xolotlán are lakes lesser in size but no less scenic: Xiloá and Apoyeque, crater lakes on the Chiltepe peninsula, a remnant volcano jutting just to the northwest of the capital; and Asososca and Tiscapa, within the city limits.
>
> There is no denying that the waters of Lake Managua are polluted by agricultural runoff and dumping. But, as unfortunate is Managua's position atop a major geological fault, equally fortunate is its lakeside situation.
>
> The lake serves as a vast, open expanse where there might otherwise be settlement and development and industry, and a buffer to the extremes of temperature on the low-lying land all around.

ON YOUR WAY TO MANAGUA, NICARAGUA

THE AIRPORT

Augusto César Sandino International Airport (formerly Las Mercedes airport, renamed for the nationalist leader who battled the U.S. Marines) is about 12 kilometers directly east of downtown Managua.

ARRIVING

The terminal building is long and narrow. It's only a few steps from your plane to immigration to baggage pickup and customs, and onward to the front door. With few flights, no backups result from simultaneous arrivals, and you'll probably clear immigration and customs quickly.

Facilities for passengers are adequate, with no frills.

An **information counter** can provide limited information about hotels and destinations.

A **bank agency** (open from 8:30 a.m.) will exchange dollars—currently cash only—for Nicaraguan currency. But you might not need this service: U.S. cash in small bills is widely accepted by taxi drivers and hotels; and street money changers occupy turf along the highway into town.

Gift shops at the airport have wares more reasonably priced than at similar establishments elsewhere. Take a look on your way in at the belts, cassettes, cigars, embroidered textiles, and all the rest, so you'll know what you can pick up on your way out of the country.

GETTING TO TOWN

Waiting **taxis** charge about $12 to downtown Managua. You can save on the fare by continuing a few steps to the highway outside the terminal. Small cabs that cruise the highway charge just $5. And if you flag down a *colectivo* taxi with passengers already aboard, you'll pay less (but your luggage might not fit).

Whichever you take, make sure you settle on the price before you get in.

Crowded local **buses** also head toward Managua. Line 117 goes straight down Pista (boulevard) Pedro Joaquín Chamorro to the eastern part of Managua, then cuts across toward the southwest. You might save a bit of money by taking this bus to someplace near where you wish to stay, and then flagging a taxi; but the buses are overcrowded, and risky with luggage. Some buses numbered 105 also pass the airport, and will take you across central Managua. Country buses coming in from the north and Tipitapa (route 266) will also stop, if there is room, and drop you at the Iván Montenegro market on the eastern end of Managua. From there, bus 118 or bus 119 will take you to the neighborhood of the Inter-Continental Hotel; bus 119 continues to the Plaza España area.

Rental cars, if you've reserved one (and you can't count on one being available otherwise), can be picked up in the lot outside the terminal building.

STAYING NEAR THE AIRPORT

The Hotel Las Mercedes is directly across the street from the terminal. You can't get more convenient. And the Camino Real is about two

STRANGE BUT TRUE
REAL-LIFE EXAMPLES OF MANAGUA ADDRESSES

- *100 varas arriba del Gran Hotel.* Translation: 100 varas above the Gran Hotel. Elaboration: "100 varas" means "one block." "Above" indicates "eastward." Further translation: One block east of Gran Hotel. Further elaboration: the Gran Hotel fell in the 1972 earthquake and no longer operates. Final interpretation: Find out where the Gran Hotel used to be, go one block east, and you'll be where you want to go.

- *Javier Cuadra, de Montoya, 2 c. al lago.* Translation: in the neighborhood called Javier Cuadra, from the statue of Montoya, two blocks (*cuadras*) north (toward the lake). This one's easy!

And here's one extracted from the phone directory:

- *Universidad Centroamericana, frente a Radio Ya.* Translation: Central American University, located opposite radio station "Ya." Obviously, you'll want to find out where Radio Ya is located, in order to find the university. So, you look it up, and read: *Radio Ya frente a UCA.* Translation: Radio station "Ya," opposite the Central American University.

Conclusion: to find out where something is, you have to know where it is already.

Or else you have to ask. Obviously, everybody in Managua knows where the main points of reference are, or they wouldn't do things this way. So fellas, don't be afraid to ask for directions. (Ladies generally need less encouragement along these lines.)

kilometers down the road toward town. Both are good choices. Look ahead for more details.

ARRIVING BY BUS

Most buses from outside Managua terminate at one of the major markets. Buses from Granada, Masaya and the southeast, and from Matagalpa and the central highlands, end up at the Mercado Roberto Huembes (or Mercado Central/Central Market) in southeastern Managua.

Buses from León and other points to the northwest along the Pacific terminate at the Mercado Lewites (or Mercado Boer) in southwestern Managua.

Buses from the Caribbean side of Nicaragua arrive at the Mercado Iván Montenegro in eastern Managua.

Buses from Costa Rica and Honduras (Ticabus and Sirca) arrive at their own terminals.

There are inexpensive hotels near both the Ticabus and Sirca terminals. There are also less attractive budget hotels near the markets, but you'll probably do better to take a taxi to a specific hotel or neighborhood selected from the listings below.

You can also get around from the markets by local city bus, but this is not recommendable when you first arrive with luggage.

FINDING YOUR WAY IN MANAGUA

ADDRESSES AS MYSTERIES

Managua is a patchwork quilt of neighborhoods, and irregular patches they are, spread over hills and along the lake's shore, each with an independent system of streets, connected to neighboring patches by winding boulevards and snaking avenues.

Street names and house numbers are rarely used. Addresses are mysteries for you to solve.

Welcome to Managua!

GETTING YOUR BEARINGS IN MANAGUA
DETAILED DIRECTIONS

An address in Spanish is a *dirección*, and in Managua (as elsewhere in Nicaragua), when you get an address, you will be literally getting a set of directions.

In the best of cases, an address will start off with a **neighborhood**. *Barrios* are downtown neighborhoods, *repartos* are more outlying districts (the term has an archaic ring that harkens back to Spanish grants), and *colonias* are near-suburban. All can be something like independent villages; each usually has its own church.

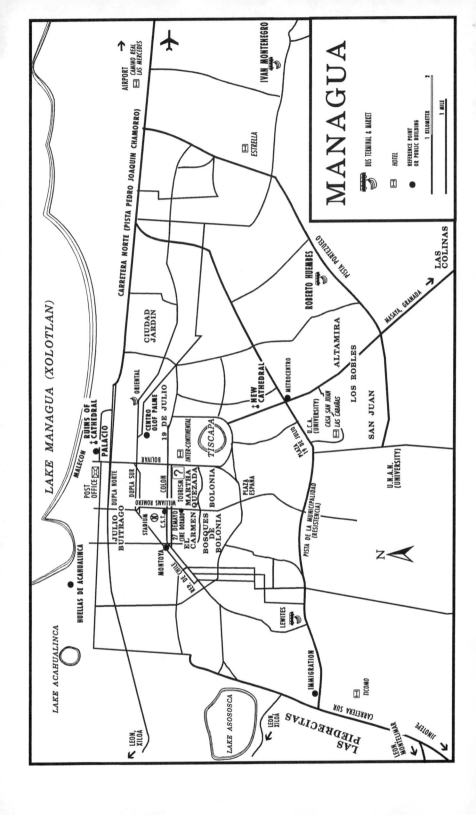

Managua

You also might have a **reference point**, which all residents know, to use as a starting point. Some are **phantom reference points**, hotels, cinemas, and houses that fell in '72, but live on in the hearts and minds of Managuans. If you're lucky, the address will say "*antiguo Gran Hotel*" ("former Gran Hotel"), giving you a clue that it's not really there.

From your reference point, you'll **navigate in a given direction**, recast from standard Spanish usage to reflect the geography of Managua: *al lago* ("to the lake") means northward, *a la montaña* ("to the mountain") indicates southward, *abajo* ("below") indicates westward, and *arriba* ("above") indicates eastward.

You'll move the indicated **distance**: *1 c.* (*una cuadra*, one block); or *100 varas* (100 varas, also a block).

And if you're lucky, you'll also have a house number, *casa 87* (house 87); or a street name, such as *Calle Colón*. *Calles* (streets) run east-west. *Avenidas* (avenues) run north-south.

In this book, I'll give addresses in the local manner, if it will help you in asking directions. But I'll add (in parentheses) some landmarks or instructions that might make more sense to you as a visitor. In many cases, this will mean getting a rough fix from the Hotel Inter-Continental , the triangular fortress-lodging on a rise above central Managua. In local parlance, it's *El Inter* (El IN-tehr, with the accent on the first syllable).

SOME IMPORTANT NEIGHBORHOODS AND STREETS

Old Managua, downtown by the lake, is the **Centro Histórico**, with the shell of the old Cathedral, the National Palace, the Rubén Darío Theater, and other significant structures. Dupla Norte and Dupla Sur are east-west boulevards through the central area, two lanes of traffic moving either way, divided by a 50-meter-wide grass strip, connecting with trunk roads beyond.

The main street leading southward from downtown toward the escarpment and the Inter-Continental Hotel, is Avenida Bolívar. It climbs and descends, with a westward fork leading to **Plaza España**, where some airline offices and travel agencies are located.

Near the Inter-Continental are several quiet neighborhoods where small hotels and restaurants are located: Barrio **Martha Quezada**, directly west of the hotel, and **El Carmen**, farther west, directly south of the light towers of the baseball stadium; and **Bolonia** and **Bosques de Bolonia** to the southwest, both bordered on the south by Plaza España.

117

NAVIGATING NICARAGUA GEOGRAPHICAL VOCABULARY

Most of these terms apply outside of Managua as well.

al lago, "to the lake," **al norte**	north
a la montaña, "to the mountain," **al sur**	south
abajo, "below," **al oeste**	west
arriba, "above," **al este**	eastward.
1 c., una cuadra, 100 varas	one block
casa	house
barrio, reparto	neighborhood
colonia	suburb
calle	street
avenida	avenue
pista	boulevard
carretera	highway
Antiguo, donde fue	"former," no longer standing

Pista Pedro Joaquín Chamorro is the airport highway heading eastward out of town across the northern fringe of the city. **Avenida Rubén Darío** becomes the Masaya highway, heading out to the southeast, while the **Carretera Panamericana**, the southern branch of the Pan American Highway, leaves Managua to the southwest.

Managua

THE TOURIST OFFICE

Visitors count in Nicaragua! The former tourist board is now a cabinet-level department, the Ministerio de Turismo, reflecting *your* importance to the economy, and the welcome that you'll receive. The ministry's headquarters are in a modest bungalow one block east of the Hotel Inter-Continental, and you are perfectly welcome to drop by, chat, pick up a map, and ask questions about lodging, sites, restaurants, and how to get from place to place.

HOTELS

There just aren't a lot of hotels in Managua, and not a lot of rooms among them. Yet, with its limited stock of accommodation, Managua has more than its share of charming lodging houses.

Store-bought, custom-built kitsch for tourists, of the kind that you can get at a price elsewhere, is not to be found. Instead, among the places where you can drop your suitcase and rest your head in Managua are a 300-cabana establishment with large pool that is more like a Central American country club than anything else, where you're likely to bump into teams of baseball players here for the championship series, or students lodged for a regional cultural meeting; a budget establishment built around a patio lined with bookshelves, where many of the rooms come with private courtyards; hillside bungalows in a private forest overlooking the town and distant and not-so-distant volcanoes; and substantial once-private houses where you get the feeling that your are, indeed, in someone's home, rather than in an anonymous establishment.

And there are also the more run-down, cheapie establishments that sell on the basis of price only, and cater mainly to locals and people from the region who have hardly any money; but if staying at a budget level is your exclusive criteria, you will do well to move on from Managua immediately, to León or Granada or one of the coastal villages, where you can find more agreeable surroundings for money not spent.

Nicaragua Guide

GROUND RULES IN THE GUIDE

Prices are given in U.S. dollars. Hotel prices include 15 percent tax. Restaurant prices include tax and service charge for a meal suitable to the establishment. All prices are accurate as of publication, and subject to change.

Not every hotel or restaurant is listed, but you'll find a range suitable to most needs. If you take exception to my advice, or make a real find, then write to me at the address in the front of the book. I'd like to hear from you.

TELEPHONING

As an example, to call the Hotel Inter-Continental,

- Dial 623530 from Managua
- Dial (02)623530 from elsewhere in Nicaragua
- Dial 011-505(2)623530 from the United States or Canada.

Some numbers are receiving an extra digit as the phone system expands. In case of problems, check with your international operator.

WHERE THE HOTELS ARE

Everywhere! You'll find the largest establishment literally across the street from the terminal of the international airport. (It's near enough to the exit gate that you can probably get your bags over without any assistance). And one of the two luxury establishments is just a kilometer away.

On the other hand, the *other* luxury establishment overlooks central Managua. Middle-range hotels are scattered both around the various neighborhoods and in outlying districts, while the budget establishments are generally closer in, a few even within walking distance of each other in the southwest part of the central area.

WHERE SHOULD YOU STAY?

For most visitors, at one price or budget level or another, there is not much particular advantage to staying in one hotel or another.

First of all, while there are some extraordinary attractions in Nicaragua, those of the capital are limited. Sightseeing in the city can easily be accomplished in a morning (or less). If you are taking tours to visit nearby towns, you can be picked up at any hotel. If you are taking buses, a taxi ride costing a dollar or two will get you from most hotels to the indicated market-terminal.

At the budget and moderate level of accommodation, some of the establishments in the Martha Quezada *barrio* (neighborhood) are convenient to stores, local eateries and travel services.

WHAT WILL YOU PAY?

Luxury hotels—the Camino Real and the Inter-Continental—charge over $100 for a double room, and are well worth what you pay.

Middle-range hotels—with perhaps a few shops and a small pool, but limited room service and no disco and only one restaurant—charge from $40 to $70 double.

Comfortable, smaller hotels in former private residences charge $30 double or less.

Budget hotels are available in central Managua and near the markets for under $10 double.

While prices have varied in local currency, the price of a room in dollars has been fairly stable for the last few years.

TO RESERVE OR NOT?

Nicaragua is not a hot tourist destination . . . not yet! Rooms are generally not hard to come by. But at holiday time when expatriates come home, or if there's any special event on, rooms will fill up quickly.

It's not a bad idea to secure reservations for your stay during a busy period; and for the first night only at other times.

NEAR THE AIRPORT

Hotel Las Mercedes, Pista Pedro J. Chamorro (airport road), km 11, P. O. Box 4655, tel. (02)631011 to 28, fax 631082, 631083. 310 rooms. $57 single/$69 double/$75 triple. American Express, Visa, Master Card accepted.

You don't have to look far to find acceptable lodging near the airport. You don't even need to take a taxi. Hotel Las Mercedes is across the street and about 150 yards from the terminal entrance. In fact, you're likely to do a lot more walking once you're on the hotel property than you did to get to the front desk.

Las Mercedes is not your chain hotel. It's something like a vestigial United Fruit Company country club. Rooms are in individual concrete or clapboard cottages, laid out in a maze occupying most of the extensive grounds, and connected by open walkways with enough overhang to divert seasonal rains. If you get lost or disoriented on the way to the pool (oversized) or the adjacent indoor-outdoor restaurant, you won't be the first. There are plenty of palms and heliconias and ginger plants along the walkways, but no open area large enough to call a garden.

In the best tropical style, the hotel flows in- and out-of-doors. A gift shop (whose wares include reasonably priced liquor) and beauty salon are adjacent to the front desk, off the air-conditioned, bare lobby. Everywhere else are hotel services and sports facilities. In addition to the large main pool with its large deck and plenteous loungers (and absence of chlorine odor), a smaller pool is tucked amid the cottages. Illuminated tennis and volleyball courts are elsewhere.

All of this is well maintained and spotless, if not endlessly updated as at pricier establishments, and the worn-in, slightly musty aspect of Las Mercedes exudes a relaxed smile that can't be bought at any price.

Not to mention that if you want to rub elbows with *real* Central Americans, Las Mercedes is the place. With more than 300 rooms and an auditorium, it accommodates several soccer teams, a convention of culturally inclined youth, and assorted travelling salesmen—all at once.

Rooms: Some visitors will require more than the adequate sleeping quarters of Las Mercedes: good-sized spaces with a king-sized or two smaller beds, television with limited satellite channels, small refrigerator (you stock it yourself), desk, individual air conditioner, adequate lighting with bare bulbs in the dressing area, hardwood headboard, industrial low-pile carpeting. The bathrooms are particularly low-tech, with shower only, tile with yellowing grout, no shampoo. You can't have it all.

Food Service: The Pérgola restaurant is modest and plain and air-conditioned, with a patio that looks through arches to the grounds of the hotel. Around the bend is El Ranchón, the prodigious covered terrace beside the pool; a bar is tucked to the side, with just a few high stools to encourage exchanges of the higher sort.

La Pérgola and El Ranchón terrace have the same menu; service may be restricted to one part or another according to the requirements of groups. The buffet is the best value at breakfast, fruits, eggs to order, a limited selection of pastries and sensual fresh juices for about $6, including tax and tip. Main courses at lunch and dinner run toward grilled meats at $8 to $10, chicken cordon bleu for less, lobster for more, though the garnished sandwich plates, such as the half-pound (!) hamburger at $4.50, are more than enough. A lunch buffet is offered most days for $10, and on Sundays, a mixed grill is prepared over coals on the terrace. Order for one and share—it's big.

Hotel Camino Real, kilometer 9.5, Pista Pedro J. Chamorro (Carretera Norte, or airport road), P. O. Box C-118. Tel. (02)631381, fax (02)631380 and 631385. Telex 1403 Posada, Cable Posada. 117 rooms. $138 single/$149 double. Visa, Master Card, American Express.

U.S. reservations: Tel. 800-327-3573.

Central America's Camino Real hotels have long set the standard in the region for excellence in service and reliability. Managua's Camino Real is suburban, set well back on a rise from the airport highway, low-lying, spread out, organized around its central pool courtyard, with ample gardens, jogging track, and tennis courts. Activities and guests regularly flow through the lobby to the open-air passageways and public areas—there's no separation of indoor and outdoor, or guest quarters from their lush green surroundings.

Rooms are all air-conditioned, comfortable and modern, if undistinguished in decor, with ample lamps and chairs. Food service is both around the pool, and in the more formal restaurant. The breakfast buffet, with many, many choices, goes for $8; main courses of standard fare of sea bass, filet mignon and chicken for $9 or so. Public facilities include a disco-bar, and a bank of slot machines.

A taxi ride to downtown costs from $5 to $10, depending on whether you flag a cab or take one parked at the hotel (which is more expensive). Shuttle service is provided to the airport.

CENTRAL AND WEST-CENTRAL MANAGUA

Central Managua offers the greatest variety in accommodations, both in size of hotels, and in price.

TOPS

Hotel Inter•Continental Managua, 101 8 Calle S.O., P. O. Box 3278, tel. (02)623530 to 623539, fax (02)625208. Telex 375 1054, Cable INHORTELCOR. 210 rooms. American Express, Visa, Master Card, Diners

U.S. reservations, tel. 800-327-0200.

Rates: lake-view rooms, $190 single/$200 double with tax, mountain view rooms $175/$185. $10 per additional person, no charge for children. Corporate rate: $164. Suites go for $370 per day.

In the midst of a bustling, recalcitrant, exciting, lively, untamed metropolis, the Inter•Continental is both a landmark of Managua and a haven from it, where standards are always maintained. Its aura and relationship to the city are not unlike those of legendary Raffles and Singapore, or Shepherd's and Cairo in the old days, when the going was good. Perhaps the Inter•Continental's fame dates to the great earthquake of 1972, when it remained erect above the fallen city—don't ever doubt the strength of a truncated pyramid. It was further enhanced during the insurrection of 1978-79, "covered" from the bar of the Inter•Continental by many a foreign correspondent. It is at the "Inter," today, that the movers and shakers get together to cut deals in the course of rebuilding the commerce of the nation.

Yet the Inter appears at first glance to have relatively modest proportions, planted as it is on a slope that continues above the city center. The façade is flat, with offset windows poking out under sheltering brows as if in a fortress, on seven successively shorter guest floors; the retreating edges suggest a stepped Mayan pyramid. A capping roof comb contains the machine room. To one side of the lobby are the pools.

Food Service: The Regency is the main formal restaurant, offering continental cuisine and luncheon buffets. Afternoon tea, a pleasant rarity, is served from 3:30 p.m., to the accompaniment of piano music. La Brasserie is more informal, open through breakfast and lunch to 2:30 p.m., and from

6 to 10 p.m. for dinner. Many outsiders, including wise travellers, come in for the buffet breakfast, served until 11:30 a.m., for about $10. Otherwise, prices are on the high side for Managua, but reasonable for the quality: soups and salads for $4 to $10, fish in garlic sauce, filet mignon or lasagna for $10 to $15, $7 for a club sandwich. Snacks are also available poolside. *The* bar is La Cita, off the lobby, complete with piano music, open from 11 a.m. to midnight, while La Cabaña serves Mexican-style snacks with Mexican-style dance music.

Rooms are centrally air-conditioned, with color television, up-to-date decor, and generous lamps, chairs and tables. Services and shops include car rental, travel agency, barber, beauty shop, handicraft store, newsstand, and meeting rooms and business center. Also available: cribs, baby sitting, 24-hour room service, safe deposit boxes at front desk. Checkout is at 3 p.m.

Mansión Teodolinda, 2 blocks south, 1½ west of Inter-Continental, tel. (02)281050. 15 rooms. $92 and up double, plus tax. Visa and Master Card.

The Teodolinda is an intimate establishment, with air-conditioned suites with television, and restaurant (breakfast $5, dinner from $10) and pool. No travel agency, shops or numerous other services that you'd find in a larger hotel, but if you need those, you can always trot over to the Inter-Continental. Good location. Some construction is still ongoing.

MODERATE

Hotel Montserrat, 4 blocks north of Inter-Continental (*de la Policlínica 1. c. al oeste*), tel. (02)668074. 10 rooms. $34 to $40 double.

A good choice for travellers looking for something above rock-bottom, a modest converted private house, with television room, and meal and bar service and protected parking. Rooms are air-conditioned, and have refrigerators, which can be stocked from the food shop next door. Persons on official programs tend to settle in here for a while, since the price is right, the atmosphere is homey, the neighborhood is pleasant, and discounts are available for extended stays.

Casa Fiedler, Barrio El Carmen, no. 1320 "*Central Sandinista Trabajadores 2 cuadras al sur, 1½ cuadra abajo*" (3 blocks south of stadium, 2 west), tel. (02)666622, 663693, 663374. 24 rooms. $12 single/$17 double with fan and shared bath, $17/$25 with air conditioning, $28/$33 with air conditioning and private bath, plus tax. No charge for children.

Dark and gloomy is the concrete Casa Fiedler, but it's clean and friendly and safe, and the residential area, about ten blocks west of the Inter-Continental, if not exactly high-toned, is unthreatening. Breakfast only is served. Take a look at the collection of pre-Columbian pieces in the reception area.

El Carmen Bed & Breakfast, Calle Colón (P.O. Box J103, Sucursal Las Jinotepes), opposite El Carmen church, tel. (02)224114, fax 224971. 10 rooms. $40 and up.

El Carmen is in the same mixed neighborhood as Casa Fiedler, and has a bar (with happy hour, no less) and basic restaurant, and more pleasant rooms and atmosphere.

Hotel D'Lido, *Centro Toyota 2½ cuadras al sur* (2½ blocks south of Centro Toyota), P. O. Box 631, tel. (02)666145, fax 664560. 24 rooms. $39 single/$51 double.

In western Managua, past the baseball stadium, at the junction of Zeledón (a main east-west street) and Paseo República de Chile. A crowded brick compound in a lower-middle-class zone, with pool, concrete courtyard, and dark, air-conditioned rooms with windows looking out only onto the courtyard. Not the cheeriest, but not the most expensive.

Fragata (Morgut), 3 blocks north of Inter-Continental, one block west, tel. (02)222166. 7 rooms. $23 single/$29 double, plus tax.

Old and musty (one of the *few* old hotels), with small rooms, but air-conditioned and with private baths, and in a central location. Just to confuse you, the newer name, Fragata, is attached to the restaurant on the parking-lot side; the old name, Morgut, remains on the main façade.

BUDGET

Tica-Nica, from Ticabus in Barrio Martha Quezada, 1½ blocks north, tel. (02)223713. 7 rooms. $6 and up.

Managua

The best you can say is that if you arrive by Ticabus from Costa Rica, you can find basic lodging here, a few blocks west of the Inter-Continental, and the neighborhood isn't bad.

Lodging Meléndez, Barrio Martha Quezada, 1½ blocks south of Ticabus, tel. (02)225704. $4 and up.
Also convenient if you arrive by Ticabus, but less attractive.

Hospedaje Quintana, from Ticabus, 1 block north, half block west. Under $10 per person.
Basic but honorable and pleasant.

MORE BUDGET BEDS

The Barrio Martha Quezada, which is the neighborhood just west of the Hotel Inter-Continental, contains a number of homes converted to sleeping quarters for guests, as well as eateries with a few rooms to let. One of the latter is **Cafetín Coco**, near Radio Primerísima.

If there's nothing obvious within view, ask for a *Casa de Huéspedes* ("KA-sa day WES-peh-des") a guest house, or *un hotel económico* (OON o-TEL eh-ko-NO-mee-ko), a cheap hotel. People will get your point. Otherwise, ask for *Cine Dorado* (SEE-neh though-RA-though), and check the streets leading eastward. Or just inquire of a passing Gringo.

Among the budget beds are several a half-block north of the Ticabus office; the Pensión Azul, two blocks east of Cine Dorado, right by Ticabus; and the Colibrí (tel. [02]227420), a half-block east of Cine Dorado, and somewhat better than the others, with private baths, and a rate of $12 or so for a room.

NEAR THE MARKETS

Since out-of-towners arrive at Managua's major markets by bus, you'll find budget lodging nearby. None of the accommodations are in terrific surroundings, and there will be fumes from buses and noise from early-morning wholesale commerce. But the locations are convenient, and the price per person is under $10—usually *well* under $10. Look for these lodgings and others when you get off the bus, but be sure to take a good look at your room before you pay.

Near the Israel Lewites market (buses from León) are the **Azul** and **El Portal**. By the Oriental market just east of downtown is **Hospedaje Oriental**. The **Mascote** and **Hospedaje Fuente** are near the Roberto Huembes market.

BETWEEN CENTRAL MANAGUA AND THE OUTSKIRTS

Hotel Estrella, Pista Portezuelo ("Semáforos de Rubenia 200 metros al norte"), P. O. Box 795, tel. (02)897010 to 13, fax (02)897212 to 13. 40 rooms. $44 single/$56 double.

Located in mixed residential and business area east of downtown, on one of the main ring roads, three blocks off the airport route. The Estrella looks like an ice cream stand, with its bright aluminum trim at streetside, but it's a perfectly adequate modern motel, nothing more, nothing less, with small pool, parking, basic bar and restaurant, and air-conditioning and cable t.v. in small rooms.

Casa de Huéspedes San Juan (San Juan Guest House), Reparto San Juan, Calle Esperanza 560, P. O. Box 5732, tel. (02)783220, fax (02)670419, 12 rooms. $14 single/$16 double/$20 triple.

Here's one of the lodgings of choice for travellers on a modest budget, a homey brick bungalow in an attractive residential neighborhood. Rooms are off passageways leading from a flowered courtyard, all with private bath, some air-conditioned (at about $5 extra per night), and many with their own private patio. Shelves in the open are full of books, and meals can be taken for less than in many city restaurants ($4 for breakfast, $5 for lunch or dinner). The owners provide a family atmosphere, and have a van available for trips to Masaya, Granada and other nearby towns. Who could ask for more?

Reparto San Juan is one of the few better-off neighborhoods within easy reach of the city center, located about a kilometer south and east of the Inter-Continental, off the Pista de la Resistencia (more recently known as Pista de la Municipalidad), one of the trunk roads that loop around the city center.

Hotel Las Cabañitas, Reparto San Juan (P. O. Box 631), tel. (02)783235. 25 rooms. $25 single/$34 double/$39 triple. Visa and Master Card.

"The little cabins" (literally) are crowded one next to another in a compound just around the corner from the San Juan Guest House, along with a small pool. Rooms are modest and the private bathrooms are basic, but with t.v., telephone and air-conditioning, the value is good.

Hotel Palace, km 2½, airport road (Banco Nacional de Desarrollo, half-block east, 1½ blocks south), tel. (02)44119, fax (02)43702. About $23 single/$34 double.
The Palace rates as a Central American businessmen's hotel, with no frills, but adequate facilities. Some, but not all, rooms have private baths and air-conditioning. Near a shopping center with a variety of stores.

King's Palace, km. 5, Masaya road, tel. (02)782456. 16 rooms. $36 double.
Adequate rooms, coffee shop, air conditioners.

SOUTHERN OUTSKIRTS

Hotel Ticomo, Km 8½, Southern Highway (*Carretera Sur*), P. O. Box 2586, tel. (02)650210, 651427, 651273, 653407, fax (02) 651529. 60 rooms. $51 single/$61 double/$75 triple. Visa, Master Card.
Head for the hills, and you'll end up at the Ticomo, a country hotel on a a shaded hillside, a kilometer back from the highway, but not all that far from the city center. Terraces, wicker rockers, a small pool and tennis courts all contribute to an away-from-the-city air. Rooms are in individual cottages, and are a bit hard in aspect, but are fairly large, and would be suites if the plywood partitions made it all the way to the ceiling. Good value for families, with t.v. and air-conditioning, restaurant and bar on-site. A taxi out this way from town costs about $6, or $10 from the airport.

Hotel César, km 8½, Southern Highway, 3 blocks east. Tel. (02)652744. 20 rooms. $65 double.
This is a sort of roadhouse-cum-executive rooms, away from noise and distractions. Rooms have air conditioners and t.v., there's a small pool as well as excellent restaurant, and fax and computer connections are available.

MOTELS

In Latin America, any establishment that calls itself a motel caters to the tryst trade. A motel is generally located on the outskirts of town; has an enclosing wall to keep out both intruders and prying eyes; air-conditioned rooms of one sort or another, but no other hotel services; rates for a few hours, as well as for the night; and maybe a parking slot with pull-down blinds or gate to hide your vehicle and license plate. A motel might have a name like Villa Amor (Love Villa), El Secreto (The Secret), or Moulin Rouge or Los Encuentros (Encounters); or it might bear a neutral name and give no clue that it's not a "respectable" main-line place. They've developed this business to suit the life-style.

I'm not particularly recommending a stay in a motel, but the price is right if you're arriving in Managua at night by car. Take a good look at the room before you check in. Who knows? You might want to stay a few days. The top rate, in **Los Laureles** (km 14½, Masaya road, tel. (02)799289) is about $40 for the night, or $12 for a few hours; but most charge less.

RESTAURANTS

Managua has a surprising number of formal restaurants, where you can sit down to a full meal, well-prepared, and served competently. Even the best restaurants aren't particularly expensive by U.S. or European standards. So you can eat quite well, without worrying too much about your budget.

If there's a problem for travellers, it's that there's not much of a middle class in Managua, so there aren't many middle-range restaurants. Trying to find a place in which to grab a light bite or a snack, without settling down to a full-course meal, can be frustrating. But there are solutions, and not just the markets and roadside stands. I'll get to them in a minute.

WHAT'S TO EAT?

When Nicaraguans eat out, often what they have in mind is a good steak, a *churrasco* grilled over the coals.

Hotel restaurants generally serve American-style food, sometimes with Nicaraguan twists, such as local vegetables . . . and the inevitable juicy and tender steak. For more details about local cuisine, see page 99.

Ethnic and foreign cuisines in Managua include Italian, German, and Chinese. And there are a few excellent French and continental restaurants.

BEST VALUE

When having a full meal, beef and chicken are your best values. Shellfish can be surprisingly expensive. Local beer and mixed drinks are inexpensive, while imported drinks and wine can bust your budget.

MORE RESTAURANTS

For more choices and recent openings, ask your fellow travellers (first!), then consult the ads in the newspapers, and in *Guía Fácil*, a bimonthly newsstand publication covering events and entertainment in and near Managua.

CREDIT CARDS

Visa and Master Card are accepted at most restaurants. Establishments affiliated with hotels, and higher-priced eateries, also accept American Express.

ORDER IN?

You came to Nicaragua to rub elbows with the locals, to break bread in the places where they break bread, to chat with the couple at the next table, to make new friends.

But sometimes, you'd just as soon stay in, especially if it's getting late, and there isn't much choice right near your hotel.

Take heart! Pizza and chicken are as far away as your telephone, or the desk clerk at your hotel who will relay your order. Pay attention to the listings below for details. Or, try one of these numbers right off to get your meal on its way: **Domino's Pizza**, tel. 782562, fax 782488; **Pollo Supremo** for roast chicken, tel. 651025 in southwestern Managua, tel. 495277 in central and eastern Managua. For fried chicken, it's **Pollo Tip-Top**, tel. 780211.

Or, try the Chinese restaurant nearest to your hotel. And don't forget room service. It's not necessarily priced out of sight.

CENTRAL MANAGUA

MEXICAN FORMAL

Los Antojitos, Avenida Bolívar, opposite Hotel Inter-Continental, tel. (02)224866.
Though the name implies light Mexican-style snack food—tacos, enchiladas and the like—and informal surroundings, and though the appearance is suburban (parking area prominent), Los Antojitos is on the upscale side as things in Nicaragua go, and not surprisingly, given its location opposite the

driveway of the Inter-Continental Hotel. Service is formal—they provide a lemon dip for refreshing your fingers, among other details.

Expect to pay $6 for enchiladas, at least $10 with tax and tip for a mixed grill (a good assortment of little pieces of chicken, pork, beef and sausage) or roast chicken, $16 for shrimp in spicy tomato sauce. And while you're here, take a look at the photos of the lost Managua of pre-earthquake times.

SPANISH

El Mesón Español, 3½ blocks south of Mansión Teodolinda, Bolonia (southwest of Inter-Continental). Spanish-style specialties include Serrano ham, mutton in brandy, and paella. Closed on Sunday.

CENTRAL AMERICAN (COMIDA TÍPICA)

La Ruta Maya is a party of Salvadoran pupusas, Mexican tacos, conversation, and, sometimes, music continuing until 2 in the morning. On Avenida Monumental, about ten blocks west of the Inter-Continental, near the baseball stadium (*de Montoya, 150 varas arriba*).

La Callecita. When Nicaraguans crave rice and beans, vigorón, nacatamales, and mondongo (tripe), they usually load up at home, or at a stand in one of the markets. When they go out, it's for a steak or foreign food. But here's your chance to sample Nicaraguan soul food without a Nicaraguan family, in indisputably hygienic surroundings. Located in the Centro Cultural Managua downtown, on the south side.

FRENCH

Café de Paris, 1 block north and 1 block west of Iglesia El Carmen (about 10 blocks west of Inter-Continental) offers standard French fare made with quality Nicaraguan beef and fresh vegetables and herbs: pepper steak, tournedos, and the like.

ITALIAN

Italia, opposite Mansión Teodolinda, 2 blocks south, 1 block west of Inter-Continental, and **Mágica Roma,** a half-block south of the Inter-Continental, are both pizza-and-pasta palaces. Italia is more formal, serves larger portions and nice salads, and charges higher prices, about $8 for a main course. **Pasta Fresca** and **Trattoria dei Tempi Nostri** are a few blocks south of these, in the Bolonia neighborhood, 2 blocks north, ½ block west of the military hospital. In addition to the usual pasta, the Trattoria has a few meat courses.

GERMAN

Bavaria Haus, 2 blocks north of Plaza España, has German-style home cooking. But don't feel you're heading into a haunt exclusively of the German community . . . the owners include a Russian and a Gringo, and for some resident foreigners, Bavaria Haus is a home away from Heim. Food is consistently good, if un-fancy. Figure about $10 for a meal.

STEAK

If you don't know what kind of food a restaurant in Managua serves, it probably serves steak, and maybe some roast chicken too. But here are a few that offer identifiable cuts, such as puntas de filete (filet tips), churrasco (charcoal-broiled steak), filete miñon, and lomo (sirloin):

La Subasta, km 8½, airport road. The name means "auction," and that's what the locale is, a restaurant on the premises of a cattle auction lot. From beast to plate, with a minimum of intervention . . . now, that's something you won't find at home. Actually, the food's quite good, with an assortment of steaks, or just a hamburger and sandwich if you wish, in cow town surroundings, with a view to the pens. Open at 11:30 a.m., with bidding scheduled for Mondays, Wednesdays and Fridays. (Call 31379 to check).

La Plancha, km 4½, northern (airport) road (closed Sunday) and **La Plancha III**, near the baseball stadium (*de Montoya, 1 c. norte, 1 c. oeste, ½ c. norte*), where they also have Chinese food.

El Gaucho, serving steaks, is near the new Cathedral, at the turn for the Masaya road from Paseo Tiscapa.

HOTELS

If you're not sure about where to eat, remember that hotels, which have to satisfy an international clientele, often are more consistent in what they offer than neighborhood restaurants. And somewhere between the appetizers and the main courses, you're likely to find a filling item at a reasonable price, such as a sandwich platter.

For more details on most of these, look under the main hotel listing, above:

Hotel Inter-Continental. The **Regency** Restaurant often has buffets, and, unusually among all the lodging establishments of the isthmus, offers afternoon tea. **La Cabaña** is an upscale cantina, with Mexican specialties, happy hours, and live music.

Hotel Estrella. Plain steaks and shrimp in the Rossini restaurant.

Also, not downtown, but in case you're heading past the airport one morning:

Hotel Camino Real, airport road. Modest but reliable restaurant; the best fare is the breakfast buffet served poolside. The inside dining room, Le Pavillon, serves steaks, lobster, and breaded shrimp.

Hotel Las Mercedes, opposite Augusto César Sandino International Airport. Good breakfast buffet.

CHINESE

There are always lots of Chinese restaurants in any Central American capital. Many Chinese looked southward, after the railroads were built in the United States, and they were no longer welcome as laborers. Others have migrated from Hong Kong and the mainland in more recent times.

If you're looking for spicy Szechuan, hot pot, dim sum, or any sort of specialty, put away your wallet. Most of these places serve old favorite Cantonese standards: *chao* mein, *chap* suey, and pork in sweet-and-sour sauce. And as a break from steak and roast chicken, it's all perfectly acceptable.

Chinese restaurants in Nicaragua are not the economy eateries that they are in some other countries. Expect to pay $8 as a minimum for a meal at any of these:

Bien Bien, *CST 1 c. al oeste* (one block east of Central Sandinista de los Trabajadores, about a block south of the stadium).

Cantón #1, *Shell Ciudad Jardín 2 c. norte* (two blocks north of Shell station in Ciudad Jardín, a neighborhood east of central Managua.

China Palace, opposite Plaza El Sol on Pista de la Municipalidad, the main ring road.

El Faisán Dorado, main street, Ciudad Jardín (*Avenida Principal Ciudad Jardín*), about 10 blocks east of the Inter-Continental.

Jardín Chino, 1 block north of Montoya (*Montoya 1 c. al lago*), about three blocks west of the baseball stadium.

Plancha III, from Montoya, 1 block north, 1 block west, half-block north (*Montoya 1 c. norte, 1 c. oeste, ½ c. norte*)

Rincón Chino, km 4, northern (airport) road.

SEAFOOD

This is the category that's often a disappointment to visitors, not because of the quality, but because the price is out of sight relative to other menu items—$15 and up for the likes of lobster and shrimp.

The usual explanation is that shrimp and lobster are export commodities, and that foreigners bid up the price. This isn't quite true, but the infrastructure isn't around to deliver fresh lobster on a wide scale, so to have it, you pay. Sea bass (*curvina*, or *corvina*) is the most common fish, while you'll sometimes be offered dorado, which elsewhere is known as mahi-mahi or dolphinfish.

Red Diamond is not far from downtown, about 5 blocks north of the Shell station in the Ciudad Jardín neighborhood.

Managua's main seafood emporium is **The Lobster's Inn**, on the southern highway (see below).

CHICKEN ROASTED

Here's a good choice for simple, nourishing, safe food at a reasonable price, especially if the Spanish of the menu and the waiter/waitress is likely to discomfit you.

Near the baseball stadium downtown, you can try **Pollo a la Canasta**, a block east and a block north of the Montoya statue.

Farther afield, **Pollo Supremo** has a location at kilometer 5½ on the airport road, next to Banco Nicaragüense (Banic), tel. 495277. Give them a ring (or have the desk clerk call), and they'll deliver to your hotel.

CHICKEN FRIED

If it's the fried product you crave, à la Kentucky but a bit spicier, **Pollo Tip-Top** has chicken outlets around town, including one near the Managua stadium about 10 blocks west of the Inter-Continental, Bello Horizonte (near Hotel Estrella), on the Southern Highway, and Altamira, toward the

Masaya Road. Better yet, have someone who speaks Spanish call 780211 to arrange delivery to your hotel.

PASTRIES

Repostería Alemana is a Konditorei—German pastry shop—more conveniently located than anything else, a block west of the Inter-Continental, then a block toward the lake. Cakes and puff pastries of various sorts, or grab a sandwich to make a light lunch. Closed Sundays.

Aurami is a chain of pastry shops catering to those who like the rich and gooey: cheese cake and strudel, along with specialty breads. There are locations on the Masaya road (km 4½), the southern highway Carretera Sur, km 7½), and at Plaza Alamo and Plaza Bolonia, the latter a few blocks southwest of the Inter-Continental.

VEGETARIAN

Ananda, back near the baseball stadium (10 blocks west of the Inter-Continental, opposite the Montoya statue), serves imitation hamburgers, salads, whole breads, and fresh juices. Open 7 a.m. to 2 p.m., closed Sundays.

MODERATELY PRICED FOOD NEAR DOWNTOWN

While the Inter-Continental and the restaurants nearby are tony, the blocks to the north and west, and to some degree the south, hold some clean, inexpensive eating places.

Cipitío, four blocks west and a block-and-a-half south of the Inter-Continental, is a favorite of younger visitors, and serves basic beef dishes and Salvadoran *pupusas* (another variation on tortillas with fillings) for under $6.

Amatl Café, two blocks south and up the hill from the Inter-Continental, and just west, is a courtyard establishment for nourishment and contemplation, associated with the bookstore next door. A set meal will cost under $5. The name refers to the huge wild fig tree.

Otherwise, head west and south from the Inter-Continental around noon, keep your eyes open, and watch where the government bureaucrats go for lunch. You can be sure that these are people who want something slightly more than basic in restaurants, but don't have a lot of money to spend.

Often you'll see them entering what looks like a private home, but if you get closer, you'll see that tables are set up in the front room, and it's really a restaurant, with no overhead for fancy signs and lights and decor.

A couple of names to look for, or ask for, are **La Sazón** (opposite Radio Primerísima) and **Dos por Dos** (or "2 X 2"), the latter a cafeteria-style luncheonette; **Bambú**, three blocks east of Cine Dorado (that is, about six blocks west of the Inter-Continental); and **Cafetín Mirna**, a block east and a half-block south of Cine Dorado. And there are others.

SNACKS

You'll find stands along some of the main streets serving quesillo (a cooked cheese product served in tortillas), hamburgers and hot dogs, but not necessarily in and around wherever you're staying. You can always pick up light food in the markets. Another choice, if you're near downtown, is to head for the **Malecón**, the waterfront promenade in old Managua. Various snack stands sell hamburgers and pizza for under $2, and roast chicken by the piece.

SOUTHWEST

Restaurante César, Southern Highway (*Carretera Sur*), km 8½, then 3 blocks east. French and Central European fare, including stroganoff, tournedos and duck à l'orange. Open 11 a.m. to 1 a.m. César is *the* place in Managua for *fine cuisine*, and it might be one of the few places where all seats are likely to be taken. So call for reservations: 652744. Dinner will cost $20 as a minimum.

El Eskimo, west side of foreign ministry (*Costado este Cancillería*) in the Altagracia neighborhood southwest of downtown. Steaks, chops and salad bar in modern surroundings, adjacent to (and owned by) the ice-cream factory of the same name.

Pollo Supremo (mentioned above, under downtown food) has a roast chicken outlet at kilometer 7 on the Southern Highway (Carretera Sur), tel. 651025, by the Shell gasoline station.

Corfu, Delta building (*Edificio Delta #3*). A sort of nouvelle cuisine establishment, with light food, including salads, and wine. Under $10.

Doña Hanna, Km 10½ on the Southern Highway (*Km 10½, Carretera Sur*), is where a family might go on the edge of town to enjoy dumplings or wurst or better, and think about the Black Forest (the one in Germany, or the one in Matagalpa).

Los Ranchos, kilometer 3½, Southern Highway, is a steak house.

The Lobster's Inn, km 6½, southern highway (*Carretera Sur*) is the acknowledged tops in this category, in price, years of service, and expansion—they have a branch in Costa Rica. In addition to the usual (curvina, shrimp and lobster), you can find snapper (*pargo*) and marinated grouper.

SOUTHEAST

Eduardo's, southeast of downtown, specializes in pepper steak, and sea bass with capers. Like many restaurants (and smaller hotels, for that matter), it's a converted substantial residence, rather than a purpose-built commercial locale, relatively intimate and charming. From the junction of Pista de la Municipalidad and Av. Rubén Darío (Masaya Road), 1 block east, ½ block south (*Rotonda Metrocentro, 1. c. al oeste, ½ c. al sur*).

La Marseillaise, main street of Los Robles, Masaya road, serves pepper steak, tournedos, and other French standards in an upscale residential area.

Sacuanjoche, Masaya road, km 8. Sacuanjoche is the yellow national flower of Nicaragua, and as the name suggests, the fare is native-style, or *típico*, to a degree, with grilled steaks and kebabs, though there are also finer preparations, such as lobster in champagne.

Asador Chino, Cine Altamira 3½ c. al norte. Your neighborhood Chinese restaurant in Altamira, past the new Cathedral and off the Masaya road. Also out this way are **Chop Suey Internacional**, Colonia Centroamérica Shopping Center (*Plaza de Compras Colonia Centroamérica*), off the Masaya highway, farther out than Altamira; and **Shangai**, kilometer 4½, Masaya road.

PIZZA

There are various local brands, mostly located in the shopping centers along all the roads that lead from Managua. Not that I have anything particular in its favor, but if you want a pizza that will more or less conform to your expectations, try **Domino's** in the Camino de Oriente shopping center, on the Masaya road. They'll deliver to your hotel, if you call 782562, or you can fax your order to 782488 direct from your personal digital assistant.

MIDDLE EAST

Bocados de Oriente, km 5 on the Masaya road, serves hummous, kebabs, schawarma, and other Lebanese-type specialties.

BARS AND CLUBS

Where do you go out at night for a drink and entertainment in a strange city?

If that city is Managua, and you need a **car** or **taxi** to get to most night places, and you don't want to be too far from your lodgings once you've had a few, you'll try the hotel bar, or one of the clubs nearby, or head to a well-established bar with music or a show. If it's something more on the edge that you're looking for, you can find it in Managua, but don't ask me.

Many bars, but not all, follow the Central American tradition of serving *boquitas* ("bo-KI-tas," snacks) with alcoholic drinks, and with enough rounds, you won't need any dinner.

At the **Hotel Inter-Continental**, the main bar is **La Cita** ("the date," or "encounter"), off the lobby, where piano music is played most evenings. For something more lively, **La Cabaña** offers Latin dance rhythms along with Mexican snacks.

Piano Bar, across the street from the Inter-Continental, offers live piano music on Friday and Saturday evenings.

Boobs are the main subject at **Josephine's Elite**, a block south of the Inter-Continental (tel. 226275). Girlie floor shows and/or the casino will be the attraction. You didn't come for the food, did you? Josephine's (along with its sister clubs in Costa Rica and Panama) is relatively clean in its business ways. Nobody pestering you to buy drinks or engage extra services. Parking is available.

Mansión Teodolinda, the hotel, a few blocks from the Inter-Continental, has a dance band on most weekends.

La Cavanga, tel. (02)281098, downtown in the Centro Cultural Managua, plays the golden oldies of Latin music—bossa nova, mambo, and more. Take a taxi—downtown Managua lacks the reassuring street life of some other capitals, but once you're in the Centro Cultural, you're fine.

> ## MUSICA VIVA
>
> Count on live music at bars on Thursdays through Saturdays. Some clubs may not be open on other evenings.

Ruta Maya, near the baseball stadium (1½ block north of the Montoya statue, tel. 225038), the restaurant specializing in Central American regional foods, has a happy hour from 5 to 8 p.m.

With a car or taxi, you can drive up to the stands along the **malecón** (lakefront) of downtown Managua. It's lively enough on weekends, with beer and snacks available all night, and enough people milling about. Likewise, there are bars and drinking terraces near the **stadium** toward the western end of downtown.

Hotel Camino Real, east of town toward the airport, holds the Oasis bar, open every night except Sunday. There's a karaoke on Thursday and Friday, with a younger clientele on Fridays. Happy hour 6 to 8 p.m.

Beyond the central area and away from the hotels are many other establishments, some of which are mentioned below. Ask at your hotel if the one you're interested in is currently in business before you head out, or, better yet, have someone call and inquire about the evening's entertainment. Many bars are open only two or three nights a week.

Chaplin, km 5, Masaya road, tel. 74375, has a karaoke. Closed Sunday.

Lobo Jack, Camino de Oriente (Eastern Highway), tel. 670123, is a night spot of long standing, with not-too-loud Latin and American music. Popular with foreigners, closed Monday and Tuesday.

El Caballito de Mar, by the Shell station at Plaza El Sol (1 block south, 2 west, 1 south/*1 c. al sur, 2 c. oeste, 1 c. al sur*), tel. 662975, is a seafood bar with guitar music on weekends.

Several bars with a youngish clientele are along Pista de la Municipalidad (ex-Pista de la Revolución) in the vicinity of Plaza 19 de Julio, opposite **UCA** ("OO-ka," the Universidad Centroamericana, or Central American University) toward the Masaya road. Among them is the huge **Carnaval,** tel. 74140, open from 5 p.m., with shows on weekends. **El Arroyito** also usually has live music.

GAMING

In addition to Josephine's, near the Inter-Continental, mentioned above, you can lose your money, among others, at:

Black Jack Club, next to Restaurant Munich, tel. 668120.

Jockey Club, downtown, 2½ blocks south of Hotel Mansión Teodolinda, tel. 667028, with slots, blackjack, roulette and baccarat; and

Pigalle, km 7½, Southern highway, tel. (02)653059, where there is also a girlie show.

Nicaragua Guide

MORNING IN MANAGUA
SEEING THE CITY

DOWNTOWN AND OLD MANAGUA

A MOVIE SET . . .

Stand in the main square of Old Managua, and gaze at the imposing Cathedral . . . the National Palace . . . the expanse of the square itself. It's all impressive, grandiose, and . . . eerie. The hustle and street bustle of a throbbing Central American capital, in the air elsewhere in Managua, is absent. The main square of Managua, the **Plaza de la República**, with a rotunda at its center, has ample parking spaces marked out on the pavement, but rarely sufficient cars to occupy them. No detritus of daily life blows through the streets or along the sidewalks, except during a political demonstration (of which there have been fewer than during Sandinista days, when the space was the Plaza de la Revolución). The Cathedral and National Palace (or Palace of the Revolution, according to which government is in power) are backdropped by empty space.

Look more closely, and see that the **Cathedral** itself is windowless and roofless. Peek inside, and you might expect to see plywood and studs backing ersatz stone facing, as on a movie set. But instead of artifice imitating life, it is life that once was.

. . . AND FUTURE CENTER

This state of affairs, which has existed for several decades in the absence of reconstruction funds, is about to change. The National Palace is being restored, and will soon be back in use. And even the old Cathedral, a solid, nineteenth-century neoclassical structure that stood up to the tremors of '72 as its roof collapsed, is being renovated, though it has been supplanted by an unusual new Cathedral in the south-central part of town. For now, you can peek inside to watch the welding.

CULTURE FIRST

West of the main square, the **Rubén Darío Theater** (Teatro Rubén Darío) is in style and function Managua's Lincoln Center, named for the nineteenth-century poet who is for many Nicaragua's national hero. The complementary statue of Darío shows him with his trademark scowl, though he did, indeed, have happy moments. Despite appearances, the theater dates from the late sixties, before the great earthquake.

South of the National Palace on Dupla Norte, the wide and not-so-busy east-west boulevard, is the **Centro Cultural Managua**, or Cultural Center. This is one of those officially conceived projects that attempts to bring together various functions in a specific locale; except that here, the locale is no purpose-built modern and sterile palace, but the shell of the dowager **Gran Hotel**, which serves as the perfect host body for the transplant. Step inside and you'll find what downtown Managua appears to be lacking, all gathered in one place: bars and boîtes, fine art galleries, studios, a book outlet, rehearsal and recital spaces, handicraft shops. Browse, shop, take a look at the calendar of events, and return at some time later in your visit.

The Centro Cultural is open from 8:30 a.m. to midnight, and has its own parking. For information about programs, dial 284045 or 281032.

Across Avenida Bolívar, the main north-south street, the **Museo de Arte Julio Cortázar** holds contemporary art works of Nicaraguans, and hosts travelling exhibitions, in a charming older building, one of the few that survived the great quakes of 1931 and 1972.

IS THERE A LAKE?

Turning northward, **Lake Managua**, or **Xolotlán** (ho-lot-LAN), is easy to overlook once you're in the city, or even if you've been living in Managua for a while. Surprisingly enough, the life of the capital and of its inhabitants has virtually nothing to do with this large and shallow and none-too-clean body of water.

The boats you'd expect on a lake of any size are not there. The beaches, or waterside parks with pools of filtered water, are likewise absent. Nobody is seen to drop a line into the waters to catch dinner, though it's said that the poor will sometimes have recourse to the creatures of Xolotlán. The banks of the lake are marshy and untrampled.

In the old, old days, before the earthquake, the lakefront downtown, the **Malecón**, was a people's gathering spot. After 1972, priorities lay elsewhere, and the old gathering spot was virtually abandoned. But in recent years, the Malecón has started to see life again, with the construction of a terrace-promenade, a truncated boardwalk, and little snack chalets, and the placing of benches overlooking the lake and the reeds along its shore. Nearby are a ferris wheel and rides. Just across the way, on a hillock, is the modern municipal library, with attendant exhibit halls.

Nicaragua Guide

BY DAY AND BY NIGHT

The old center of Managua is a fascinating remnant of the way things used to be in Managua, and it endures as the emotional focal point and cultural, political and psychological crossroads of Nicaragua, where major political demonstrations are held as a matter of obligation, and where the government still convenes.

Though lightly trafficked by vehicles and pedestrians, it is as safe as most other city centers in the region, and perhaps *safer*, with open fields of vision, and few crowds or hidden nooks into which purse snatchers and pickpockets might vanish.

By night, however, Old Managua is another place entirely. The open, unlit, grassy spaces along the wide boulevards are an invitation to pedestrians to stay away. Prostitutes appear at dusk in Spandex shorts to thumb for pickups along the main east-west streets (you didn't think they were hitchhiking, did you?). A certain amount of drug-dealing and assorted illicit exchange prevails, as anywhere. It's no surprise that it takes place, only *where* it takes place. Visitor, wander elsewhere of an evening, unless you take a taxi to an exhibit, or have a car and use the guarded parking lot at your destination.

GOVERNMENT BUILDINGS

Between the lake and the Inter-Continental Hotel, along or near Bolívar, is a cluster of official buildings. The tower is the **Banco Central de Nicaragua**, the central bank, formerly the Bank of America. Next to it, at reduced elevation, is the **National Assembly** (Asamblea Nacional). Least prominent is **La Presidencia**, the presidential offices. A wall surrounds the compound of newer buildings, and casual visitors may not enter.

At the intersection of Avenida Bolívar (the main north-south street) and Dupla Norte (the east-west boulevard), are two fountains, not particularly notable, except that red dye is regularly dumped in the water of one, and black in the other. The results are gray liquid spouting on one side and pink on the other; but everyone gets the point. Red and black are the colors of the Sandinistas, currently out of power, but with many supporters.

BASEBALL

Out toward the western part of central Managua is the **Estadio Nacional (National Stadium)**, with its distinctive, freestanding light towers illuminating the night. Ask at your hotel about scheduled games. Seat prices start at less than $1.

NATIONAL MUSEUM

A dozen blocks east of the old center, along the lakefront, the small **Museo Nacional (National Museum)** is housed partly in a mansion that survived the '72 quake. Pre-Columbian earthenware is on exhibit inside. Hours are 8 a.m. to 4 p.m. Monday through Friday, closed on weekends. In a complementary, newer building is the **Escuela de Arte (Art School)**, with the same hours.

MEETING PLACE

The **Olof Palme Convention Center (Centro de Convenciones Olof Palme)**, less than a kilometer northeast of the Hotel Inter-Continental, near the junction of 15 de Septiembre and Av. 10, is everything a modern meeting with thousands of delegates and support personnel could wish for—plenary hall, meeting rooms, simultaneous translation system and the rest. Opened in 1987 for an international meeting of parliamentarians, the center has hosted a range of personages from presidents and monarchs to humble Guatemalan indigenous luminary Rigoberta Menchú. Its name honors the late Swedish prime minister.

With the change of government, and the center's new obligation to pay its way with more than prestige events, you're more likely to run into a wedding party, teen celebration or bar mitzvah. Or to book a room yourself, at $30 and up. Wedding in Managua? Listen, you can get a deal.

INTER•CONTINENTAL

Peeking out at central Managua from its hillside perch to the south is the Hotel Inter-Continental (or Inter•Continental), the armored Mayan pyramid that withstood the '72 earthquake and became the legendary hangout for journalists who covered the Insurrection against Somoza from its bar. As previously mentioned, the "Inter" is the major reference point for visitors; at least, it's one of the few that makes sense.

All around the Inter-Continental are neighborhoods of one-story houses and low-lying buildings containing restaurants, government offices, and businesses of one sort or another, in the *barrios* (neighborhoods) of Martha Quezada and El Carmen, immediately to the west; and Bolonia and Bosques de Bolonia (up the hill, and then down and westward).

LAGUNA DE TISCAPA

Avenida Bolívar, the street that passes the Inter-Continental, rises and then descends to a "Y" junction north of the hotel. To the west (the right, leaving downtown) is Plaza España, currently being torn up, around which many airlines and some travel agencies have their offices. To the left, Paseo Tiscapa takes a loop around Laguna de Tiscapa (Tiscapa Lake, or Mirror Lake, to translate the Nahuatl exactly), a treasured bit of fresh water that looks somewhat like a filled sinkhole or quarry. Watching from above is an oversized profile of Augusto César Sandino, wearing his trademark campaign hat.

THE NEW CATHEDRAL

Much of the area to the immediate south of Plazuela España and Lake Tiscapa is set aside for parks, or is open. One of the major highways out of the city, to Masaya, starts from near Tiscapa, and along it is the new **Cathedral of Managua**, (or Catedral Metropolitana de la Purísima Concepción) consecrated in 1993.

By day, the Cathedral has an appearance that suggests not at all its universal Catholic vocation. It is a squarish building with dozens of nippled domes, and if any religion comes to mind, it is that of the mosque; though the curious mounds could also be taken, without much imagination, for the tanks of a soft drink or chemical plant protruding through the roof. If not identified to the casual visitor, this is a building that will be bypassed and unnoticed.

Unexpected, then, is the metamorphosis of the Cathedral into a ruler of the night. Humdrum multidomed square transforms into a beacon. Light gleams from its arched entry, and beams heavenward through the tips of its multiple cupolas. Alone it shines, unchallenged and unrivaled by any civic building, any authority. If there were ever a symbol of renewal, of the promise of a journey upward, it is this temple. Behold the reward to come.

FOOTPRINTS BACK INTO TIME
HUELLAS DE ACAHUALINCA

One of the odder and more rewarding sites in Managua lies three kilometers west of the city center, in the middle of a poor *barrio* of shacks and industry. **Las Huellas de Acahualinca** ("las WAY-yas thay a-ka-wa-

LEEN-ka," The Footprints of Acahualinca) are one of the oldest signs of human presence in Nicaragua, impressions of scurrying feet left in mud that solidified into rock. The fossilized prints were discovered in 1874 in a quarry on the site.

Visitors can descend to an excavation in a basement-like shelter to view the line of foot impressions, along with those of animals, marching lakeward in straight lines on a lava bed, and, unseen, onward through the earth.

The footprints were first studied scientifically in 1941, by Francis Richardson of the Carnegie Institution. Additional prints were discovered in a new excavation in 1978.

Richardson dated the prints at 6000 years of age, and suggested that they were made by a culture that hunted, fished, and gathered fruit. There was no particular human tragedy à la Pompei, according to Richardson. Lava from an eruption had probably cooled, to that point that humans and beasts trod upon it in its soft state, before it solidified completely.

But other savants have suggested the picturesque tragedy of refugees fleeing an eruption, and overtaken by the lava in which their prints are eternally embedded, though their earthly beings vaporized.

Whatever the actual details, volcanic ash covered the prints, and protected them from the dirt that later filled in the area.

VISITING LAS HUELLAS

The Huellas are in the Acahualinca neighborhood—named for a small lake in the district—which stretches along the lakefront to the west of central Managua. Take a taxi or a guide to the site; even if you have a rented car, it would be easy to lose your way, as street names are not posted, though the city map available from the tourist office could get you there. The entry to the museum and excavation looks like a large home, somewhat out of place in its modest surroundings; there is no easily visible sign.

Entry fee is about $1.50.

THE HEART OF COMMERCE
MARKETS OF MANAGUA

Managua's **public markets** are the lifeblood of the city.

In a country where food chains and superstores have not taken over the avenues of distribution, they are the main sources of supply for many Managuans. In them you'll find fruits and vegetables and cereals and hanging slabs of meat and tin pots and cheap "western" clothing and lots of old-fashioned goods, such as stovetop pressing irons made in China, that could easily make for off-beat souvenirs. And there are handicrafts as well.

And not incidentally, the markets are also informal social clubs, news centers, transport hubs, clusters of eateries, and, of course, of course, geographical reference points.

If you think that Managua lacks a center or centers, look at the markets, dummy!

Most of the markets are vast, and appear, at first glance, to be disorganized and intimidating. But everything has its place. There is the section for inter-city buses, with parking lots, and ticket counters and benches under roofs. The commerce in goods goes on in vast inside galleries, and these are more sedate than one would guess from the scurry of bodies and jam of traffic outside.

Merchants in each specialized section cooperate as much as compete. If a stall owner is called away, the neighboring merchant will fill in. If one market lady doesn't have quite what you're looking for, she'll point the way to someone with additional stock. In these close quarters, where sellers have face-to-face contact every day, it's the only way.

SPECIFIC MARKETS

Managua has five major markets. Most have two names—the traditional one, and the name attached in the Sandinista period. Usually, the Sandinista name has been officially "repealed," but is still in popular use.

Mercado Oriental ("Eastern Market"), on the eastern edge of downtown, is within walking distance of some hotels, but is smaller than other markets, though it looks pretty big if you're not used to this sort of shopping. **Mercado San Judás**, in southwest Managua, is off the beaten track for most visitors.

The huge **Mercado Roberto Huembes** ("mehr-KA-though ro-BEHR-to WEM-bes"), or **Mercado Central**, is in southeast Managua on Pista Portezuelo, one of the main ring roads. The Huembes market has the largest handicraft section. Visitors using public transport will find buses here for Granada, Masaya and Matagalpa.

Mercado Iván Montenegro, or **Mercado San Miguel**, is in far eastern Managua, and is the terminal for buses to Chontales and the Atlantic area of Nicaragua.

Mercado Israel Lewites, or **Mercado Boer**, is southwest of downtown on Pista de la Municipalidad (a.k.a. Pista de la Resistencia), a major ring road, and serves as the bus terminal for León and points west.

SHOPPING AND NAVIGATING

If you're looking for crafts to take home, the starting point in Managua is the **public markets**. There are plenty of **crafts** in the section devoted to **artesanías** ("ar-teh-sah-NEE-yas"), though much of what's to be found is intended for daily use, rather than as souvenirs: belts, jewelry, handbags, plates, and the like. And make no mistake, these items are not regarded as cutesy or folkloric, but are a living part of Nicaraguan material culture (as the professors would say).

How do you **find your way**? Don't try too hard! All of the fun in a great public market is to wander around in awe at how commerce functions when computers are not predicting and dictating demand. Merchants are bound to solicit your business—want a shirt?, need some fresh-caught fish for dinner?—and send you toward their cohorts who have the right goods.

THE MERCHANDISE

A few words to describe specific crafts will come in handy. *Artesanías* ("ar-teh-sah-NEE-yas," handicrafts) are the starting point.

Among the crafts that might interest you are *hamacas* ("ha-MA-kas," hammocks), *bolsas* (bags and purses), *collares* ("ko-YA-res," necklaces), *sombreros* (hats), *aretes* and *joyería* (earrings and other jewelry), *artículos de madera* (woodware), *cotonas* (formal cotton shirts), *cerámica* (ceramics), *cinturones* (belts), *muñecas* (dolls), *mecedoras* (rocking chairs), *esculturas* (statuettes), and much more.

But there's much, much more. Virtually all the handicrafts made in Nicaragua (see page 94) make their way to the capital.

GROUND RULES

Prices are by no means fixed in the markets, but Nicaragua does not have such regular hordes of tourists that inflated amounts are requested by sellers. You probably won't be quoted much more than what a Nicaraguan would be asked to pay. Bargain, but don't be too insistent once you find the seller's line of resistance.

Cash is the medium of exchange in markets, with prices set in córdobas, rather than in dollars (as in hotels), so forget the travellers checks and credit cards, and keep your cash in a pocket inaccessible to wandering fingers.

Nicaragua Guide

STILL MORE SHOPPING

Remember, I said the public markets are just the starting point for your shopping excursions (didn't I?). This most rewarding of activity for visitors may be continued in many quarters of Managua.

One good place to browse is the **Central Cultural Managua** in the ex-Gran Hotel, downtown, on Dupla Norte. **Ceramics** will be found in outlets there, ranging from small to substantial. Some feature traditional designs, others are glazed avant-garde pieces that have been fashioned into lamps. Oyanka is the name of one outlet with a large stock.

On the outskirts of the city, Cerámica por La Paz is at kilometer 9½ on the new León road.

Another store outside the markets that also has clay, leather, wood and ceramic products is La Casa del Artesano, next to Banco de Préstamos.

If you're a craftsperson yourself, or have aspirations, you can check out the supplies of raw materials in the public markets.

Antique **furniture**, and reproductions of antiques, along with crafts, are found at La Querencia ("The Longing"), in the old center, Pancasán IV etapa, no. 77, open Wednesday, Thursday and Friday only.

In a decentralized city, the shops at the **airport** represent one of the more convenient craft outlets. Prices are not particularly high, and there's a good selection of carved stone and wood, leather craft, and fabrics. Do not leave without a heavyweight, unbleached cotton t-shirt bearing the likeness of Augusto César Sandino. Current price, with a little haggling, is $5 or less.

ON THE OUTSKIRTS

ASOSOSCA

On the western outskirts, and visible from the Pan American highway, Lake Asosocsca ("blue water" in Nahuatl) serves as a reservoir of drinking water for Managua. A pictograph believed to represent Quetzalcoatl, the feathered-snake god of the Aztecs and other peoples of Mexican origin, has been found on a rocky outcrop here. South of Asososca is Lake Nejapa ("ash-water"), a salt lake that once was a center of mineral treatments.

The easiest place from which to view Asososca is **Las Piedrecitas Park** (Parque Las Piedrecitas), a children's play area on a rise above western Managua, off the Pan American Highway leading toward Jinotepe and the southern coast.

Managua

LAKE XILOA

Around the bend of water directly before the city to the northwest is the Chiltepe Peninsula, and on the peninsula, about 20 kilometers from downtown, two lakes formed in craters of a remnant volcano. **Apoyeque** ("salt water" in Nahuatl), with its surrounding vertical cliff-walls, is unassailable even by the most intrepid of visitors; but its non-identical twin is a lake more pristine and attractive and swimmable than Lake Managua itself. Xiloá (hee-lo-A, "lake-in-back" in Nahuatl), reached on a branch road from the route to León, surrounded by hills, is a favorite weekend spot for Managuans, with light-blue, slightly mineral waters. At two by three kilometers, it is a relative puddle, dimensionwise, in lake-blessed Nicaragua.

Centro Turístico Xiloá is the public park that stretches along the shores. There are play areas, picnic shelters, rough lawns, and a bit of shade under trees, as well as a grassy beach. The ensemble is something like many a state park, with a maintenance budget that has suffered cutbacks.

Beyond the park are vacation houses and suburban residences.

Facilities include snack stands, and one more formal restaurant, the Kalúa, which serves steaks at about $8 per shot. The H♥tel Xilá, adjacent, with its car slots furnished with concealing blinds, is not to be confused with tourist accommodations.

COLD SPRINGS AND WARM SPRINGS

At kilometer 20 on the west side of the highway northward (passing the airport) is **Centro Turístico El Trapiche**, a suburban park with picnic shelters, swings, a large meandering swimming pond, snack stands, a floating restaurant, lovers intertwined on benches (look, there's no place to go in Managua!), and, best of all, the plenteous shade trees that are missing in so many other public areas in or near the capital.

Though the waters appear to be diverted and dammed from Lake Managua or surface streams, they actually originate in springs, so, despite the absence of a chlorine odor, a dip in their waters will do no harm.

A few kilometers beyond, on the way to Tipitapa, are the **Tipitapa Thermal Baths** (**Baños Termales de Tipitapa**), where the water comes from underground hot mineral springs. Dip your toe in pools at your choice of thermostat setting, from lukewarm to steaming.

ZOO

The **National Zoo (Zoológico Nacional)** re-opened not too long ago, and in modest form, at kilometer 16 on the Masaya road. Signage is limited, cages are still being set up, and most of the constrained budget goes to keeping the animals fed. Parties interested in concretely aiding the development of the zoo can contact the Wildlife Department of the Ministry of the Environment and Natural Resources (Departamento de Fauna del Ministerio del Ambiente y de Los Recursos Naturales), Km 12½ Carretera Norte Hacienda Santa Elena, fax (011-505-2)31596.

OUR PATRON SAINT, AND OTHER PARTIES

In case you miss it, religion, and especially the Catholic religion, are part of the makeup of Nicaraguans, and their devotion, based partly on deeply ingrained pre-Columbian practices and beliefs, often turns toward the adoration of specific saints.

In Managua, *the* saint, or patron, is St. Dominic, or **Santo Domingo**, and though he has sometimes dealt hard blows by not protecting against earthquake and flood, he has seen to the survival of the city and most of its people, and it is in his honor that Managuans celebrate each year, from August 1 to 10, in a party-cum-religious-devotion that is impossible for anyone to escape.

The principal expression of devotion at fiesta time is the fetching of the tiny statue of Santo Domingo de Guzmán from his shrine in the Managua hills south of town, the execution of which task serves as a pretext for dancing in the street, and fireworks, and horseback processions of cowboys, and amplified blarings of roving marimba bands, and masked parades that have as much to do with the tradition of carnival as with anything originating in Rome.

And at other times of the year, Managuans join in celebrations that span Nicaragua. As in many Latin countries, Christmas is not a holiday, but a season of holidays, starting with the Purísima festivities at the beginning of the month, which end on the night of December 7; followed by processions that recall the wanderings of Joseph and Mary in search of shelter.

With the change of government, the Fiestas Patrias (National Independence Holiday) on September 14 and 15 are the main civic celebration, though mass gatherings of workers still take place on May 1.

ART SCENE

Amidst humble circumstances, political sea-change, a rebuilding capital city, uncertainties of every sort, art and traditional crafts are mainstays and handholds for many Nicaraguans.

In how many capital cities do you see classified ads offering instruction in traditional ceramics? Galleries devoted to native primitive painters? Persons of all social levels buying and using hand-made belts and tableware? A constrained public purse that has given priority to building a cultural center and theater? In how many poorer cities are there art competitions with first prizes of $1000, $2000 or $5000?

Here are some of the locales where the creative arts can be appreciated:

- **Centro Cultural Managua**, in the heart of Old Managua, on Dupla Norte (a wide east-west boulevard) holds several galleries (Códice and others), bookstores, painters' studios, and coffee shops. Travelling expositions are regularly booked. Nearby, **Teatro Rubén Darío** (Rubén Darío Theater) also hosts expositions. See page 142.

- Casa de los Tres Mundos, Los Robles (Masaya Road), 2½ blocks north of La Marsellaise, tel. 670304.

- Galería Solentiname, 6 blocks south of UNAN (National University) transfer point, tel. 70939, specializes in primitive painters, especially, of course, those on the Solentiname Islands in Lake Nicaragua. Sometimes they have jazz or other musical events as well.

- Galería Praxis, from Plaza España, 2 blocks north, one block west, half block north, tel. 663563.

- Escuela de Artes Plásticas, Col. Dambach

- Galería Contil, Calle principal Colonial Los Robles, casa 193.

- Galería El Aguila, km. 6½, Carretera Sur (southern highway), tel. 650524, features contemporary paintings and sculpture.

. . . and, of course, there are the markets and handicraft shops (see page 148).

MANAGUA MINUTIAE

BANKS AND EXCHANGE HOUSES

Like everything else, banks and exchange houses are dispersed in the island-neighborhoods of Managua. If there's none evident in the vicinity of your hotel, ask at the front desk, look in the vicinity of Plaza España, or check the list below.

Before you head for a bank, read the advice on *Managing Your Money,* page 61. In general, there is no particular advantage, at the moment, in using an exchange house (*casa de cambio*) over a bank.

In fact, there may be no particular advantage in using either. Hotels usually give a rate of exchange not too different from that of banks, and credit cards, especially Visa and Master Card, are widely accepted.

Banks can have longer lineups, but are more plentiful than **exchange houses**. Some locations are mentioned below, in case you have to arrange a money transfer or cash advance.

- Banco Mercantil, Plaza España, one block south, tel. 668228, fax 668024.

- Banpro, Plaza España; and km 4, Carretera Norte (northern highway/airport road).

- Banco de Crédito Centroamericano (Bancentro), km 4, Masaya road, tel. 782777, fax 786001.

- Banco de Préstamos (Banpres), opposite west side of Hotel Inter-Continental, tel. 283046, 283048, fax 283057, telex 1268.

→The bank at the **airport** *does not*, at the moment, accept travellers checks.

Exchange Houses (*casas de cambio*) are something like neighborhood check-cashing shops for Nicaraguans. They'll convert remittances from relatives abroad, and sell money orders. They'll also take your U.S. cash or travellers checks, with positive identification, such as a passport. A few names are:

- BICSA (Buró Internacional de Cambio), 2 blocks south of Plaza España, tel. 663296, fax 663418.

- Cambiocentro, km 4, Masaya road, tel. 782637, fax 681791.

Managua

- Multicambios, east side, Plaza España, tel. 668407, fax 663163.

TRANSPORT IN MANAGUA

LOCAL BUSES

City buses—*buses urbanos*, or *urbanos colectivos*—are old, crowded, and sometimes in poor repair. If you stay in Managua for a while, you might get to know the routes, but for a first-time visitor, the system is confusing, given the lack of street numbers, the multiple names and assorted ways of referring to landmarks, and residents' perception of their city as island-neighborhoods—colonias, repartos and villas—rather than as a whole spreading out from downtown. Many bus routes avoid the center of the city altogether, which, for a visitor, is just no help.

All in all, taxis are a better way to get from point to point.

But if you have more time than money, or wish to see Managua from a Managuan point of view, by all means take an urban bus trip. Or, once you're in your lodgings, ask about which local bus will take you to the central area, or to the nearest market.

Service on most routes starts at about 5 p.m., and continues until about 10 p.m. Fare is the equivalent of about 15 cents.

Some of the main routes are:

102   Villa Progreso (east end) to Acahualinca (west of downtown, along lake).

105   Sierra Maestra (extreme southwest) to Unidad to Propósitos (extreme northeast). Some buses continue toward airport.

106   Sierra Maestra (extreme southwest) to Mercado Oriental (Oriental Market, just east of downtown area)

109   Reparto Schick to Parque Central (main square in old downtown); route includes Avenida Bolívar between the Inter-Continental and the lake; and the Roberto Huembes market and bus station southeast of the Inter-Continental.

110   Lewites market to Metrocentro shopping center and junction to Montenegro market.

RECOLLECTIONS OF THE THIRD WORLD VANGUARD

It wasn't too many years ago that Nicaragua was an outcast in Uncle Sam's eyes; and, to many, many others, including some U.S. citizens, a nation in the vanguard of the struggle for the self-determination of peoples, and against international hegemony, the excesses of capitalism, unequal distribution of the rewards of labor, and social injustice in general.

Whatever your views of the heroes and villains of recent Nicaraguan history, the vestiges of the Sandinista period make for a fascinating museum of east-bloc scenes and revolutionary trivia, the likes of which are to be seen nowhere else in the hemisphere, except in Cuba (to which Nicaragua bears many other resemblances).

In the course of the next few years, some of the evidence of the revolutionary period will erode, or be covered or erased. But much will remain indelible, as Nicaraguans move on, and reconcile with themselves.

Here are some examples of the moment:

- The **Olof Palme Convention Center** honors the assassinated Swedish prime minister who kept the lines of trade and communication open, and provided development aid of the sort that was cut off by other nations during the Sandinista period.

- The **fountains** at the intersection of Avenida Bolívar and Dupla Norte in central Managua, their waters regularly colored red and black by Sandinistas

- The **Tomb of Carlos Fonseca Amador**, in the heart of old downtown Managua, near the National Palace, honors one of the co-founders of the Frente Sandinista de Liberación Nacional (Sandinista National Liberation Front). Fonseca died in 1976.

- The **Museo de la Revolución (Museum of the Revolution)**, adjacent to the Roberto Huembes Market in southeastern Managua. With the change in government, it is now an *ex*-museum, closed to the public, a modern, concrete square waiting to find other uses. But with its situation adjacent to a people's market, rather than in some toney neighborhood, you get the idea of who came out on top of the class struggle in '78. For now, you can still see the wrecks of jerry-built armored vehicles in the dirt yard.

- **Lada taxis** were imported in quantity from the Soviet Union, when western vehicles were not to be had, and they're still rollin' along in their second and third incarnations, dented, patched, repaired, and painted several times over. Canadians might be familiar with the vehicles, but not Americans: bug-sized and bug-prone, they're virtually identical to the obsolete Fiats of a few decades ago. If you were in Italy at the time, it's déjà vu all over again.

  Likewise, the buses of Managua are largely a tribute to Soviet-bloc manufacturing standards.

- **Military hardware** is no longer as easily glimpsed as it once was in Managua. It used to be that planes landing at Augusto César Sandino airport proceeded along a row of Significantly parked Soviet helicopters with characteristically vulnerable belly motors. No more. The hardware is deployed more discreetly these days, though you can still spot Russky choppers behind walls along the airport highway.

  Likewise, you might glimpse a Soviet armored car; but more likely, the Russian equivalent of a Jeep, large and clunky.

- **Cubana**, the Cuban national airline, has interrupted its service to Managua. But **Aeroflot**, "la línea aérea con las mejores tarifas del mundo" ("the airline with the best fares in the world") counts Managua among its destinations.

- The **Iranian cultural center** on the Masaya road (kilometer 4½, tel. 75742). You won't find many of these in the western world.

- The **Iranian embassy,** Las Colinas (Masaya road), Vista Alegre E-93, tel. 75190. A less uncommon species.

- The **embassy of Cuba,** Las Colinas (Masaya road), tel. 71182.

- The **embassy of Libya,** practically in the shadow of the Hotel Inter-Continental, tel. 668540, and the Libyan cultural center.

- The **embassy of Palestine,** Las Colinas (Masaya road), Las Flores 136, tel. 670720. Still a rare find.

- The **ex-embassy of the Soviet Union,** now the Russian embassy, Las Colinas (Masaya road), Vista Alegre 214, tel. 799460.

- Most moving, south of the old center, looming over Lake Tiscapa from a hilltop perch, is the oversized, full-body cutout of **Augusto César Sandino**, complete with trademark wide-brimmed hat, an ineradicable presence, despite changing administrations.

116   Seminario to Villa Progreso (roughly east-west through central Managua), passing Inter-Continental Hotel and Iván Montenegro market. Bus 101 also runs between the Inter-Continental and the Montenegro market.

118   Los Laureles to Las Piedrecitas (park overlooking Managua), east to southwest through Central Managua, passing Plaza España and Lewites bus station.

119   Includes the stretch from Plaza España southwest of the Inter-Continental to the Roberto Huembes market and bus station to the southeast and Iván Montenegro market in eastern Managua.

TAXIS

Managua has a plentiful supply of **flea-taxis**, Russian-built Ladas that cruise the main streets and are ready to take on people, cargo, and anything else that will make a trip worth the trouble. Fares are low—anywhere from $1 for a short trip of a few blocks, to $5 for a ride out to the international airport.

You can pay even less if you pick up a *colectivo* cruising one of the main roads of Managua. How do you know a colectivo? If a taxi stops and it has people in it already, they're flat-rate passengers, and you'll be charged a flat-rate fare as well.

Wherever you're going, make sure you set the fare before you get in and the driver takes off. And don't take it as a ploy to get your tourist money when the driver quotes you a fare in dollars—that's the way many prices are figured. You convert to córdobas when you pay up—the driver isn't really interested in cash dollars.

In addition, there are **taxi stands** that host vehicles with a fixed address. These more dignified conveyances charge more, whether you approach them at their stands, or call them to your hotel, or wherever you happen to be. For example, a ride into town from the international airport, or from the taxi stand of the Hotel Las Mercedes, across the street, goes for about $12.

You should have no trouble flagging down a cab on a main street, but if it's late and you have to call a cab, here are some numbers: Hotel Inter-Continental, 223469; Chamorro (downtown), 224872; 25 de Febrero, 225218; Chávez, 225700; 2 de Agosto, tel. 631512. Or, ask your hotel desk to call a nearby taxi stand.

Managua

BUSES TO OTHER TOWNS

Bus terminals for different parts of the country are located at the public markets.

- **Mercado Roberto Huembes (Mercado Central)**: Buses for the **east** and **northwest** regions of Nicaragua (Estelí, La Concepción, Granada, Masaya, Masatepe, Matagalpa, Nueva Segovia, Rivas, Ticuantepe, Veracruz). Service ranges from continuous in the case of Masaya and Granada to every 30 to 40 minutes. The last bus for highland towns usually leaves at 4 p.m. For lowland towns to the east, about 6 p.m.

- **Mercado Iván Montenegro (Mercado San Miguel)**: Buses for the eastern area, beyond Lake Nicaragua: Boaco, Camoapa, Juigalpa and Chontales, Lóvago, Nueva Guinea, Rama, San José de los Remates, Santo Tomás.

- **Mercado Israel Lewites (Mercado Boer)**: Buses to Pacific-west and south-central Nicaragua: Carazo, Chinandega, El Crucero, El Tránsito, La Paz-Centro, León, Masachapa, Nagarote, San Rafael del Sur and Pochomil,

BUSES TO CENTRAL AMERICA

Sirca and **Tica Bus** provide service on alternate days to San José, **Costa Rica**, and Tica Bus has service to Tegucigalpa, **Honduras**, as well, and sometimes to San Salvador and Guatemala City.

There's always a chance that you'll be requested to show a **ticket out of Costa Rica** once you reach the border of that country. (This is more likely the younger you are.) The bus companies will be happy to sell you the necessary ticket, if you don't already have an onward air ticket.

To inquire about departures, call:

- Sirca, Altamira (southeast of downtown, Avenida Delgado 2 blocks south of Vicky store), tel. 673833 or 75726. Departures three days a week, recently Monday, Wednesday and Friday at dawn, with a stop in Rivas. Slightly cheaper than Tica Bus.

- Tica Bus, Bolonia (seven blocks west of the Inter-Continental and one block south, or two blocks east of Cine Dorado), tel. 222096. Recent scheduled departures Tuesday, Thursday and Saturday at 7 a.m.

If schedules don't suit you, head out on the first domestic route going your way. For Costa Rica, take a Rivas bus from the Huembes market, then continue to Peñas Blancas.

For Honduras, take a bus for Somoto or Ocotal from the Roberto Huembes market, then find an onward bus to the border at El Espino or Las Manos. Or, travel via Chinandega in the lowlands.

DRIVING

Kids wash windshields unbidden at every stop light in Managua, and people of all ages peddle razors, shoe laces, and whatever they can make a market in, to whomever they can stop. Even people who are not selling wander into the street without any idea of looking to see if a car is coming.

Aside from creating a serious safety hazard, there's a security issue, whatever your sympathy toward their circumstances. **Keep your windows rolled up.** It takes but seconds for a hand to enter and snatch anything loose, or even something not so loose, like a necklace.

Just remember, taxis are inexpensive.

EMBASSIES AND CONSULATES

Most of the addresses below are for consulates. For those not listed, look in the phone book under "Embajadas." Most are open mornings only, and some operate only a few days of the week. Call before you visit for detailed directions, if needed, and hours.

- Argentina, Sandy's, Masaya Road, 1 west, 2 north, 1 east, tel. 781581, fax 678406.
- Austria, Plaza España, 1 north, tel. 663316, fax 663424.
- Belgium, tel. 223202.
- Brazil, Carretera Sur, km. 7½, tel. 651681, fax 652206.
- Bulgaria, Reparto Las Colinas, Calle Los Mangos 195, P. O. Box 1941, tel. 72274, fax 73888.
- Canada, opposite north side of Zacarías Guerra post office, tel. 287574, 281304.
- Chile, Carretera Sur, P. O. Box 4541, tel. 660302, fax 660181.
- Colombia, Los Robles main entry, 2 west, ½ north, P. O. Box 1062, tel. 780058.

Managua

- Costa Rica, IBM building, Montoya 2 north, 1 east, El Carmen, west of Inter-Continental, tel. 663986, fax 663955.
- Cuba, Las Colinas (Masaya road), 4 blocks in, tel. 71182.
- Denmark, Bolonia, southwest of Inter-Continental, tel. 668095, fax 286351
- El Salvador, Las Colinas (Masaya road), Ave. del Campo no. 142, tel. 71734, fax 74892.
- Finland, Hospital Militar 1 north, 1½ west, tel. 663415, fax 663416.
- France, 1½ blocks west of El Carmen church, tel. 226210, fax 281057.
- Germany, Plaza España, 1½ blocks north, P. O. Box 29, tel. 663917, fax 667667.
- Guatemala, km 11½, Masaya road, P.O. Box E-1, tel. 799609, fax 799610.
- Honduras, Planes de Altamira no. 64, tel. 670182, fax 670183.
- Iran, Las Colinas, Calle Vista Alegre 93, P. O. Box 27, tel. 75190, fax 74183.
- Italy, Av. del Guerrillero, 1 block north of Montoya statue, tel. 666486, fax 663987.
- Japan, Hospital Militar, 1 north, 1½ west, tel. 668668, fax 668675
- Libya, Mansión Teodolinda 1 south, P. O. Box 867, tel. 668540, fax 26563.
- Mexico, km 4½, Masaya road, P. O. Box 834, tel. 784919 (consulate, 75886), fax 782886.
- Netherlands, Terraza, 1 north, 1 west, tel. 661175, fax 660364.
- Nicaragua, tel. 666175.
- North Korea, Shell Las Palmnas 1 north, 1 west, no. 109, P. O. Box 1693, tel. 661480.
- Norway, Plaza España 1 west, tel. 664199, fax 663303.
- Palestine, Las Colinas, Calle Las Flores 136, tel. 760241, fax 670720.

- Panama, Reparto Pancasán, 1 block north of Hotel Colón, P.O. Box 1, tel. 781619.
- Russia, Las Colinas, Calle Vista Alegre 214, P. O. Box 249, tel. 760374, fax 760179.
- Spain, Las Colinas, Av. Central no. 13, P. O. Box 284, tel. 71321, fax 760937.
- Sweden, Plaza España, 1 block west, 2 blocks north, ½ block west, P. O. Box 2307, tel. 660085, fax 666778.
- Switzerland, kilometer 6½, Northern Highway (Carretera Norte), tel. 492671.
- United Kingdom, Reparto Los Robles (southeast of Inter-Continental), tel. 780014, fax 784085.
- U.S.A., km 4½, Carretera Sur (south highway), P. O. Box 327, tel. 784912, embassy; 75886, 666010 consulate, fax 663865.

Rarities in the list above are Bulgaria, Cuba, Iran, Libya, North Korea, and State of Palestine. Others may be found in the phone book. Is Angola still represented? Whatever the change of political circumstances from those under which they established their diplomatic links, most of these entities are not about to give up their local representation.

ENTERTAINMENT

Movies just never came back after the 1972 Managua earthquake. Though a few of the large cinemas survived the tremors—and can be seen to this day amid the open spaces of Central Managua—the population dispersed, videos came into fashion, and there was no lively center from which to draw a walk-in clientele.

So . . . you can count your chances for viewing movies on a few fingers. Cinemas 1 and 2 are in a shopping center (Centro Comercial Camino de Oriente) on the way out of town toward Masaya. Cine González operates in the old downtown area, and Cine Cabrera is not far from the Intercontinental (two blocks toward the lake, four blocks west). Cine Imperial El Viejo is a block north of the Esquipulas church in the El Viejo barrio. Others are in outlying residential neighborhoods, or in shopping centers.

And, most interesting and most convenient at the same time, Cinemateca Nacional, downtown, regularly schedules classics (address: Barrio 19 de Julio, 75 varas north of Teatro González). Showings are in the evening, with late-afternoon matinees on weekends, and the ticket price is about $2. They have a bar and protected parking. Call 223845 for program information.

There are also weekly showings at Alianza Francesa (Alliance Française) in Planes de Altamira, off the Masaya road on the outskirts of town, tel. 281032, 284045.

The **National Chamber Orchestra of Nicaragua** performs regularly at the Teatro Rubén Darío, university halls, and in cultural centers around the country.

Theater groups perform at Centro Cultural Managua, Teatro Rubén Darío, and on university stages and at cultural centers around the country. Consult the *Guía Fácil*, available at newsstands, for listings.

IMMIGRATION

Migración is headquartered on the south side of Pista de la Municipalidad, the main ring road, near its junction with the southern highway toward León and Jinotepe (Carretera Panamericana Sur). Visit in the morning to clear up any problems, such as overstaying your entry period. Or, inquire first, tel. 650014. Bus 118 for the Lewites market passes nearby.

POST OFFICE

The main post office (Telcor) is located in central Managua, a couple of block west of the Plaza de la República. Look for the building with antennas and satellite dishes on the roof. Hours, as with most central city offices, are until sunset, or 7 p.m.

Domestic and overseas calls can also be made from Telcor, and there are fax facilities as well.

COURIER ALTERNATIVES

For important documents, there are several courier services. See page 104 for some names.

TELEPHONES

Many public phones in Managua, when you can find them (often in the lobby of hotels), work with magnetic cards, rather than coins. The cards can be purchased at post offices (Telcor, or PTT).

Long-distance calls can be made from the Telcor (post and communications office) in Central Managua, just west of the main square.

For more details about telephone service, see page 105.

WATER

Water in Managua and in most other towns is chlorinated, and is generally considered safe to drink. Just to be safe, you might want to stick to bottled drinks. In Managua, bottled drinking water is available at some supermarkets and gasoline stations. (Just as in the United States, this is not an indication that the local water will kill you, at least not quickly.)

WEATHER

Managua is *warm*. The city slopes upward from its lakeside elevation of about 40 meters above sea level to about 120 meters in the surrounding hills, so there's some variation in conditions. But in general, temperature throughout the year ranges from 27 to 32 Centigrade (80 to 90 degrees Fahrenheit). During most of the dry season, from November to March, when the rays of the sun are not so direct and days are slightly shorter than during the rest of the year, temperatures range from 24 to 28 degrees Centigrade during the day (75 to 82 Fahrenheit).

By April and May, the dry-season breezes have stilled, the rays of the sun become more direct and humidity hangs dramatically in the air in wait of the climax of the first rains. Daily temperatures can reach from 32 to 35 degrees Centigrade (90 to 95 Fahrenheit).

Temperatures fall somewhat during the rainy times. And, given the lack of natural barriers to clouds, when it's not actually raining, skies are generally clear and open.

LEAVING MANAGUA

BY AIR

To go anywhere by air, you'll head for Augusto César Sandino International Airport, about 12 kilometers east of Central Managua.

If you're returning a **car** to the airport, you can't get lost. Follow the lakeside boulevard, Pista Pedro Joaquín Chamorro, eastward.

By **taxi**, the fare is only $5 or so if you flag a mini-cab on the streets, but as much as $12 if you call a cab from a taxi stand or in front of a hotel.

By **bus**, the journey is more daunting, especially if you have more than carry-on baggage. Buses 116, 118 and 119 pass the Inter-Continental Hotel going eastward to the Iván Montenegro market, from which buses leave for Tipitapa, passing the airport. Some buses numbered 105 cut across Managua from the southwest toward the airport; others terminate in Unidad de Propósitos near the Hotel Camino Real; from the turn from the main road, you can flag a passing cab or any other bus heading eastward. Keep an eye on your luggage, of course, for which you might have to buy an additional seat.

CHECK IN

For **domestic flights** to the Caribbean region and the Corn Islands, use the annex at the western end (toward Managua) of the terminal building.

For **international flights**, check in with your airline in the main terminal. Visit the **souvenir stands** now—it's your last chance. The **bar** and a basic **restaurant** are upstairs, but if you want something more substantial, and have some time, walk across the highway to the Hotel Las Mercedes.

There are *no facilities for re-purchasing dollars at the airport*, so spend your local currency to the degree that you can, and use cash dollars for your last expenses.

When you're ready to say goodbye, go through immigration and pay your **exit tax** ($12) in U.S. cash. The **duty-free** shop is in the departure lounge, and opens for all flights, even midnight charters.

AIRLINES

Scheduled service to Managua is currently provided by:
- **Nica**, Plaza España, tel. 663136, fax 663153.

- **Aviateca**, Málaga building, Plazuela España, tel. 662313, fax 663147.
- **Taca**, Plaza España, tel. 31422.

The above three airlines have a joint sales office at Centro Comercial Delta (Delta shopping center), módulo 18, tel. 663136.

- **Aeroflot**, Plaza España, Málaga building, tel. 660565, 660162, fax 663178.
- **Lacsa**, Camino de Oriente shopping center, tel. 668268, fax 668271.
- **American Airlines**, Plaza España, 3 blocks south, tel. 663900, fax 663911.
- **Aviateca**, Plaza España, tel. 662898
- **Continental Airlines**, Plaza España, tel. 631030/31/32/33, fax 631034.
- **Cubana**, Masaya road, tel. 661702
- **COPA** (Costa Rica and Panama), Planes de Altamira, tel. 670045, 675597, 675438, fax 670387.
- **Iberia**, Plaza España, Málaga building, tel. 664440.

Airlines with **representatives** in Managua include Air France, Plaza España, tel. 662612; Alitalia, Bolonia, tel. 664685; KLM, tel. 668052, fax 664629 : Ladeco, Plaza España, Málaga bldg, tel. 667011; LTU, Bolonia, tel. 667734; Lufthansa, tel. 668411, fax 668972; Varig, tel. 666615, fax 662611.

Domestic services are provided by:
- **Avionic**, tel. 631999.
- **Nica**, tel. 631929.
- **Alas de Nicaragua**, tel. 301126
- **La Costeña**, international airport, P. O. Box 2363, tel. 631228, fax 631281.
- **W+G Aero Servicios**, international airport.

AUTOMOBILE RENTAL

Before you rent, see page 83 for a discussion of driving. In general, you'll get a better rate if you reserve before you travel, through the toll-free number of one of the chains; but there are always exceptions.

Among the rental companies operating in Managua are:

- **Targa**, tel. 224875 (Intercontinental), 31176 (airport) 224881, fax 224824 (main office).

- **Budget**, 1 block west, 1 block south of Montoya statue, tel. 666226

- **Hertz**, Kilometer 4, Carretera Sur (Southern Highway) Automundo building, tel. 668399.

- **International**, Sol building, Reparto Serrano, tel. 782622.

- **Lugo**, Central Sandinista de Trabajadores 5 blocks south, 1 block west (west of Inter-Continental), tel. 665240

- **Toyota Rent A Car**, tel. 663620, 661381 (Hotel Camino Real), 32192 (airport), 284132 (Montelimar), (046)33204 (Ometepe).

BY BUS

See page 159 for bus services from Managua. For specific information about service to any destination, inquire at the tourist office, a block west of the Inter-Continental.

TRIPS FROM MANAGUA

Where can you go in a day from Managua?

By public transportation, tour, taxi or rented car, the following destinations are within easy reach:

- Masaya Volcano National Park
- The town of Masaya
- Colonial Granada
- The shores of Lake Nicaragua, and the islands
- The "White Towns" of the heartland of Nicaragua
- The people's amusement parks, Hertylandia and Las Vegas Jr., near Jinotepe

Nicaragua Guide

- The Pacific beaches at Pochomil and Montelimar
- Old León, and the volcano Momotombo

If you're driving, virtually any beach or town on the Pacific slope of Nicaragua, from the border of Honduras right down to Costa Rica, is within range; though the bays of San Juan del Sur and nearby are certainly worth a few days of your time.

For more information, just read the next chapter, or check the index to point you to the proper place in this guide.

TRAVEL AGENCIES

You're already in Managua. Why would you need a travel agency?

- to arrange a tour, especially to a volcano or the islands of Lake Nicaragua, or some other place that you can't reach by public transportation.
- to find out about new hotels and excursions
- to book a ticket home, or a flight to the Caribbean or the Corn Islands.

These are the major companies offering travel services in Managua. The larger ones, such as Careli, have personnel who can speak English, so you don't have to worry about wasting your time if you call from abroad.

- **Nueva Tur Nica**, 2½ blocks south of Plaza España (*Plaza España 2½ c. sur*) tel. (02)660406, 661387.
- **Ecotour**, tel. (02)664719, 660718.
- **Sol Tour**, ½ block west of Policlínica pharmacy (*Farmacia Policlínica Nic. ½ c. al oeste*), tel. (02)663913/4, 661059.
- **ICN Tours**, 1 block east, 2 block north of Villa Fontana post office (*Telcor Villa Fontana 1 c. al este, 2 cs. al norte*), tel. (02)71694, 70995.
- **Senderos**, ½ block west of Inter Continental main entry (*del costado sur Inter Continental ½ c. al oeste*), tel. (02)224326, 224208.
- **Careli Tours**, 3 blocks south of Plaza el Sol, Colonial Los Robles, tel. (02) 782572, fax 782574. Careli is one of the larger and more experienced of travel agencies oriented to visitors from outside. U.S. mail drop: P.O. Box 52-7444, Miami, FL 33152-7444.

- **Central American Tours**, 1½ blocks east of La Femina, Ciudad Jardín (*de La Femina, 1½ c. arriba*), tel. 413566.
- **Continental**, km 4½, Masaya road, 1 block west of Kathi shop (*de la tienda Kathi, 1 c. al oeste*), tel. 781233

SAMPLE TOURS

Among the usual tour offerings and what you might pay:

- Day trip to Montelimar, including all meals, drinks, and use of sports facilities, $60.
- Masaya Volcano, $40.
- Granada and Las Isletas (islands), $50.

9
HEARTLAND OF NICARAGUA
TOWNS, LAKES AND
BEACHES NEAR MANAGUA

Southeast of Managua, under the watch of Mombacho and Masaya volcanoes, is the heartland of Nicaragua: rolling hills cut by deep valleys, carpeted with coffee plantations and fields of grazing cattle, spotted with depressions filled with blue waters, bordered by the Great Lakes of Central America and Pacific waves.

Though Spanish rule in this area was anchored in the city of Granada more than 400 years ago, the ways of the ancestors of todays Nicaraguans were never successfully suppressed.

Here is the greatest concentration of villages in Nicaragua, many still bearing their indigenous Chorotega names: Masaya, Nindirí, Niquinohomo, Diriamba, Nandaime, and many, many others. Others are named for the saints of the Spaniards—San Marcos, San Juan, Santa Teresa and others—who blended with, but never replaced, traditional gods.

And, though the region covers a square no more than 25 kilometers by 25 kilometers, it holds several days' or even weeks' worth of destination travel, including:

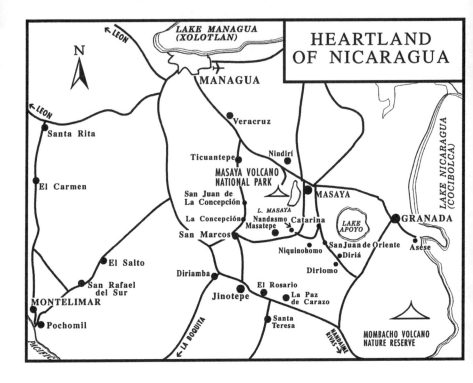

- **Masaya Volcano National Park**, and the more rugged Volcano Mombacho.

- The **lakes** of **Apoyo** and **Masaya**, and the inland sea that is Lake Nicaragua, with its hundreds of islands

- The **Pueblos Blancos**, the "white towns" that are a journey into the past of Central America, each with a craft specialty, an aged church, and traditions that stretch back into time.

- **Granada**, the colonial city of cobbled streets and dignified houses, where horse-drawn carriages are the preferred means of transport.

- **Pacific beaches** that include Central America's premier all-inclusive resort.

Accommodations are concentrated in Granada, Jinotepe, and down on the coast. Plan to stay the night in these places, or to return to Managua.

Heartland of Nicaragua

TO MASAYA, GRANADA, AND LAKE NICARAGUA

For most visitors, the route through the heartland leads from Managua to Masaya, and on to Granada.

The way out of Managua is a well-cared-for two-lane road, ascending and descending through rolling fields of yucca, corn and fruits and vegetables, lush or sere, depending on the season, lined by almond trees, palms, and madrone trees. Traffic is rarely heavy, but is sometimes slow, when forced to creep behind a truck proceeding at a stately pace on a winding stretch.

MASAYA VOLCANO NATIONAL PARK
PARQUE NACIONAL VOLCÁN MASAYA

THE VOLCANOES

Masaya Volcano National Park comprises a double volcano—Masaya and Nindirí—that grew in stages, successively exploding, settling, growing again out of the original crater, then branching off into new craters and a second cone as later eruptions found alternative paths of lower resistance to the surface. Its multiple orifices, craters and enclosing ridges are not unlike those of some imagined, deformed, inverted, omnipotent Being.

Indeed, Popogatepe, The Growing Mountain, as Masaya is called in the Chorotega language, was venerated and appeased with human sacrifices in ancient days by the native peoples of Nicaragua.

The Spanish conquerors of Nicaragua knew Masaya as *La Boca del Infierno*, the Mouth of Hell, and their own appeasement was the erection of a cross, in the 1500s, while they excavated the slopes in search of gold.

In the historical record, Nindirí last erupted in 1670. The San Fernando crater of Masaya burst out in 1772, sending a fire-river of lava down slopes that remain largely bare and unadorned by vegetation to this day. The Santiago crater appeared in 1852 between the peak of Masaya and Nindirí, and remains active, while the San Pedro crater, also formed in the last century, is quiescent.

VOLCANIC VALUE

Central America's premier volcano for visitors is within commuting range of Managua. Not only is it awesome and easier to get to than any other volcano in the region (and, as far as I know, *anywhere*), but it offers *five*—count 'em, *five*—volcanic cones for a single five-córdoba (70-cent) ticket price. Not to mention a first-class museum of volcanology, ethnology, folklore and ecology; hiking trails; caves; restaurant; and spectacular views.

Now that's value. In fact, for many visitors, Masaya Volcanoes Park in itself is worth the trip to Nicaragua.

THE PARK

Masaya Volcano Park, founded in 1974, extends over 54 square kilometers, and was the first national park established in Nicaragua.

All of Masaya volcano is included in the park. The very peak of the volcano is protected absolutely, while there is a successive transition through recovering and regenerating forest in a buffer zone, to a cultivated zone near the base, where agriculture is permitted under park control.

ACCESS AND HOURS

The turnoff to Masaya Volcano National Park is at kilometer 23 on the Masaya road. Any Masaya **bus** (from the Roberto Huembes market in Managua) will drop you at the entry, but that's as far as you can go by public transportation. Traffic to the craters is scarce, so don't count on hitching a ride; and the walk, though only about 5 kilometers, is hot and arduous, over exposed ground with only low-lying vegetation.

In a rental **car**, it's a quick drive from Managua or Masaya to the crater; and a **taxi** is economical if shared by two or three persons (remember, these are mostly cramped Ladas), at maybe $25 for an excursion of a few hours. Most travel agencies have **tours** to the volcano park, for about $40 per person, or less in a larger group.

The park is open from 9 a.m. to 5 p.m., to 6 p.m. on weekends. The phone number at the gate is (052)5415.

FLORA AND FAUNA

Flora in Masaya Volcano Park runs the range from scruffy bushes that can barely cling to life in the steam and sulfur blowing up from active Santiago crater to lava and ejecta breaking down into soil and tenuously covered with hesitant vegetation. Much of the park is covered with low brush, wildflowers that bloom in the dry season, dozens of types of orchids, and intermittent trees, most notably the yellow-flowered Sacuanjoche, or Nicaraguan frangipani.

While the slopes of Masaya Volcano are not especially lush, the park provides an expansive refuge in the most densely populated slice of Nicaragua, and **wildlife spotting** and **birding** can be rewarding. Rabbits, deer, and monkeys are sometimes seen by visitors, while coyotes and cats, including panthers, come out at night, after visitors have departed.

If you're up at the summits in the late afternoon, you might spot *chocoyos coludos* (green parakeets) flying back to their nests in cracks in the crater walls, safe from the predators amid fumes that don't ruffle their feathers—just one of the remarkable examples of specialization you'll run into in Nicaragua. Also around, in less noxious places, are magpies, turtle doves, hawks, woodpeckers, and chachalacas.

PARK SITES AND SIGHTS

Entry past the gate house takes you onto a road that winds up gentle slopes, to a visitors' center and museum, with snack stand and parking area. The road continues farther up to the edges of the five craters (including red-hot glowing Santiago), parking terraces, and lookout points. Departing from the road are 20 kilometers of trails, leading off to caves, and down to Lake Masaya. The terrain is bare lava or grassy, with mild slopes, sprinkled with boulders, and scattered flowering trees.

Sendero de los Coyotes—"Coyote Trail"—runs 4.5 kilometers from the entry road, below the visitors' center, through regenerating seasonally dry tropical forest, past dry lava rivers that were thrown out of the volcano is a series of eruptions that started in 1670, and rock formations, to the shores of Lake Masaya (Laguna de Masaya).

Nicaragua Guide

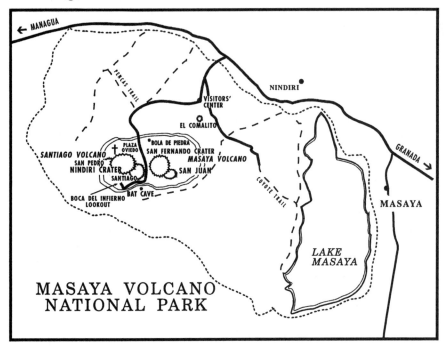

The Visitors' Center (Centro de Visitantes) contains not only exhibits on volcanology and Masaya volcano in particular (with a model of the mountain), but a comprehensive yet human-scaled **museum** devoted to the people of Nicaragua: where they originated, how they live, and what they have achieved culturally, along with flora and fauna, and the natural zones of the country. Even if volcanoes leave you yawning (and this one won't!), the museum, one of the best on the isthmus, will awaken your interest.

In rooms circling a courtyard, visitors are drawn to a series of prints showing the changing profile of Masaya over the years, as successive eruptions blew off and reshaped its top; a collection of artifacts of the autochthonous peoples of Nicaragua, including their pottery, and paintings of their ceremonies; and illustrations of native flora and fauna, such as the sea turtle.

In short, it's a human-scale natural history and archaeology and ethnology museum, by far the best of any museum in the country.

Also here are a picnic area and restaurant.

Heartland of Nicaragua

- *Guided **walks** through the visitors' center, at no charge and lasting 30 minutes, are offered most days at 10 and 11 a.m. and 2 and 3 p.m. These and other tours offered by the park are in Spanish, of course.*

  El Comalito ("The little griddle"), up the road from the visitor's center, is a volcanic cone with steam outlets at its base. Beyond it, **Sendero de las Pencas**—"Nettle Trail"—runs over solidified lava flows, back toward the base of the volcano.

- *The park offers a free 45-minute **nature walk** around El Comalito, starting on most days at 10:30 a.m. and 2:30 and 4 p.m. This is an ecologically oriented excursion, with discussion of how plants and animals of the seasonally dry tropical forest interact with the volcano.*

From the trailhead, the paved road climbs more sharply upward, toward the craters, passing the **bola de piedra** ("stone ball"), a huge boulder that exploded out of San Fernando crater. At **Plaza de Oviedo**, a plateau named for one of the scientists who explored the volcano, is a parking area with a lookout point affording views into Santiago crater directly ahead, and Nindirí and San Pedro craters to the west (right), while the San Fernando and San Juan craters still loom atop Masaya, to the east.

A crater is not a crater is not a crater, as even a quick glance by the acrophobic will attest. **Santiago** crater is 570 meters across at its widest, a hellish pit that descends 180 meters to a platform, then drops another 120 meters in an inner pit, to openings that spout sulfuric gases and acids. Uniquely in the hemisphere, Santiago periodically experiences a welling up of lava, which remains visible in molten form for several years before subsiding, to a relieving burst of gases. Adjacent is the plateau of **Nindirí** crater, 590 meters above sea level, active at the time of the Conquest, but now extinct, and filled in with cooled lava runs, bare and unvegetated. Farther on is **San Pedro** crater, a deep, extinct funnel.

Ruling over the three lower craters is the wooden **Cruz de Bobadilla** (Cross of Bobadilla), exposed on a high point. Hold onto your hat and watch your footing as you climb the 184 steps through permanent wind currents to the base and a higher lookout point. You could *easily* be blown right off the steps and down the steep slope. But it's worth it, for the spectacular view all the way to Managua and Xolotlán in one direction, and neighbor-volcano Mombacho in the other.

From the Plaza de Oviedo, the paved road winds upward and across the slopes of Masaya, with its **San Fernando** and lesser **San Juan** craters.

San Fernando marks the peak of Masaya, at 635 meters above sea level, and is 650 meters across, with a drop of 200 meters inside. Inactive for two centuries, its lava broken down by rain and pioneer vegetation, it now supports a hidden forest on its floor.

- *A 30-minute **walk** into San Fernando crater is given at 11 a.m. and 2 and 4 p.m., at no charge.*

But these are only the main craters. On the slopes below are El Comalito and other primitive openings, covered over by tangled vegetation, but visible to any practiced eye that can detect the telltale surface alteration.

On the south side of the craters, at the end of the road, is the **Mirador Boca del Infierno** (Mouth-of-Hell Lookout), on the edge of the Nindirí abyss, affording another view into the inferno, and beyond toward sulphur-colored sands. **Watch your step** while you gaze into the depths! This area is not for the faint of heart. Protective barriers are intermittent and winds are strong.

Beyond the lookout, down the south slope, a trail banked with concrete ties leads through an area strewn with lava boulders to the **Cueva de Murciélagos** (Bat Cave, or Caverna Tzinancanostac), a sinkhole formed in the once-molten lava.

- *Guided cave walks, at a nominal fee and lasting 30 minutes, are given at 10 a.m., and on the hour from noon to 4 p.m. These are your best and probably safest way to explore underground.*

BACK ON THE ROAD

Nindirí, just off the highway near the turn for Masaya volcano, is a village generally unnoticed but for its colonial church, and the **Tenderí Museum** (Museo Tenderí), a collection of ancient sculpture and pottery turned up in caves and under fields in the area.

Past the lake, on the north side of the road, the fortress of Coyotepe (along with its impressive water tank), once a redoubt of the National Guard, and later of the Sandinista army, sits atop a small mountain. Feel free to alight from your bus, or park your car, and hike up the hill for another view of Masaya and the volcano. The fortress is in the process of being converted into nothing more sinister than a community center.

MASAYA

- *29 kilometers from Managua*

Local color, old ways, tradition . . . they're all built into the way Nicaraguans view Masaya, the City of Flowers.

Masaya is where all the crafts of Nicaragua come together. What do they make in San Juan de Oriente? Ceramics. What is the craft specialty of Masatepe? Leather. In San Marcos? Cotton clothing and embroidery. In Masaya? Everything . . . hammocks and carved masks, and hemp hangings and purses and fans, wrought silver and jewelry fashioned from shells and coral, hammocks and earthenware plates and pre-Columbian ceramic reproductions and *cotonas*, native-style formal shirts.

Oh, you'll see an occasional Guatemalan belt or weaving in the Masaya stands and markets, but nowhere near the predominance of imports that passes for souvenirs in Costa Rica. Mostly, when you buy a trinket in Masaya, you're buying, and supporting, authenticity. And the price is right.

Masaya was not devastated in the way of Managua in the 1972 earthquake, but damage there was, and fighting during the Insurrection of 1978 left public buildings in ruins. Some remain as roofless, crumbling walls. Among the casualties was the centerpiece of the city, the solid market building, dating from 1891, which occupied a site used by Indians for trade since pre-Columbian times. Plans are being developed to re-install the market in its traditional location.

Masaya is a busy place, but busy with horse-drawn wagons, rather than motorized traffic, which lends part of the town the air of the old west, an effect not at all decreased by the mission-style church in the main square with its smoothly curving façade, a ringer for the Alamo.

GETTING THERE

Bus service to Masaya from Granada and Managua (Roberto Huembes Market) is almost continuous during the day. The drive from the capital takes from 30 to 60 minutes, depending on whether you're stuck behind a slow truck.

THE MARKET

Shopping for crafts is the main attraction in Masaya. The traditional market, just east of the square, is only a set of walls; vendors have relocated their stalls to a location about ten blocks east of the main square. The market has *everything* that Masayans need and don't need in their daily life, from rice and beans to Michael Jackson cassettes. As you walk through, helpful people will offer, "*¿Qué busca?*" ("What are you looking for?") Answer "*collares*" (necklaces), "*hamacas*" (hammocks), "*sombreros*" (hats) or something similar, and you'll be pointed toward the endless crafts. If you don't end up with a few dolls, or stones shaped into figurines, or huge hardwood salad forks, or tortoiseshell earrings, or a mother-of-pearl pin, then you can ignore a bargain.

Prices are negotiable in the market, but the sellers are proud people, so don't expect to chop the first price in half.

THE MALECÓN

West of Masaya's main square (the opposite direction from the market), is the promenade, or Malecón, above Lake Masaya (*Laguna de Masaya*), a pleasant strolling area bordered by concrete balusters. The trees along the walkway are the *malinche* (delonix recia), common in this area, with lacy leaves similar to those of the acacia and other dry tropical forest species.

Ancient steps hewn in rock in pre-Columbian times lead down to the water; a glance upward reveals the slopes of Masaya volcano.

Along the Malecón is CECAPI, a government-sponsored artisan training school, cultural center, and **handicraft exhibition**, housed in a colonial-style building with tile roof, central courtyard, and covered walkways. Items available here tend to be of finer quality and more substantial than those found in the market. Prices are fixed.

Examples of CECAPI wares are clay figurines, tables of guanacaste wood, carved-stone statues from San Juan de Limay, near Estelí, stuffed alligators, embroidered dresses, marimbas, rocking chairs, piñatas, hardwood tableware, and black pottery from Matagalpa.

In the same neighborhood, along the street parallel to the lake, are many shops selling brightly colored hammocks of rough hemp fiber.

LAGOON

Lake Masaya (Laguna de Masaya) is the lowest part of the depression that surrounds Masaya volcano, filled with runoff and ground water to a depth of 80 meters. Congealed lava rivers run down the slopes of the volcano, and continue under the lake's waters. Some of the surrounding rocks were carved with petroglyphs by the ancient inhabitants, who knew the lake as Tenderí.

Masaya-the-lake is much regarded as a scenic treasure, but otherwise hardly touched by Masayans, except for occasionally boating.

WHERE TO EAT

El Filete, a steak house at kilometer 26 on the Managua-Masaya road, is a large establishment catering to travellers and meetings, with a reputation for serving some of the finest red meat in Nicaragua.

Otherwise, there are several eateries near and even in the main square of Masaya, with set meals to offer at lunch. **La Alegría** is a couple of blocks to the north of the square, while **El Sándalo**, off the southwest corner, is a substantial old house with popular (inelegant) food.

STAYING

Masaya is usually a day trip from Managua or Granada. If you're driving, the **Hotel Cailagua**, on the highway at kilometer 29 (tel. 052-4435), has rooms with air conditioning for about $35 double. Hotels in town are not attractive, but the **Regis**, tel. 052-2300, four blocks north of the square on the road toward Managua, is better than others, at about $10 double sharing bath.

ART SCENE

Among locales of interest to collectors of art are the Centro Cultural Alejandro Vega Matus; and the Galería Monimbó, two blocks from San Sebastián church, toward the cemetery.

TOWN FAIRS

If you're in Nicaragua in February, try to take in the Masaya fiesta, on the Sunday of Lazarus. The high point is a procession to Magdalena church... headed by dogs in costume.

But the main celebration in Masaya, and indeed the major town fiesta in all of Nicaragua, in honor of St. Jerome (San Jerónimo), takes place on September 30, and always includes dances of pre-Columbian origin, among them the Negras, Diablos, Torovenados and Aguizotes.

TOWARD GRANADA AND THE PAST

Past Masaya, the volcano Mombacho looms, saw-ridged and ever more imposing, off in the distance toward the south. The character of the scattered buildings visible from the main road begins to change. There are more red tile roofs, among the rusting corrugated metal sheets, and even a few of thatch. Thick-walled buildings of adobe and plastered rubble begin to predominate.

The straightforward explanation is that one has moved beyond the zone of damage of the 1972 earthquake, and things here are as they have always been. But the impression is that one is gradually moving back into time.

GRANADA

- *45 kilometers from Managua; population 120,000.*

On the shore of Lake Nicaragua, Granada is one of the oldest cities in the Americas, founded in 1524 by the Spanish conqueror Francisco Hernández de Córdoba, adjacent to an indigenous town called Jalteva. Port, terminal for commerce over the lake-and-river route to the Caribbean, agricultural center, ecclesiastical bastion, Granada grew steadily in importance, always a rival of León, its Conservative politics a mirror image of those of the Liberal capital.

But Granada's position was never secure. Daring pirates penetrated Spanish defenses and sailed up the San Juan River to attack the Spanish bastion. And though the ongoing competition with León after independence seems quaint in this age of uniformization, it was a serious business that was exploited to the disadvantage of both by American adventurer

William Walker. First in the pay of the Liberals, he set up his government in Granada with the connivance of local Conservatives, whom he later jilted. In the end, a retreating Walker burned Granada in 1856; and eventually, Granada and León both lost out, when the capital was permanently settled in Managua.

Other cities on the continent are equally long-lived, but Granada preserves the past not only in memory sometimes stubborn and always proud, and in heritage colonial-baroque buildings and graceful plazas that appear unaltered over the centuries, but also in the ways in which Granadans go about their daily tasks. Horse-drawn *diligencias* (carriages) are a means of common transport, and a horse-drawn hearse is the means of exit from this world; swaying in a rocker on a solid, stone-platformed porch facing the cobbled street is a respectable way to bide one's time; clay wares and hammocks and furniture crafted by local artisans are preferred over factory products.

GETTING THERE

Buses leave for Granada from the Roberto Huembes market in eastern Managua. In Granada, the terminal for Managua buses is about nine blocks west of the Hotel Alhambra, and two blocks north (a block north of the hospital). Departures are about every 20 to 30 minutes until 7 p.m., fare about 60 cents U.S. There is also regular service to Rivas and smaller towns nearby from a stop about four blocks south of the Cathedral, by the market.

An alternative bus service to Granada with reserved seats is available several times a day from opposite the UCA (Universidad Centroamericana). Inquire at the Piñata store.

WHERE TO STAY

Hotel Alhambra, facing the west side of main square (*frente costado oeste, parque central*), tel. (055)6316 and 4486, fax (055)2035. 48 rooms. $18 to $35 single/$21 to $38 double. Visa, Master Card.
Best-located of the city's hotels, a modern, concrete building whose two stories and terraces do not overwhelm Granada's picturesque square. Rooms are off pleasant, planted courtyards, and come in several strengths, from fan to air-conditioned to air-conditioned-with-balcony-and-t.v. Floors are of tile, decor is plain but inoffensive, bathrooms have showers only,

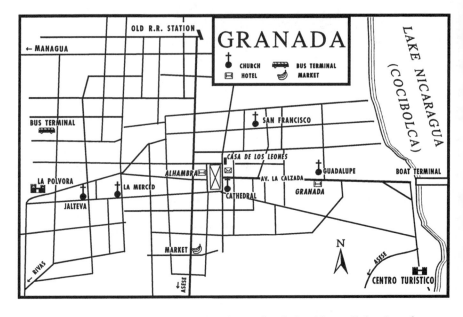

and illumination varies from barely to flooded with sunlight. In other words, look first, you can get something fair, or a lot of room for the price.

Hotel Granada, Calle La Calzada, tel. (055)2978, 2974. 60 rooms, from $23 single/$30 double plus tax.
Located along the long street that leads from the main square to the lake and dock, opposite the Guadalupe church. The hotel is unpretentious and charming, behind an archway, with cool and sheltered flowered central courtyard, parquet ceiling tile in public areas, and interior archways framing views of Mombacho volcano. Rooms, in rows along the courtyards, are somewhat dark, but with adequate wooden furnishings, and air conditioning. Coffee shop, bar, meeting rooms, safe-deposit boxes, and assorted seating areas, including one furnished exclusively with child-sized rocking chairs.

Cheaper Lodgings are not hard to find on Calle La Calzada, the street that leads from the center of Granada to the lake. Hospedaje Vargas and Hospedaje Cabrera both have simple rooms off courtyards for under $10 per person.

WHERE TO EAT

The **Hotel Alhambra** is the preferred eating spot in the center of Granada, with its bar-restaurant spilling from the premises onto a sheltered terrace. Breakfast costs about $2, and a complete lunch of standard grilled steak or chicken from $6 to $10.

Across the street, the restaurant in Granada's **cultural center** offers sandwiches, coffee and tea, and often a soothing background of music.

Your alternative, for a sit-down meal, is to head to the **Centro Turístico** for a terrace meal overlooking the wind-swept waters of Lake Nicaragua. See "Lakeside Food," below.

For roast chicken, consider **Rostichería Pollos del Monte**, on Calle Atravesada, one block north of Framacia Rosario.

On the way to the lake, the **"Drive Inn" El Ancla**, across from the Hotel Granada, offers sandwiches and basic meals.

SEEING GRANADA

THE MAIN SQUARE

I don't think there's a lovelier main square than that of Granada, a stand of tall palms and figs, interwoven with benches and refreshment kiosks, a coupola'd bandstand in the center with lions depicted in its trim, and a fountain to one side; lined by red horse-drawn carriages awaiting custom; surrounded by stately buildings with delicate flutings in their plasterwork, and pavements flagged in volcanic slates.

At the southeast corner stands the plain tan **Cathedral** of Granada, with dome and double towers, and neoclassical pediments, a latter-day addition to the city's inventory of otherwise distinguished temples.

One of the more attractive architectural sets hereabouts is a complex along the east side of the square, including the yellow-painted Colegio San Antonio, a girls' secondary school, two stories high (the maximum elevation in Granada), its upstairs porticos sheltering part of the sidewalk below.

Attached, and integrated into a continuous façade, is the **Casa de los Leones**, a fine, restored colonial building named for the lions in the stonework of its portal, and now housing a cultural foundation (the Casa de los Tres Mundos, tel. 055-4176). You may enter, and admire the carved wooden ceilings, varnished louvers, stairways, and inner courtyards. Local crafts, including lace and art prints, are sometimes on sale.

At the north end of the square, the building painted red was the home of William Walker before he abandoned and set fire to Granada in 1856.

CONVENT OF SAN FRANCISCO

Granada's imposing San Francisco convent and church dates from 1529, when construction was started under Brother Antonio Benavente, one of the army of Franciscans who constructed the ecclesiastical order that accompanied the Spanish civil regime even in the most remote quarters of the Americas. One of the important churches of the city it remained, even serving for a time as the base of Father Bartolomé de las Casas, protector of the rights of Indians in the Spanish domains. It achieved notoriety in 1856, when William Walker set up shop in the church, and used its rooms as prison cells. Set afire as Walker beat his retreat, it was later reconstructed in altered form.

After the Walker depredations, the convent became a school, and like schools elsewhere, never had enough funding to prevent deterioration. But in 1988, with Swedish assistance, restoration work was started, and is ongoing.

A visit to the church and convent today is, as in so many parts of Nicaragua, a trip into the last century. Opposite, and all around, red-tiled roofs extend over and shelter the sidewalk. Horse-drawn carriages pass by, and perhaps a glassed-in black funeral coach, followed by mourners. Not a motorized vehicle is in sight.

The convent literally provides a look *inside* colonial ecclesiastic architecture, through the broken walls of stone-faced rubble, roofless interior rooms, and beamed ceilings undergoing consolidation, repair and reconstruction. In a rear courtyard, unexpectedly, stand rows of tall palms.

Within the convent walls are two museums. The **Museum of Anthropology and History of Granada (Museo de Antropología e Historia de la Ciudad de Granada)** contains changing exhibits from Granada's long history, and for a casual visitor, might be as interesting for its lovely restored main courtyard surrounded by tile-roofed passageways supported by massive hardwood columns, as for anything in the long, narrow, high-ceilinged exhibition rooms.

Out in back, in a section of courtyard shielded by a shed roof, is the **Zapatera Statuary Collection** of 28 pieces unearthed over the years on Zapatera island in Lake Nicaragua, and brought to this location in 1970. Most originated in the sites known as Punta de las Figuras and Sonzapote. They obviously demonstrate the high artistic achievements of the ancestors of today's Nicaraguans, and as such, were not looked upon kindly by the Spaniards, who destroyed native "idols."

An aura of mystery surrounds these statues. Superficially, there are resemblances to the sculptures produced by the Olmecs of pre-Conquest Mexico: some of the statues have rounded, squat bodies, and human faces with expressions clearly of pleasure. But there are also animal heads and glyph-like markings that relate clearly to the statuary of the Maya, though they show nothing of Mayan stylistic rigidity. Perhaps the artistic expression of both peoples arose from a common tradition.

Among the statues are those with heads of a jaguar, a turtle, an alligator, eagle, and coyote. Most are on rectangular bases, carved in basaltic rock using tools made also of basalt, or of a harder rock: the use of metal tools was unknown to the pre-Columbian peoples of America. When such rock is carved today, it must be kept continuously wet, to prevent cracks from developing.

The three broad classes of sculpture are anthropomorphic, showing only a human head; sculptures of objects; and those showing both a human and an animal. In the last cases, the animal may be supported atop the head of the human, or the animal may show a human head in its jaws. In Mesoamerica, even today, humans are often thought to have a *nagual*, or animal co-spirit.

The association of the statues with fertility is obvious: one alligator figure exhibits what are clearly male genitals. Since most of the carving is on the front, and the sides and backs are squared, there is speculation that they served as inset columns in some sort of temple. Plumed serpents and crosses found on some statues indicates a strong connection with cultures to the north; the plumed serpent, of course, is emblematic of the Aztecs of Mexico, and the inhabitants of the region at the time of the Conquest spoke a language related to that of the Aztecs.

The Zapatera statues were brought to public attention by Ephraim Squier, an American diplomat who travelled extensively in Honduras and

187

Nicaragua, who came upon them in 1849. Hundreds of other statues have been found on Ometepe Island, and in the Chontales region on the far shore of the lake. The Chontales statues show personages in positions usually associated with South American Indian art.
Entry to the premises costs about $1.50.

GUADALUPE CHURCH

The Guadalupe Church is a neoclassical structure, less distinguished and less aged than other churches in Granada, with severe geometrical lines and molding plaster. Bell towers are capped with pyramids, and on the whole, the structure is a precursor of the simpler and in many respects less pleasing ecclesiastical structures that appeared as reinforced concrete came into use. General-Presidente William Walker used Guadalupe as his last base in Granada.

LA MERCED

The Church of La Merced (Our Lady of Mercy), dating from 1781, two blocks west of the square, is one of the premier structures of Granada, built in the Central American adaptation of the Churrigueresque style, massive and squat, of thick walls of brick and rubble, concentrating the mass of the building low to the ground, to minimize vibrations in the earthquakes that regularly shake the land. The rather perfunctory architecture is elevated with barely controlled decoration, flutings on columns, outset trim running all around the façade, niches in place of windows, and plaster designs. La Merced has a characteristically low, Moorish-style bell tower, and columns inset into the walls. Unusually, statues are absent, and shutters cover window openings. The interior of the church, which was restored in 1862, is rather humdrum.

JALTEVA

Another long block west from the square, the Jalteva ("hal-TEH-va") Church, dating from 1895, is of no particular interest.

FORTRESS

Two blocks beyond, at the edge of town, is **La Pólvora** ("The Gun Powder"), an ex-garrison with massive walls slit for gun emplacements. Partially restored, its interior remains in ruins, but is due to be renovated to house a museum of arms.

Six blocks north of the square is the abandoned **railroad station**, awaiting a new vocation.

VENERABLE BUILDINGS

Elsewhere in Granada, there are many old buildings, and though few are of particular architectural merit in themselves, many are of a style rarely seen in towns or surviving anywhere in the isthmus for that matter. Particularly interesting are the hacienda-style houses with front porches elevated on a stuccoed platform of brick and rubble about a half-story above street level, of a height to protect the genteel occupants from mud that splashed up from street level in the days before paving. And there are many nineteenth-century buildings with pediments and cornices and stone-encased, deeply inset windows with iron grilles, tile roofs, massive wooden beams, wide eaves that provide shelter from the rains, and decorative lintels, all characteristic of the pre-independence period. Family life generally goes on behind closed doors, in the Moorish tradition, but sometimes the street entry is ajar. In that case, take a quick glance. Maybe the courtyard inside is austere; or maybe it's bedecked with plants and statuary, or even a running fountain.

SHOPPING

Embroidery, wicker furniture, and leatherwork are amoung the specialties of Granada. Antiques can be found in several shops, among them Antigüedades Granada, a block north of the Merced church; La Bocona, two blocks north of the same church; Mercedes Morales, two blocks south of the church; and Borgen, a half-block east of San Francisco church. Wicker furniture can also be found along the entry road into town. But how to get it home? El Palenque art gallery is on Calle El Palenque. Lace, art prints, and other fine pieces are sometimes available at the Casa de los Leones on the square.

While the central part of Granada is placid and little trafficked, the area around the green **market** building, three blocks to the south of the square, is another story. Carpenters, fruit merchants, jewelry vendors and shoemakers operate from shops and sidewalks, and vendors spill out into the roadway. The market is filled with bras and socks and hair spray—not goods of interest to visitors—but the energy of commerce might be worth a look.

COCIBOLCA
LAKE NICARAGUA

The great lake of Nicaragua is at the doorstep of Granada.

Look at a map, and the geological history of Cocibolca (the traditional name for the lake) leaps up at you. Large, shallow, lapping at islands formed by the unbroken chain of volcanoes marching down the edge of the isthmus, separated from the Pacific by a sash of low-lying, undulating plain, it seems clear that the bottom once contained the salty waters of the great sea, but was separated from it in one of the great volcanic upheavals that are still shaping the land. What better proof of an ancient opening of its waters to the oceans, than the presence of fresh-water sharks whose ancestors must have been marooned when the cataclysmic final closure occurred?

And yet, according to geologists, it did not happen that way at all. Upheavals and reshapings there were, but such as to bring about a gradual lowering of the central plain, as the shifting and sliding of tectonic plates to seaward bore down on the plate under the mainland; so that the Camastro and Oyate and Mayales and Tecolostate and other watercourses that once unburdened themselves in the Pacific conjoined their watery burden into a gradually deepening young puddle, which grew into a lake, which eventually diverted their outflow to the other side of the continent, through the San Juan River; and left the coastal strip parched for so much of the year.

All this happened in the pleistocene era, elsewhere known as the Ice Age.

So much for appearances.

SERVICES

Cortel, the **post office** and **telephone agency** (PTT), is on the main square, across the street from the cathedral. A **bank** is across the street. A **tourist information** office is located on the ground floor of the Hotel Alhambra, entered from the street.

A COACH RIDE

Few places in Granada are more than a dozen blocks from where you are; and you can hire a motorized conveyance (a.k.a. taxicab) should the need arise; but you will be missing out on the spirit of the city, and part of your time excursion, if you do not avail of the services of a horse-drawn carriage (fiacre, hackney) to hie thee forthwith,

FIESTAS

Granada celebrates its town fair on August 15, in honor of the Virgin of the Assumption, with horseback parades and bullfights. And the pre-Christmas celebrations, especially the Purísima, culminating on December 7, are widely observed.

GRANADA-BY-THE-LAKE

While Managua largely ignores its waterfront, Granada celebrates the placid beauty of its own lake. A grand and stately boulevard, La Calzada, leads from the center of the city to the shore. A pier is the departure point for regular lake steamer service to the island of Ometepe, and to San Carlos at the lake's outlet into the San Juan River.

CENTRO TURÍSTICO

A large park, the Centro Turístico, meanders along the shores, its grassy beach lapped by ocean-sized waves during the windy dry season, placid under intermittent rains in the Nicaraguan winter, frequented by herons and other avian species. There are plenty of shady spots under trees, play areas, and picnic spots, as well as horse-carriage rides and the inevitable baseball diamond. Entry with a car through mock castle ramparts costs about $1.50. For most of the week, the park is lightly used, but weekends bring day trippers from Managua.

LAKESIDE FOOD

The Centro Turístico has several eateries, ranging from snack stands to sit-down patios such as **Terraza La Playa**, which serves standard fare of

LAKE NICARAGUA PARTICULARS

Area	8264 square kilometers (surpassed in Latin America only by Lake Titicaca in Bolivia)
Surface altitude	31 meters above sea level
Dimensions	160 kilometers by 60 kilometers
Islands	390
Basin	Drains 28,000 square kilometers; in periods of heavy rain, Cocibolca receives the runoff from Xolotlán (Lake Managua), via the Tipitapa River.
Denizens	Notable species in Lake Nicaragua include bull shark, swordfish, tarpon, guapote (tropical bass) and turtles, along with frogs, toads and lizards along the banks.

thick and tender filet mignon or chicken in wine for about $7, sandwiches for slightly less, credit cards accepted. The food's good, but the pleasure is in watching the waves, distant hazed shores and volcanoes, and grazing horses, and naming the birds flocking to waterside, while trying to keep your napkin from taking to the air in the steady breeze. **La Vista** and **La Garsa** are also said to be good establishments.

BOAT SERVICES

Boats depart from Granada's long concrete pier, near the entrance to the Centro Turístico, on Monday and Thursday at 2 p.m. and 4 p.m. for San Jorge (near Rivas), Ometepe and San Carlos. The return trips are on Wednesdays and Saturdays. Fare to San Carlos is about $3, and tickets can be purchased right at the pier. Call the port office to verify schedules, at (055)4313.

Russian-built hydrofoils are coming into service, which will shorten voyages considerably.

MOMBACHO

South of Granada, above the shores of Lake Nicaragua, rises the volcano Mombacho (1363 meters). Dormant since early in the Conquest, when it exploded and buried an Indian village, its ancient ash fertilizes coffee plantations on its slopes. The very peak of Mombacho is a reserve of cloud fore
st, that tropical wonderland of oaks and ferns and moss and begonias, teeming with the songs of birds and the growth of plants nourished at all levels in an eternal round of decay and fertilization.

If you're interested in climbing Mombacho, inquire at the tourist office in Granada. Several roads service the coffee plantations on the slopes; but if you approach without guidance, it's easy to reach a dead end in the cloud forest.

ASESE AND THE LAKE ISLANDS

A road cuts inland to the south from Granada, crossing the neck of a lake peninsula in the shadow of Mombacho volcano, darting under bridging trees in seasonally dry tropical forest, to **Asese**, a lake harbor lined by rushes and reeds and basaltic boulders. There is no immediate village or settlement, but low-key pastimes of a scenic and natural sort are plentiful.

WHAT'S THERE

There's one restaurant atop a volcanic rock terrace, a pleasant open-air establishment under a bamboo-lined tin roof supported by tree trunks, overlooking the lily pads of the sheltered byways. Great waterside trees trail vines into the water, and, of course, birds too numerous to catalog here flit about.

In the water are boats, boats, and boats: rowboats belonging to inhabitants of nearby islets, private power cruisers, half-sunken wrecks offshore, and, most typically, brightly painted lake cruisers, long, narrow, pointed and open. These will accommodate a dozen passengers or more in safety on a custom-fashioned ride through islands near and distant.

The rate for a **boat ride** is about $10 for a half hour, $17 for a full hour. The fare is usually shared among a group, and there is little bargaining.

GETTING TO ASESE

The road to Asese runs from near the Centro Turístico. It's a drive of about 6 kilometers.

A **bus** leaves Granada at 6 a.m. for Asese, to pick up people coming in from the islands by boat for the market. Departure for Granada is at about 7 a.m. Another bus leaves Granada at about 11 a.m., and leaves Asese for the return trip at 1 p.m.

WHERE TO GO FROM ASESE

LAS ISLETAS

Las Isletas are 350 islets (or maybe it's 354 or 365—the Authorities differ) formed of volcanic ejecta from ever-hovering Mombacho, directly to the south. The same material formed the peninsula in the lake that separates Ysese from Granada.

Some of the islets are no more than rocky outcrops in the water where plants have laid claim to the surface; others hold vacation houses, and some are recreation areas. Still others are occupied by fishermen who make their living catching guapote, a tropical fish that is often compared to the lake bass of North America.

Between the water and the fish and the vegetation that provides shelter and nest-building material, **birds** are among the most evident inhabitants of the islands, and birders, especially, find an excursion rewarding.

The **Fortress of San Pablo**, on one of the distant islands, was built in the eighteenth century to protect Granada from pirates and English expeditions. It's currently being restored.

Masate Island has a simple restaurant, and there is another on **Isla Coyolito**. Both are within a few minutes of Granada.

Tahiti is a privately owned island-cum-recreation center, complete with palms, mango trees, and ever-vigilant herons and oropendolas. Casual visitors can use the pool and restaurant (a buffet makes things easy for the linguistically challenged), and there are four sleeping rooms for overnight stays. Call 78-1580 in Managua to make arrangements if you plan to spend the night, or if you have it in mind to rent the whole island for the weekend.

Nicarao Lake Resort is another private lake getaway for individuals and groups. (Yes, the name is in English only, for whatever cachet that

> **MORE OF THE LAKE**
>
> Ometepe Island, see page 235.
> San Carlos, see page 256.
> Solentiname Islands, see page 257.

affords). Located on El Morro island, 15 kilometers from Granada, it consists of thatched shelters, a swimming hole, barbecue area, and facilities for water sports, including pedal boats, water skiing, kayaks and locally made dugouts. Lake fish and local fruits are on the bill of fare. Accommodations are planned for the future, but for now, you can ask your boatman to include a stop during your lazy excursion around Las Isletas. For more information, write Nicarao Lake Resort, P. O. Box 2285, Managua, tel. (2)281316, fax (2)222706, or stop by their offices in Centro Comercial Managua, in downtown Managua. The boat ride to El Morro takes about a half-hour.

ZAPATERA ARCHIPELAGO NATIONAL PARK

Zapatera Archipelago National Park (Parque Nacional Archipiélago Zapatera), takes in Zapatera Island, where numerous pre-Colombian carvings have been discovered. The most significant pieces have been removed for protection to Granada's Convent of San Francisco; but some ancient tombs, an altar and stone stairs can be viewed, and sometimes active excavations can be visited.

At **El Muerto Island**, in the park, is a basaltic plateau with extensive ancient inscriptions.

A boat ride to Zapatera from Ysese takes about 90 minutes. Visitors may enter freely, but as yet, there are no special facilities or services.

THE WHITE TOWNS

Los Pueblos Blancos—the White Towns—are the villages that cluster in the rolling countryside south of Masaya, before the land descends to the coast.

This is picturesque Nicaragua, a region of villages sometimes no more than two or three kilometers apart, set amidst cattle pastures and plantations of waxy-leafed coffee bushes, backdropped by the volcanoes Masaya and Mombacho, overlooking the crater lake of Apoyo, or steamy river valleys. There are still many, many tile-roofed, whitewashed adobe buildings of the type that gave the region its nickname. And every town has a venerable colonial church facing a dusty main square, with bandstand or benches or kiosk. Motor vehicles are rarities, and, except for the inevitable advertisements for beer or headache remedies, each town looks much as it did in the last century.

Old-time ways are more than appearance. Leatherwork, embroidery, and ceramics flourish. Ceremonial dances with roots in pre-Columbian times and the Spanish conquest are performed at town fiestas. Oxcarts transport goods on unpaved tracks, and horses transport people.

TRAVELLING TO THE WHITE TOWNS

An automobile is the easiest way to go from town to town, tarrying as long as suits you in each. A taxi is easily arranged, as well. Or, you can start off from Managua by bus for Masaya or Granada, and then stand by the road to pick up local buses to take you onward.

JINOTEPE

Head town of the department (province) of Carazo, Jinotepe ("hi-no-TEH-peh") thrives on servicing the coffee plantations of the vicinity—there's a large *beneficio*, or processing plant, on the outskirts. There are no particular sights to see—the town church is an oversized neoclassical turn-of-the-century structure of limited merit—but there are good **lodging** and a couple of **dining** choices. If you're meandering around the Pueblos Blancos, Jinotepe makes a good stopping point for the night.

STAYING

Hotel Jinotepe, tel. (041)22514, 22947, fax 22657. 30 rooms, from $25 double.

The Hotel Jinotepe is an older edifice in front, with high ceilings, and additional add-on tiers with most of the rooms in back. The central courtyard is large and breezy and lined with banks of flowers, and the red roof tile lends a colonial aspect. White wicker rockers are the seating in the lobby, and old movie posters—James Dean, Bogie, Miss Monroe—go perfectly with the predominant faded '50s air. Rooms come in all shapes and sizes; many have balconies with views over the tin and tile roofs of town (in Jinotepe, the two stories of the hotel are soaring). Furnishingwise, the hotel is provincial eclecticism embodied, with industrial carpeting, and chairs and beds gathered from here and there over several eras. Bathrooms have electrically heated shower only. Bar, restaurant, private baths. Located a block and a half from the square.

The Hotel Jinotepe is managed by the Ministry of Tourism, and serves as a hospitality training school.

EATING

Pizzeria Colisseo is one block west of the church, and is pleasant and clean with, of all things, tablecloths—and food several cuts above what you might expect to find in a provincial head-town. Pizzas come in three sizes and assorted decorations, for $4 to $10, and lasagna and spaghetti are served as well, for $3 to $4. Credit cards accepted.

FESTIVAL

Jinotepe celebrates its town fair on July 25, in honor of St. James the Apostle, with the traditional dances known as El Toro Huaco, Las Inditas, and El Viejo and La Vieja. The last, unusually, involves couples; other celebration dances are performed by groups of a single gender.

Nicaragua Guide

HERTYLANDIA
HOME-GROWN AMUSEMENT

Hertylandia is one of Nicaragua's pleasant surprises.

Sited on the edge of Jinotepe, on a quondam coffee farm, it is part **amusement park**, part **botanical garden**, decidedly in good taste, and entirely Nicaraguan, yet set apart from the daily world behind mock castle ramparts and turrets. Most of the huge site remains in a green state.

The immediate attractions for **kids** are a miniature train, and a palace full of mechanical and video **games**, watched over by an oversized concrete monkey. There are also **rowboats** on a small lagoon; a **snack bar**; a **zoo** with peccaries, peacocks, monkeys, ducks, and similar examples of Nicaraguan fauna; and a section of plants and trees, duly identified (cashew, ginger, heliconia, banana, chilamate, Spanish cedar, etc.); and **motocross** track. A free-range zoo has ducks, geese, monkeys, and more. Traditional ceramics are crafted in adobe *ranchos*. Concrete paths embedded with ancient Amerindian glyphs connect all the parts.

And then there's the centerpiece, the stockade that encloses Western-style Fort Levitin, accurate in at least some of its details (the 50-star U.S. flag and the coffee bushes in the background wouldn't pass prop muster). Apaches and cavalry (known here as *federales*) regularly battle it out for the benefit of visitors, among teepees and covered wagons. An old rural house at the center of the stockade has been converted to a house of horrors, with snakes, skeletons, and rushes of cold air. In a jolt back to reality, just outside lie buried fighters and victims of the '78-'79 insurrection.

MEET THE HUMAN SPECIES

Why visit Hertylandia? In the absence of an official botanical garden, and with the Managua zoo in the process of rebuilding, this could be the best place to familiarize yourself with the native plant and animal species, as well as to get close to the workings of a coffee *finca*.

It's also a top-notch place to get to know the *human* species of Nicaragua. You know the problem . . . You visit a country, and the only people you meet are waiters and tour guides and taxi drivers. Maybe you can make contact in a bar, but where are the *real* people? Hertylandia is one place in which to rub elbows with them.

Heartland of Nicaragua

Admission to Hertylandia costs about $2. Hours are from 9 a.m. to 7 p.m. on Friday, Saturday and Sunday *only*, but will undoubtedly extend to other days once facilities are expanded. Games and rides are ticketed separately from the entrance fee, at 75 cents to $1.50 for a "train" (motorized cart) ride or a 15-minute horseback ride.

A **hotel** is under construction, and a pool, water park and miniature golf are on tap. For inquiries about current hours, the numbers are tel. (041)22155, fax (041)23080.

As for the name . . . "Herty" is not particularly redolent of Spanish or Chorotega heritage, but is a local family of political and commercial renown.

LAS VEGAS JR.

Yet another, more modest amusement area is Las Vegas Jr., situated on the road for Santa Teresa, which branches south from the main highway east of Jinotepe. Despite the name, this is another reduced version of Disneyland, with a collection of animals and birds (macaws, monkeys, turtles, geese, peacocks, deer, you name it), rides, a house of mirrors, a rubber-ball play pen such as is found in an IKEA store, and snack bar.

Admission is about $1, and hours are from 9 a.m. to 6 p.m. during the week, with a later closing on weekends. There are plans to add a hotel.

DIRIAMBA

Sister town of Jinotepe, and just three kilometers away, Diriamba is something of a cradle of traditional dances, inclding El Gigante, El Toro Huaco, and especially El Güegüense ("gweh-GWEN-seh"), or Macho Ratón, a folk-comic opera of a production in which the dancers, dark-skinned in the majority, dress up in costumes decorated with mirrors, be-ribboned hats and masks that burlesque the pale skin and great noses of the Spanish overlords. The church is a turn-of-the-century structure, more interesting on the inside than the outside, with blue-pastel-painted woodwork and old paintings.

Why two towns of fair-sized populations (several thousand) so close together? Their names hold a clue. Diriamba is a Chorotega word, while

Jinotega is Nahuatl, and in the days before the Conquest, their peoples were not exactly on speaking terms.

The town fair in honor of San Sebastián (St. Sebastian) culminates on January 20, while the day of Santiago (St. James the Apostle) is also widely celebrated, on July 25; both with the famous regional dances.

Accommodations are available at **Hotel Dirianquen**, on the main street through town, about $10 per room, limited facilities.

LA BOQUITA

One of Pacific Nicaragua's more easily reached beaches is 30 kilometers from Diriamba via a good road. Look ahead to page 211 for details.

SAN MARCOS

What a pleasant little town is hilly San Marcos. Plaster saints top the corners of its old church. The central square is decorated with a bandstand. A general state of good repair, lacking in the villages of the vicinity, prevails.

COLLEGE, U.S.A.

One of the more unexpected sights you'll come across in the Pueblos Blancos is the Latin American Campus of the **University of Mobile** (Alabama), a tropical U.S.-issue college campus with everything from library to computer lab, where programs, signs, and instruction and administration are in English. Even the students, mostly from places like Managua and Masaya and Guatemala City, have that southern California air, sporting designer jeans, backpacks, and Pittsburgh Penguins caps.

The University of Mobile is Baptist-affiliated, and took over this campus from a teacher training school a couple of years ago. There are about 3000 students, a couple of dozen of whom are actually from Mobile.

If you'd like to look around, check in with the guard at the gate. If you're interested in the program, see more details on page 92.

FIESTA

San Marcos celebrates its fair on April 24, highlighted by the meetings of processions of the images of St. Mark, the Virgin of Montserrat, St. Sebastian, and St. James. Traditional dances, including Las Inditas, La Vaquita and La Gigantona, are performed.

SHOPPING

La Cotona sells outfits of *manta*, traditional rough homespun cotton cloth. The same wares are sold in hotel shops in the capital, and at the airport.

MASATEPE

About eight kilometers east of San Marcos, Masatepe ("ma-sa-TEH-peh") is a town of agricultural workers and artisans. Sweets from Masatepe are known throughout Nicaragua. but more interesting to visitors are the durable wares exhibited at several spots along the road through town.

The pre-eminent craft outlet is the former **railroad depot**, west of the town center. Anywhere else, this gem of a building, with its generous roof overhangs and great interior spaces, would be turned over to a quasi-municipal corporation, to be rescued from neglect, painted, re-wired, gentrified, and occupied by boutiques, at enormous rents. In innocent Masatepe, humble sellers have simply moved their wares onto quays next to walls with peeling plaster still daubed with faded slogans of the revolution, for which privilege they pay tribute to the municipal administration in the amount of $11 per month.

You *do* need a car to carry off some of the treasures to be found here: willow rockers, hardwood bookshelves, tables and assorted other furniture. But the basketwork leather shoes can go into your shoulder bag or right onto your feet.

NANDASMO

The village of Nandasmo lies about three kilometres to the north of the road that runs eastward from San Marcos. Its plain, tile-roofed church looks colonial, but dates from 1913. Nothing much happens in Nandasmo. Continuing eastward, turn at San Bernardo for Vista Alegre, a hamlet with views over the valleys to the north, and up to Masaya volcano.

La Bendeja, on a hillock on the south side of the road, is a popular weekend eating spot, with country cooking.

NIQUINOHOMO

Niquinohomo ("ni-ki-NO-mo") would be a stopping place for visitors in any case, with its fine tile-roofed eighteenth-century **church** with uncommon exterior buttresses, its oxcarts, and its modest, traditional, thick-walled houses, many with grilles rather than glass in their windows.

But Niquinohomo is also the **birthplace of Augusto César Sandino**, hero of the struggle to establish the control of Nicaraguans over their destinies in the 1930s, when U.S. Marines occupied the land.

At the northwest corner of the *parque* (main square), is the blue-and-cream family home of Gregorio Sandino, Augusto's father, unmarked, now a town library, and formerly a museum. It is a well-cared-for traditional town residence, with worked wood pillars, and central patio hung with plants, appropriate to the status of Gregorio, a prosperous coffee planter.

On the opposite corner is the house where Augusto César Sandino was born in 1895. Though the illegitimate child of a servant woman, he was acknowledged, taken into the Sandino family, and educated. Sandino went on to a distinguished career as soldier and insurgent, and was on the way to achieving many of his aims, when he was murdered in 1934.

Niquinohomo celebrates its town fair on July 26, in honor of St. Ann.

CATARINA

Catarina and its region raise many ornamental plants on a family scale. Baskets are woven here as well; but the main interest is yet another view, from the lookout point three blocks east and uphill from the town center.

VIEWS OF LAKE APOYO

Here, from an ever-windy rampart, unfolds a vista a thousand feet downward to the waters of Laguna de Apoyo (Apoyo Lake), the villages of Diriomo and Diriá and San Juan de Oriente, and onward to Granada and across Lake Nicaragua.

Lake Apoyo is a large cup of ground water, 180 meters above sea level and as much as 110 meters deep and nine kilometers across, covering 28 square kilometers. It probably formed as an ancient volcano exploded, collapsed and imploded. It has no known outlets, but its waters seep underground to join those of Lake Nicaragua. Lagunero, guapote and mojarra are fished from its waters, but recreational use is limited (fortunately).

A trail from the lookout point leads down to the lake shore through scrub and regenerating forest; another way to the lake is by a jeep trail that branches at kilometer 37 on the Masaya-Granada route.

A visitors' center at the Catarina lookout has some food stands, and there are plans to improve the installations with a more formal restaurant and overnight accommodations.

SAN JUAN DE ORIENTE

Pottery is the craft specialty of San Juan de Oriente, a village of adobe houses and cobbled lanes clinging to steep hill slopes among banana and coffee groves. It's said that nine out of ten village families work in the craft, and everywhere one treads are home-based shops that invite the visitor. Pre-Columbian styles and designs are faithfully reproduced or cleverly adapted to the needs and shapes of the modern kitchen. Especially characteristic is red-hued ware.

The largest workshop is the Cooperativa Productora de Cerámica, located a winding two blocks downhill from the church. Here all the processes in making earthenware can be observed, from the mixing of clay from many sources, to turning pots, polishing, painting, incising pre-Columbian motifs, and firing. Typically, an outer, dark-colored layer is incised to reveal the cream-colored layer underneath.

The ware made at the co-op include fruit plates, urns, plant pots and tableware, all fired in a great brick kiln.

But don't look for these items in the markets of regional towns. Because of the time and effort that go into production, much of the co-op's output can't be sold in Nicaragua at a price to make the effort worthwhile. So you have to purchase it right in San Juan de Oriente, or look for it in London or New York.

DIRIOMO AND DIRIA

Diriomo, with its tile-roofed white church and brick houses more substantial than those of its neighboring villages, is noted for the sweets manufactured in its home-based plants, and the skills of its folk healers, or *curanderos*. Diriá is its poorer twin, with an unusually lo-o-o-ong church.

DOWN TO THE SEA
NICARAGUA'S PACIFIC BEACHES

GOOD NEWS!

The good news is that most of Pacific Nicaragua is a strip of black volcanic sand, usually of extraordinary depth. Around Montelimar (the resort most easily accessible from Managua), at low tide, there's room for a couple of football games played end-to-end, with waves lapping one set of goalposts. Just inland is wild, seasonally dry tropical forest, thick with vines and drenched with the squawks and songs of macaws and toucans, and the roars of howler monkeys.

Farther south, toward the border of Costa Rica, in the vicinity of San Juan del Sur, the coast breaks up into a spectacular series of bays and coves, each a horseshoe of sand bordered by sheltering promontories. Some contain fishing villages and accommodations, and are reached by road; others are completely deserted, except when visited from time to time by . . . you.

In the stretches where the beach is broken by a river entering from the higher country, Pacific Nicaragua is blessed with estuaries and marshlands, nesting and hunting areas for aquatic birds both native and migrating.

Heartland of Nicaragua

GUARANTEED SUN

For more than six months of the year, there is guaranteed sun during daylight hours, and dry air, along with cooling and refreshing sea breezes. By happy coincidence, the **sun season** coincides with winter in the northern temperate zones.

The rest of the year, roughly from May through October, is Pacific Nicaragua's **green season**. It's still sunny most of the time. But on almost every day, you're guaranteed that rain clouds will blow through on their inevitable march toward the volcanoes of Nicaragua's backbone. They'll shed some of their moisture and continue on their way. But there is **never a rainy day** in the sense of the temperate zones, no endless drizzle. The sun always returns.

Inconveniences caused by the rain are of short duration. And there are major advantages. **Lush greenery** is the most evident characteristic of the so-called rainy season. The other plus is that where resort hotels exist (and we'll get to that in a second), **prices drop**, not because of difficult conditions, but because demand falls during the northern winter.

BAD NEWS?

The bad news, if it is, indeed, bad news, is that accommodations along the Pacific are limited. If you're interested in the beach, it would be a good idea to check with a travel professional in Managua during your visit. Plans are under way to increase the range of accommodations, and some hotels that fell on hard times in recent years are currently being upgraded.

Currently, the major resort destination for visitors from abroad, with much justification, is **Montelimar**. Nearby **Pochomil** serves day visitors from Managua. A beach and fishing village, with a few basic hotels, is **San Juan del Sur**, toward the Costa Rican border. Poneloya and Las Peñitas, near León, have off-beat budget accommodations to interest backpackers. And there is any number of beach villages that can be visited for a few hours if you have a car available, but which do not yet feature attractive overnight accommodations.

NEAR MANAGUA

Most visitors from abroad need look no farther than Montelimar to find a comprehensive, reasonably priced, inclusive resort vacation.

TWO ROUTES

The road from Managua toward San Marcos and Jinotepe ascends and dances along the highest ridges in the heart of Nicaragua. To the north are the greener valleys where coffee grows; to the south, the dry hills that range down to the Pacific. Fog rolls up from the coast and socks in the main highway for hours at a time, and a steady wind blows across the stunted vegetation in the highest stretches.

At about kilometer 20 is the so-called *casa embrujada* (haunted house), an abandoned, stuccoed, dollhouse-style residence on the east side of the road, which nobody dares enter at night.

Near the crossroads for Pochomil, at **Las Nubes**, the green-and-white Hotel Capri offers lodging and meals.

From Las Nubes, a branch road winds down from the windy ridge, then up, over and down successive hills, the crest of each affording seaward views. It is a scrubby, seasonally dry tropical forest that is traversed, devoid of rain for half of the year, where cattle are left to wander through cleared stretches in search of sustenance. There are few agglomerations of people along the way—San Rafael del Sur is the main village. One large section of these wide open spaces has been fenced in for the operations of Nicalit, a cement and roofing works.

Where the flats are reached, not far from the water, sugarcane is planted on more gentle slopes.

The **easier route** from Managua joins the road just south of San Rafael del Sur. Longer, but less winding, and therefore less interesting, it involves travelling toward León by the southern route (Carretera Sur), and turning off at Santa Rita. Of course, the intrepid traveller at the wheel of a rented car will descend by one route, and ascend to Managua by the other.

POCHOMIL

Just inland from the beach is the village of **Masachapa**; beyond is Pochomil, the strand where Managuans go on weekends, a government-sponsored development of play areas, canals, picnic shelters, and restaurants, spread along more than a kilometer of the land's edge.

The best that can be said of Pochomil is that a cash-strapped government has put its resources elsewhere. The once-picturesque canals are overgrown with tangled vegetation, the concrete of the public structures is pitted and covered with mold. A visitor down this way with a car might chance one of the accommodations, but otherwise, it's a daylight destination.

Nearby are all gentle scenes associated with a beach village: fishermen repairing their nets at roadside; children bicycling with strings of fish wound about their handlebars.

Pochomil is generally deserted during the week, crowded at holidays. **Buses** run about every hour from the Israel Lewites (Boer) market in Managua. If you're driving, the fee for entry to Pochomil is about $1.50.

ACCOMMODATIONS AT POCHOMIL

The **Bajamar** has bungalows each with four guest rooms, holding a queen and a single bed, for $33 with air conditioning, $22 with fan. There's no phone to call ahead and reserve. This is your best bet, and will do if you're down during the week and the place is uncrowded. Less attractive is the **Altamar**, at about $15 for a room, for however many fit in.

FISHING

Angling is said to be good for snapper (*pargo*), sea bass (*corvina* or *curvina*), Spanish mackerel (*macarela*), sole (*lenguado*) and other species known more for their good taste than their fighting qualities. Boats can be found for hire in Masachapa. Fishing for larger species is based out of San Juan del Sur, farther down the coast.

MONTELIMAR
NICARAGUA FIRST-CLASS

- *59 kilometers from Managua*

Up until 1978, Montelimar was notorious, rather than famous; it was here that Anastasio Somoza chose to locate his beachside retreat. And for good reasons, among them guaranteed dry weather for much of the year, gentle sea breezes, ample flat lands to carve out a landing strip, and hardly a settlement nearby.

All of which is why in the post-Somoza era, Barceló International, a Spanish enterprise with master expertise in providing all-inclusive vacations in idyllic settings, snatched up the property to create Nicaragua's

GOOD VALUE?

The wise traveller will ask if there is some spanner in the works. In return for putting all your money down and agreeing to take whatever services and facilities are offered, might you perhaps be accepting something less than top-notch?

On the one hand, when you book an all-inclusive, you give up the opportunity to sample restaurants and bars and entertainment off the property, unless you're ready not to use what you've already paid for.

On the other hand, in the case of Montelimar, there just *isn't* much else nearby. There are some basic eateries and hostelries a couple of kilometers away at Pochomil, but if a visitor wanders over to these, it will surely be just to see what's out there.

As it happens, I once travelled from Managua northward on a charter flight where I was the only person who had *not* taken a package to Montelimar. Talk about captive interview subjects! Those I chatted with agreed, unanimously, that Montelimar had provided excellent value—good food, lots of activities, attractive surroundings. The staff were considered eager to please if a bit undertrained and amateurish (perhaps because of the young age of the property—then two years).

The occasional contretemps—balky air conditioning and the like—were dealt with as soon as the front desk was called, even in the middle of the night.

Litmus test: nobody reported stomach trouble, and all would consider a return trip to Montelimar, or to a hotel of the same chain.

---

premier beach resort. But, whatever name is officially attached to it, in the shorthand of international travellers it will forever be known as **Somoza's Place**. The details:

Barceló Montelimar. 202 rooms. (200 additional rooms under construction), Municipio San Rafael del Sur. Tel. (02)71911, fax (02)673022 in Managua.

U.S. reservations: Barceló Award Hotels, 150 S. E. 2nd Ave., Miami, FL 33131, tel. 800-858-0606 (800-336-6612 from Canada), fax 305-539-1160.

Rates: $69 to $79 per person per day, according to season, including room, meals, unlimited bar consumption, entertainment, and use of all sports facilities. Children's rate (sharing room with parents), $19 to $24. Transfer from Managua, $42 per person. Daily day-use rate, including everything except overnight accommodations, $50 per person (must be prearranged with Managua office).

In general, Montelimar is the reason for a good chunk of the international tourism that Nicaragua is currently receiving. It is a world-class all-inclusive resort where the price of accommodations includes virtually *everything*.

The village—and that's what it is—consists of dozens and dozens of tile-roofed cottages clustered on an expanse of land sloping gently to the Pacific. The main building is La Casona ("the great house," suggesting an hacienda), with its gourmet restaurant and night club. But the centerpiece is the meandering swimming pool, claimed to be the largest in the region; and at the center of *it* is a circular bar with restaurant and disco.

Part of the vast property consists of open lawns and grassland, but there are also lush tropical gardens of ferns and begonias, sheltered by palms and banana plants. Walkways meander through it all, and bridges span the ponds.

And of course there are several kilometers of nearly deserted beach directly in front.

Guest rooms are air-conditioned and cheery, in bungalows that are well shaded from the sun by generous roof overhang. All are equipped at luxury level, with two large beds, phone, mini-bar, television, and safe-deposit box, and all have terraces.

Food is served mostly buffet-style, and is available at virtually all hours; though the gourmet restaurant provides a more formal setting, and offers specifically Nicaraguan fare and French and Spanish specialties, to supplement the American-type food and nightly theme meals of the main restaurant.

Facilities include restaurants, four bars, coffee shop, night club, and whirlpool. And there are handicraft shops, a travel agency for local excursions, car rental, and a beauty parlor. Convention facilities accommodate 500 (in case you're planning an event). Medical assistance is available 24 hours a day, and motorized transportation is available around the property.

Nicaragua Guide

NO UNINVITED GUESTS

Did you ever wonder what it was like to stay in a Soviet V.I.P. compound, where officials and their guests lived the high life behind walls and out of reach and out of sight of the local populace?

Neither did I, until the first time I tried to enter Montelimar, and found a ring of security at the entry to the parking lot, shielding still *another* ring of security beyond, which shielded the guests from my presence, and me from the party.

Montelimar is by no means the only beach resort that enforces its exclusivity; but it has refined the concept. If you just show up at the gate, even with money in hand, you will be invited, politely but firmly, to leave. And the more insistent you become, the firmer they will get. The guards have their instructions, and in Nicaragua, nobody wants to lose his job for the sake of a gringo visitor.

To stay at Montelimar, reserve through your travel agent, through Barceló hotels in Miami, or through the Managua office. If you want to come down for the day and enjoy all the facilities, book through a Nicaraguan travel agency, or the Managua office.

Once you make it in, it's a nice place.

Sports, in addition to the pool, include a full gym, and four clay tennis courts, sailboats, windsurfers, table tennis, volleyball, basketball, baseball, as well as activities-for-a-fee (see below).

What's Included: All food, beverages made with local liquors, wine with meals, some sports, night-club entertainment, and daily programs such as aerobics, dance lessons, and theme parties. You can also use the casino at no entry fee, but it will probably end up costing you.

What's Not: horseback riding, jet skiing, scuba diving, deep-sea fishing, all-terrain vehicles and motorcycles carry additional charges.

What's coming: Expansion plans for Montelimar include 200 guest rooms, 18-hole golf course, marina, and private airport.

Package Tours: Tour wholesalers, mostly in Quebec and Europe, regularly buy chunks of accommodation at Montelimar and re-sell them to the public as inclusive packages, with charter air transport and ground connections thrown in. Considering the lower cost of charter air travel (not to mention the point-to-point convenience), you'll often pay less than if you made all the arrangements separately and reserved through a scheduled airline. If you live in Ontario or Quebec, or in the northeastern United States, ask your travel agent to look into the availability of one of these packages for Montelimar.

NORTHWARD

El Velero, up the coast from Montelimar and reached by a road through Puerto Sandino from the old (Pacific-side) Managua-León highway, is a wide beach with limited facilities for day use. Overnight accommodations, managed by the social security institute, may be used by drop-ins on a space-available basis. To the south of El Velero, **El Tránsito** also handles day visitors from the capital.

SOUTHWARD

LA BOQUITA

The beaches are wide at La Boquita, Casares and Huehuete, seaside villages easily reached by a road running down from Diriamba, and the surfing is said to be excellent. La Boquita has a paved promenade and basic eateries, and is somewhat more pleasant than the more frequented village of Pochomil up the coast.

One adequate hotel, **La Casona**, functions here, at about $20 for a double room.

Buses run to La Boquita from Diriamba, and from the Israel Lewites market in Managua.

ISOLATED BEACHES

Farther down the coast, reached by a track running just inland from the water, are the beach villages of **Veracruz**, **Astillero**, **Casares**, and others. There are no facilities for visitors, but with camping gear and food, one can stay near the water with no hassles.

TURTLE HAVEN

Chacocente, a beach near Astillero, is a reserve for Ridley and leatherback **turtles**, which lay their eggs in September and October. On nesting nights, armies of turtle mothers swim and crawl ashore, clumsily paddle and sweep and struggle to excavate cavities in the sand, lay their eggs, cover them, and crawl off, barely able to reach the sea. The eggs hatch two months later, and the hatchlings waddle through a gauntlet of lizards and raccoons and swooping birds. Only a small fraction make it to safety in the water.

Humans, too, are major turtle predators. Aside from the tastiness of turtle eggs, they're said to fortify sexual abilities, and thus are highly prized. But with limited protective personnel, the establishment of reserves such as Chacocente, new regulations, and educational campaigns, the outlook for the turtles is more promising than in the past.

MORE BEACHES

For additional seaside places, see the coverage of Poneloya, northward along the Pacific, near León (page 228); and San Juan del Sur (page 237), southward, accessible from Rivas.

10
LEÓN AND THE NORTHWEST

TWO ROUTES TO LEÓN

Two highways join Managua with the tradition-filled city of León. One route cuts southward from the western edge of the capital, following the southern branch of the Pan American Highway, then branches up over a ridge of hills, and onward through undulating and unchallenging countryside. This used to be the less desirable of the two ways to León, but the road has recently been repaired and upgraded. With fewer towns along the way, it's now the quicker way to go—less than 100 kilometers, under two hours in travel time.

THE LAKESIDE ROUTE

The main route to León climbs from the western end of Managua over bordering volcanic mountains, past the turn for Lake Xiloá (see page 151), and onto a bare plateau taken up with storage lots, the Colgate plant and its cousins, an electrical generating station, and love motels. The land is too poor, and too valuable at the same time in the commercial sense, to be left in cultivation, and so it ends as a mixed-used no man's land.

Beyond, the flatlands are edged by Lake Managua, by the perfect volcanoes Momotombo and Cerro Negro, and by lesser conical mounds not tall enough to appear on many maps, but occasionally angry enough to blow off steam, or even more. This is ranch country, porous soil blown up and out from the earth's interior, rich in the rains, bone-dry when the rains are absent, covered by grasses that are left in the fields as standing fodder. Corn and beans and soya are planted in some lakeside plots, for harvest year-round.

NAGAROTE

Nagarote, a roadside town, bears more than a passing resemblance to a cattle settlement in northern Mexico. Its houses are well separated and set back on individual lots on wide, dusty streets dotted with pickup trucks, in place of the clustering adobes of the classic Central American mold.

Nagarote's claim to fame is an ancient tree, said to be one of the oldest standing in Nicaragua.

Beyond Nagarote, as the road rises and dips, it is crossed and paralleled by the perfectly level embankment of Nicaragua's now-phantom national railway. With a regular rhythm imposed by the realities of economics and the accessibility of a clandestine scrap market, the disappearance of the track can be measured at a finite daily rate.

REFRESHMENT

Restaurante Campestre El Paisaje, at the Volcano Momotombo lookout point, kilometer 32, is one of the few stopping points on the route, and has a kids' play area.

PUERTO MOMOTOMBO AND OLD LEÓN

A graded dirt road branches from the highway, 54 kilometers from Managua, winding on a northeasterly loop over the hills and seasonally dry beds of streams that descend from the slopes of looming, multi-coned Momotombo volcano. The roadbed deteriorates rapidly to a rutted track, but it is mostly wide, and, without notable grades, it is passable in a sedan driven at a sedate pace.

The main crater holds its secrets from view, but lesser vents tilt to reveal views of their inner edges, even from below. An abandoned hacienda house lends a ghost-town air, but there's an even larger ghost town ahead.

Puerto Momotombo is the village attained unexpectedly at the end of this seemingly untrafficked road. It is another collection of wind-blown brick houses with tile roofs on dirt lanes, with a solid brick school. Follow the signs at all cutoffs for *Ruinas de León Viejo* (Ruins of Old León), and you'll reach your destination.

OLD LEÓN

Old León was founded by Francisco Hernández de Córdoba in 1528 under orders of Pedrarias Dávila, one of the more notorious of the Spanish conquerors. The site lay right in the middle of a number of Indian villages, a move that afforded the Spaniards plenty of skilled if unwilling labor during the truncated life of Nicaragua's first capital.

And labor aplenty was required, for in this spot remote from the metropolis, a new Spain was created not in miniature, but in full-scale imitation of the original, with churches and plazas and a palace of government, and mansions to house the Spanish masters. And, since they were starting from scratch, the conquerors improved on the original, with wide, straight streets to replace the winding byways of their homeland.

León functioned as the center from which agricultural domains were ruled, and from which the extraction of gold from the mountains and streams of Nueva Segovia was supervised; and the focus of proselytization of the natives, to put a euphemism to their forced conversion; and, inevitably, as the stage on which were played out the intrigues and jealousies of Spaniards vying for influence and riches. The climaxes were bloody on more than rare occasions. It was in the plaza of León that Francisco Hernández de Córdoba himself was beheaded, convicted of treason.

The town of León flourished, as more buildings were erected, more trade flowed through. Not so the natives, who succumbed to smallpox and venereal diseases and assorted other ravages of their overworked bodies.

But in the end, the land had its revenge. In 1609, the earth trembled, and León shook and collapsed. The inhabitants salvaged their belongings, abandoned the cursed site, and set "their" Indians to re-erecting the head Spanish settlement on another site, to the southwest.

THE RUINS

The ruins of Viejo León are about four blocks south of the present-day town of Puerto Momotombo. The admission fee is about 75 cents.

No intact buildings remain, but the foundations of the original Spanish civic and religious buildings, and the lower sections of their brick walls, topped with a protective layer of mortar, can be appreciated in a rough-cut field.

Among the notable monuments and public spaces:

The **Plaza Mayor**, now a grassy square, was the principal public assembly area of the first León. Along its edges were erected the major public buildings of the capital.

The **Cathedral** was founded in 1528 by Pedrarias Dávila. The building had three naves and a sacristy.

The **Casa de la Fundición**, covering 831 square meters, was damaged several times in quakes and fires, and was last reconstructed in 1544.

The **Church of La Merced** (Our Lady of Mercy), originally built in 1528 with a thatched roof, rivaled the Cathedral as the major temple of the town—a situation that was not uncommon in the Spanish colonies, where church-building by religious orders hungry for power sometimes exceeded immediate needs. A tile roof went on in 1530. Pedrarias the conqueror was buried in this church in 1531.

Various **houses** have been identified from archival research. The house of Ana Jiménez borders the plaza, and other houses of notable families are elsewhere. But obviously, the spaces between the buildings were not empty, as they appear to today's visitor. Some of the building foundations lie still untouched since the destruction of Old León; while others were built entirely of wood and reeds and thatch, and left no traces once they fell and their materials rotted.

THE IMABITE MUSEUM

Back in the village, the Imabite Museum (**Museo Imabite**) is an offbeat, human-scale collection of artifacts from pre-Columbian times to the turn of the century, small enough to be housed in a single room, and to be appreciated without overwhelming. As a community-based project, it provides the casual visitor a window on the pride with which small-town Nicaraguans look upon their history and their heritage.

Admission is by contribution. Five córdobas per person will do. An attendant recites a non-stop description of the most significant items.

Most of the archeological pieces exhibited at Imabite were found in the surrounding area. Some came from the banks of the lake, others turned up

> "Imabite" is the native Chorotega word for the original village that stood here on the banks of Lake Xolotlán, perhaps deriving from *nimbu* (water) and *ite* (drink), or indicating a stone shaped by water.

in a riverbed near the ruins of Old León. Still others were unearthed right in the village.

According to Spanish records, the area immediately around the first Spanish capital was the province of Nagarando, densely inhabited, probably by Chorotegas related in language and culture to the Aztecs of Mexico. Plentiful water and fish probably figured in their choice of this site.

Some of the artifacts on exhibit at Imabite are ceremonial, such as incense burners, and funerary urns in which the bones of chieftains were reburied after a decent period of decomposition; but most are domestic, and include items like grinding stones (*metates*) that indicate the importance of the cultivation of corn, axes, ocarinas, and stones that were used in the manufacture of paper.

Pottery of styles associated with what are today Honduras and El Salvador indicate that Imabite was on a long-distance trade route.

Humanoid basalt sculptures about a foot high—some found right in the lake—are particularly characteristic of the ancient inhabitants. One is fashioned with an incense burner in the head. Some might have been representations of local nobility; one shows earlobe cuts of the kind associated with warriors.

Ceramic vessels from the early period of Spanish occupation are an indication of the population of the area by Indian laborers. Though household items, which families had to furnish on their own account, they were more than merely utilitarian: figures such as the faces of turtles are worked into their designs. Some polychrome fragments indicate Spanish influence on pottery styles, and one human figure is European in facial characteristics.

Old León was abandoned in 1609, and passed out of written history for more than two centuries, until in 1882 a site near the old capital was chosen as a lake port and terminus for the Nicaragua Pacific Railway. The railway opened on January 27, 1884, and Puerto Momotombo became something of a boom town. Relics in the museum from this period include a Victrola, part of a railway undercarriage, and farm implements. But the glory was short-lived; a lakeside rail route all the way to Managua left Puerto Momotombo to wither. Its museum, the ruins of Old León, and the

Nicaragua Guide

tilting walls of the wooden hacienda house of General Zelaya serve as reminders of importance bypassed.

EATING AND SLEEPING IN PUERTO MOMOTOMBO

Ask at the museum about modest rooms, available at under $5 per person for the night. The Bar Gaby down the street can provide basic eats. An open-air stand near the entry to the Old León site, decorated with hanging plants, is a pleasant stopping area.

TRANSPORT

Buses operate to Puerto Momotombo from La Paz Centro on the highway between Managua and (present-day) León. The first bus leaves at dawn, the last at about 3 p.m. The last bus out of Puerto Momotombo leaves at 3:30 p.m. To reach La Paz Centro, take a León bus from the Israel Lewites (Boer) market in southwestern Managua; or a Managua-bound bus from León.

The site is reached more conveniently in a rented car, or by taxi.

MOMOTOMBO VOLCANO

Towering over Puerto Momotombo is the ever-smoking volcano of the same name ("Ruling above the waters" in Chorotega), rising to 1230 meters (4100 feet). And an angry deity it can be. According to an oft-repeated tale, missionaries in the sixteenth century attempted to scale its heights and baptize it with a Christian name; but Momotombo rumbled and sputtered and sent the priests scurrying.

So reliable is Momotombo's activity that a plant at its base harnesses its fiery gases to generate a fifth of Nicaragua's electricity. Because of the plant's strategic importance and lingering security-consciousness, casual visitors are not allowed onto the volcano; but climbers can obtain a permit by contacting the state energy company, Instituto Nicaragüense de Energía, public relations department, Pista de la Resistencia, Managua, tel. 674379. Birding is good in the protected area around the volcano, especially for aquatic species.

Monte Galán, on the lower slopes of Momotombo, is the collective name for three small lakes full of sulphureous water, and inhabited by crocodiles. Closer to Puerto Momotombo is **Tigre** ("Tiger") Lake, also known as **Tecuacinabia**, in an extinct crater.

Momotombito ("Little Momotombo", also called Cocobolo) is the volcanic island in the lake directly east of Big Momotombo. Once an indigenous shrine, to judge by finds of statues, it is still largely forested.

LA PAZ CENTRO

La Paz Centro (never referred to as simply "La Paz") is another dusty town of brick houses well separated on dirt lots. Many roadside stands sell *quesillo*, a regional specialty, consisting of boiled rennet with cream and onion, often flavored with chile. Other stands sell the craft specialties of La Paz Centro, red pottery and incised cow horn.

LAND OF RICHES

Past La Paz Centro, farther from the shores of Lake Managua, the countryside becomes less severe, covered by fields cultivated more densely in the rich, porous, weathered volcanic soil.

This is the center of large-scale agriculture in Nicaragua, on the blessed plain undulating down toward the sea, from the ridge of periodically eruptive volcanoes. Dry and parched for half the year, the northwestern plains have somewhat of the aspect of the Central Valley of California; but they bloom without irrigation in the rains that arrive reliably from May through October.

Sesame is planted in places, but white gold—cotton—is king, going into the ground in June, growing in the rains, then maturing into a snowy blanket over long, sunny days that the weevils hate.

Of course, the plains were populated long before Spanish was spoken here, by the Subtiava and Nagrandano peoples, related in language and culture to the peoples of Central Mexico. The Subtiavas retain their identity even today, in one poor but proud neighborhood of the city of León; while all the names of the towns of the area—Chinandega, Chichigalpa, Posoltega—recall the ancient heritage now submerged in the Hispanic culture that radiated throughout the colonial period from the Spanish base at León.

LEÓN

- 90 kilometers from Managua

While Nicaragua is a venerable land, it is León, not Managua, that is its venerable city, along with Granada. Founded on its present site in 1609, after the first capital was destroyed by an earthquake, for most of the centuries of Spanish dominion, and well into independence, León was the major city, trading center, ecclesiastical seat, and focus of learning in the land.

It was from León that the Hispanization of western Nicaragua—the destruction of the indigenous way of life and its replacement by Spanish towns and Spanish administration and Spanish religion and Spanish trade —was carried out. After independence, León was the seat of the Liberals, the party that originally stood for independence from Spain, secular administration, and freedom from Government restrictions.

Like Granada, León is a city that exudes the air of the past. The rivalry between León and Conservative Granada was settled to the advantage of neither, when the capital settled in Managua in 1852, halfway between the two. But León never lost its position as a university center.

And having been stripped of its political importance, it retained the grace of its peninsular ways. Built on hills, its low-lying houses are almost universally roofed in red tiles, with generous eaves, substantial doors, and hidden courtyards and arcades that suggest the Moorish side of the colonizers. The Cathedral, towering in gleaming white, might well have sat untouched since the last century. A great tree in a one-time outlying Indian village recalls the execution of an indigenous leader, as if it had taken place yesterday.

But a closer examination reveals painful details of recent events. Bullet chinks and monuments to the fallen speak of fighting during the 1978 *insurrección* against Somoza. And on a hilltop overlooking León is a fortress whose garrison kept the area subdued.

WHERE TO STAY

Hotel America, 1 block east of central market, tel. (0311)5533. 9 rooms. From $10 per person.
In a traditional building with tile roof, not a particularly good value, but conveniently located, the América attracts young travellers.

Hotel Europa, 3 Calle Noreste, 4 Avenida (P. O. Box 24), 3 blocks north of Cathedral, 4 blocks east. Tel. (0311)2596, 6040; fax 2577. 29 rooms. $13 single/$18 double with fan, $22/$24 with air conditioning. Master Card, Visa.

The location of the Hotel Europa near the train tracks doesn't look promising, but it is, in fact, one of the better places in which to hang your hat. Rooms are a bit gloomy, but are tidy, opening from outside passages rather than inner hallways. Some of the lower-priced units share baths. The courtyard is flowered and attractive. Protected parking. Look for the Lucky Strike sign.

Hotel Colonial, half-block north of university main building, tel. and fax (0311) 2279. 16 rooms. From $22.

A modern, two-story structure with no particular attraction conceals the older and more charming structure where most of the guest rooms are located. Some rooms are air-conditioned, and breakfast is available.

WHERE TO EAT

El Sesteo, right on the square, is a plain, open-to-the-street eatery serving both complete meals and snacks, and though it isn't fancy, the food is good. A large pepper steak costs about $6, beer less than a dollar, and fruit drinks are served. Some claim that this is an excellent place for watching co-eds.

La Cueva del León, a half-block north of the university, and a couple of blocks north of the square, serves fish from the nearby coast, as well as the usual beef-and-chicken assortment.

Restaurante Sacuanjoche, just east of Colegio Lasalle on the street leading from the square toward the Darío house, is more formal than most restaurants here (indeed, more formal than most restaurants in Nicaragua), with tablecloths, attractively prepared steak and chicken courses, and even a few wines.

Unlike most other Nicaraguan towns, including Managua, León has many, many **snack** places where one can order something less than a full meal in benign surroundings. This is largely due to the student population, which is the main market segment. If you're looking for a pizza, a sandwich, a bowl of soup, take either of the streets that run north from the square, and look in every other door or so. The **Libro-Café La Casona de Colón,** a block north from the northwest corner of the square, is a good choice, with books

Nicaragua Guide

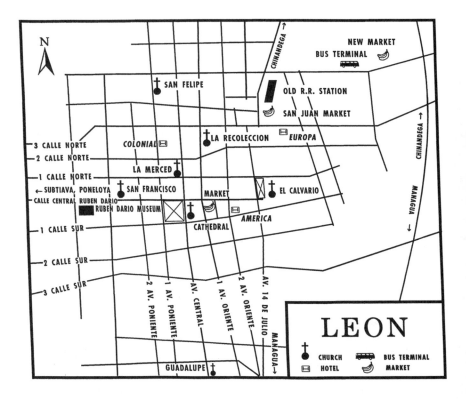

on sale as well as corporeal sustenance. Or, try a roast chicken shop. **Rosticería El Dorado** is 1½ blocks east of the San Felipe church, which is five blocks north of the square.

GETTING THERE

From Managua, **buses** for León leave from the Israel Lewites market near the west end of the city. Service is every half-hour or more frequently, until about 6 p.m.

Buses for Managua leave about every half hour from the new market, on 6 Calle Norte toward the eastern outskirts of town. There is also frequent service to Chinandega and the port of Corinto; and several buses a day head cross-country past the volcanic chain toward San Isidro in the highlands, between Estelí and Matagalpa. This last trip takes about three hours.

SITES

Start at the *Parque Central*, or main square, an open, bare expanse surrounded mostly by centenary buildings, some of them galleried in the Spanish tradition.

CATHEDRAL AND MAIN SQUARE

León's Cathedral (Catedral) was the largest in all of colonial Central America, bespeaking perhaps the aspirations of the colony, or perhaps something else. According to scholars, the plans for Leon's major church got mixed up with those for Lima's on the voyage out from Spain. If a mistake there was, it was never corrected, and construction got under way in 1747. Not until more than 100 years later was the building completed.

Whatever its origins, the grandeur of León's central rococo church is indisputable. Two lions emblematic of the city (*León* literally means "lion") guard its portals. Its altars, statues and oil paintings are all treasures of colonial art. And it is the resting place for prominent Nicaraguan generals, ecclesiasts, and men of letters, including national poet-hero Rubén Darío, mourned by yet another lion.

The entire Cathedral was restored with the assistance of Spain in time for the five-hundredth anniversary of the landing of Columbus in the Americas; and the original construction techniques were duplicated in every step of the process.

On the south side of the square is a set-piece of nineteenth-century Latin American formal architecture, the perfectly neoclassical Colegio Asunción, with its grilled windows in stone-block casements, rectilinear moldings, and tile roof.

MARKETS

Behind the Cathedral is León's traditional **central market**, run-down, its commerce spilling over into the streets. Another, larger market, the Mercado San Juan, is four blocks north and three blocks east of the Cathedral, by the former railroad station; while an even larger market and bus station lie on the outskirts of town, six blocks north of the Cathedral, and about five blocks east.

CALVARY

Four blocks east of the Cathedral, **El Calvario**, another effusively styled Churrigueresque gem, like almost all churches so named is situated on an elevation, though slight in this case. The interior is especially graceful and modest, with an intricate woodwork ceiling supported on slim columns with floral decorations, under a large dome.

The small park in front of the church holds a monument to Edgardo Munguía Alvarez (known by his nom-de-guerre, Ventura), who died in the fight against Somoza. A plaque on the church itself commemorates civilian protesters who were shot by the National Guard in the bell tower in 1979.

A block north of the little park, a plaque in the wall of an adobe house marks the birthplace of Gen. Máximo Jérez, Liberal leader of Nicaragua in the last century.

Another four blocks northward, the **Church of San Juan** is mostly new in body, though its original spirit remains in the surviving eighteenth-century façade.

The **San Juan Market** wraps around the church and extends northward, toward the former railroad station.

LA RECOLECCIÓN

Two blocks west and one block south, La Recolección is another magnificent colonial church, with a squat bell tower constructed beside, rather than atop, the main section. This architectural adaptation was common in Central America after the first experiences with earthquakes. Spanish architects decided that they could minimize damage by concentrating the mass of structures as low to the ground as possible, to reduce vibrations; and by grounding potentially lethal superstructures, such as bell towers.

UNIVERSITY

In the vicinity of La Recolección are many of the buildings of **UNAN**, the **National Autonomous University of Nicaragua**. Education is the main industry of León, which has a medical school on its outskirts, a technical college, and several private secondary schools. And with the large local student population, it was a center of subversion against the Somoza government, which attempted to keep a tight lid on the town. Bullet pocks in the cement plaster of many a building remain as a reminder of the 1979 fighting.

A block north of the western end of the square, and to the west, is the **Galería de Héroes y Mártires** (Martyrs' and Heroes' Gallery), commemorating key figures in the Anti-Somoza campaign.

LA MERCED

La Merced (Our Lady of Mercy), a church two blocks north of the western end of the main square, is simpler than some of the other old churches of León, but in better repair. Like La Recolección, it has a a bell tower anchored at ground level. La Merced is attached to one of the university buildings. Three blocks farther north is the plain **San Felipe Church**, in neoclassical style, with a plain wooden ceiling inside, and gilt altar decorations.

The **Laborío Church**, a few blocks southwest of the square, is a plain neoclassical structure with tin roof, said to date from the seventeenth century.

MONUMENT TO A POET

Two blocks west of the northwestern corner of the square is the house known as Cuatro Esquinas, now the **Rubén Darío Archive and Museum**.

Rubén Darío, born Félix Rubén García Sarmiento, son of an army officer in obscure Nicaragua, rose to world literary stature. He is celebrated as one of the first poets in Spanish to use external correlatives to represent the workings of the mind, somewhat in the manner of Emily Dickinson. He earned fame with *Azul*, published in Chile in 1888, and went on to edit newspapers in El Salvador and Guatemala.

Though he represented his country as a diplomat, and travelled to Argentina, New York and Europe, he returned triumphant to his native city at various times in his life, and lived in this traditional town home with its interior garden.

Photos, furniture, editions of Darío's poetry in several languages, and his possessions fill the surviving rooms of the house (part has been replaced by newer structures), revealing the many sides of his personality. He had two wives, but was a lifelong romantic rover, and found the love of his life, Rosario Murillo, in Spain in 1899. She was a gardener's daughter, and the two lived together without priestly blessing.

Darío died in Nicaragua in 1916.

One other major church in León is that of **Guadalupe**, five blocks south of the Cathedral, and in poor repair.

PAST IN THE PRESENT

Colonial houses will be found still standing here and there in León. Thick walls with deeply inset windows, iron grilles, tile roofs, massive wooden beams, carved decorative lintels, balconies well above the level of the streets and their squishy mud in days of yore, and generous eaves are all characteristic of construction in the pre-independence period. If a door has been left open, take advantage to steal a look into the hidden world of the inner courtyard, usually bedecked with plants, a sanctuary from the world outside.

SUBTIAVA

About a kilometer west of León's Cathedral is **Subtiava**, once a separate township of Indian artisans, now a part of the city, but still humble and traditional in its ways and outlook, with the air more of a rural village than of a neighborhood.

On Subtiava's bare and quiet main square is its mission-style **church**, dating from the seventeenth century (or 1530, before the founding of the relocated León, according to some sources), its façade dwarfed by its huge adjacent bell tower. Curiously, the side walls show the figures of entwined snakes, evidently an indigenous motif adapted by native artisans to ecclesiastical architecture, perhaps to symbolize the Christian search for eternal life. The interior depiction of the sun might have a similar origin. The altar is a prized survival from the earliest days of the colony.

Again in traditional fashion, ecclesiastical and civic structures dominate this public space: the parish house, a tile-roofed building with porch arcade, and an old peoples' home.

A few blocks to the south, ask for the way to the **Tamarindón**, a centuries-old tamarind tree from which the native chieftain Adicac was hanged by the Spaniards for rebelling against their authority and withholding information as to the whereabouts of gold—a fate much repeated in those days. The tree, surrounded by an iron fence, stands in the courtyard of a carpentry shop, where decorative furniture and caskets are produced.

SOMOZA'S CITADEL

About a kilometer south of Subtiava, atop a basaltic dome with a commanding view of the vicinity, stands **El Fortín**, once a garrison of Anastasio Somoza's Guardia Nacional. Special attention was paid to keeping the reins on León, with its potentially troublesome student population, and this redoubt was one of the measures, a squat concrete bunker with gun turrets, occupied by Sandinista forces after the *Triunfo*, and now abandoned.

Access to the Fortín is by a poor road that steadily deteriorates as it climbs through suburban fields—if you're driving, park your car before the top. You're free to walk through the ghostly garrison, past the cells; and also to admire the spectacular views to León and its red tile roofs and white Cathedral, the march of volcanoes toward Honduras, and the edge of the blue Pacific. A peek below reveals that the town dump is on the far side of the hill, just below the crest.

SHOPPING

León is less noted for handicrafts than some other central Nicaraguan towns and cities, but two specialties that are notable are *cotonas*, the formal shirts made of homespun cotton; and embroidered cloths.

Look for these at several general merchandise stores, or at the markets, as León is innocent enough to have nothing that even approaches being a souvenir shop. The San Juan market is four blocks north and four blocks east of the Cathedral on the main square; and the main market, another block north of the San Juan market, then three blocks farther east on 6 Calle Norte.

FESTIVAL

León celebrates in honor of St. Jerome on September 30, with a procession from the church in Subtiava to the Cathedral of León. The September 24 fiesta honors the Virgin of Mercy (Virgen de Mercedes) while traditional dances are performed during pre-Christmas celebrations on December 7.

TO THE COAST

NATURAL AVIARIES

A good paved highway runs from León, down to the Pacific at Poneloya, crossing low-lying wet spots that are excellent spots for birding in the dry season. Once again, this is largely grazing country.

Toward the coast, the Telica River branches into lazy, winding fingers, separated from the waves by barrier islands and peninsulas, forming salt marshes and mangrove estuaries that serve as breeding grounds and nesting areas for fish and birds. The estuaries and bays all along this stretch of coast also make for fine birding and wildlife observation at any time of year.

PONELOYA

Just 20 kilometers from León, and fewer than 20 minutes by road, Poneloya is a village of the rich and the modest. Substantial houses and inexpensive inns stand side by side along the road that runs just back from the waves, and the beach is wide and empty. There's little traffic of people here; on some days, the major activity consists of hogs and chickens rooting in the fallen fronds of palms. You wanted to get away?

Facilities are limited, and most visitors will want to visit for the day with a car, to enjoy the beach, and for the excellent birding opportunities in the estuary just north of the village. Boats can be hired for exploring by arrangement with local fishermen.

ACCOMMODATIONS IN PONELOYA

La Posada, relatively new, has about 13 plain but air-conditioned rooms going for about $20 each, and is your best bet for a night. There are more basic places, including **Hotel Lacayo**, tel. (0317)307; and **El Palomazo**. And there are several snack stands.

Las Peñitas, adjacent to Poneloya, is a group of vacation houses without much of a town, though there's an eatery right at the end of the road, overlooking mangroves and another estuary. Again, look to hire a boat if you're interested in exploring by water.

Buses run to Poneloya and Las Peñitas from central León; service is most frequent on weekends.

LEÓN TO CHINANDEGA

At **Telica**, on the road to Chinandega, is the junction for a branch road across the spine of volcanoes, toward the uplands of central Nicaragua. Along the way, about 25 kilometers out of León, are the **San Jacinto hot springs** (Hervideros de San Jacinto), craters of boiling water bubbling up amid spouts of sulphureous gas. The springs are fed by waters that originate in the fuming Telica volcano, and can be heard flowing underfoot.

San Cristóbal (1750 meters) is the volcano that towers to the northeast of Chinandega. Reigning Nicaraguan volcano in terms of height, it last erupted in the seventeenth century, in time to guide a pirate raid on the port of El Realejo, followed by a surprise attack on León. It has been fuming again since 1971.

At **Chichigalpa**, northwest of León, is **San Antonio**, a sugar mill and the major rum distillery in Nicaragua.

CHINANDEGA

Chinandega is the major city in a cotton-growing area, more modern and less charming than León.

WHERE TO STAY IN CHINANDEGA

The **Hotel Cosigüina**, tel. (0341)3636, fax 3689, a half-block south of the square, has rooms from about $20. Some are air-conditioned, with televisions. There are also a bar and restaurant, and meeting rooms, and credit cards are accepted.

Cheaper are the **Glomar**, tel. (0341)2562, a block south of the market, $10 with some air-conditioned rooms and private baths; and the **San Antonio**.

Aside from the Hotel Cosigüina's restaurant, standard beef and chicken fare is available at the Corona de Oro, a half-block west of the bank on the square.

Buses run directly to Chinandega from the Israel Lewites market in Managua, as well as from León.

El Viejo, a few kilometers to the northwest of Chinandega, draws pilgrims every year to an image of the Virgin, guarded in bejeweled raiment in its church.

GULF OF FONSECA

The Gulf of Fonseca is shared with neighboring Honduras and El Salvador; Nicaragua's sentinel over the waters is **Cosigüina volcano**, 807 meters, at Nicaragua's Land's End. Now placid, with a lake imprisoned in its crater, Cosigüina was once a tiger. In 1835, its cone, then several times higher than it is now, rumbled and blew apart, in the **greatest eruption ever recorded in the hemisphere**, heard as far away as Quito in Ecuador.

If you're interested in climbing Cosigüina, look first for a guide in nearby Potosí.

Just to the east, where the gulf laps the volcano, are the marshlands of the delta of the **Estero Real,** or "Royal Estuary", where the Tecolapa River lazes toward the sea, wrapping around the island called **Mangles Altos** ("High Mangroves"), set aside as a natural reserve. To explore the mangroves, inquire in Potosí about renting a boat.

Potosí is Nicaragua's port, or outpost, on the Gulf of Fonseca, at the end of the road and 66 kilometers from Chinandega. Ferry service to El Salvador could be restored at any time.

EL REALEJO AND CORINTO

El Realejo, southwest of León, was the major port of Nicaragua in the colonial period, when the shallow estuary gave shelter from storms, if not always from pirates: on the main square are the ruins of a church laid waste in a raid in the 1600s. A colonial shipyard still survives as well. In 1855, it was at El Realejo that William Walker and his band of 57 adventurers and misfits first set foot on Nicaraguan soil.

Toward the end of the nineteenth century, when Nicaragua was opening to commerce with the world, especially in coffee, El Realejo was inadequate for large, modern ships. The lighterage of cargo from ships anchored offshore into the estuary was seen as a hindrance to commerce.

So in 1875, construction was started on a pier at a site on the bar opposite El Realejo. With the completion of a lighthouse, and of a bridge in 1882, **Corinto** supplanted El Realejo as Nicaragua's main port.

In its way, Corinto was ahead of its time. Up and down the Caribbean and Atlantic coasts of Central America in the present century, the ports of San José and Barrios in Guatemala, and Puntarenas and Limón in Costa Rica, have only in the last few decades been supplanted by newer facilities.

Basic lodging is available in Corinto at the Hotel Central, tel. (0342)380, opposite the port office.

Guasaule, 205 kilometers from Managua via a road that cuts north from the Pacific plain through the breach between San Cristóbal volcano and the Gulf of Fonseca, is the southern highway border crossing for Honduras. The road onward crosses the narrowest part of Honduras to El Salvador; a branch road leads northward to Tegucigalpa.

11
THE SOUTHEAST

ON THE ROAD

Nandaime, in the shadow of Mombacho volcano, 65 kilometers from Managua, marks the limit of the hilly, highly populated coffee region south of the lakes Managua and Nicaragua. Nandaime is a farm center, with a juice plant and silos, and colonial church.

To the southeast is savanna: flatter, grassy, relatively dry country. Sugarcane fields line the road in areas, and there are mills in which cane juice is converted to granulated sugar. Melons and papaya, the classic produce of sun-drenched, loose soils, are offered at roadside stands. Where irrigation is available, the deep green of waving rice plants extends into the distance. Elsewhere, the plains stretching to Lake Nicaragua on one side, and to a fringe of hills along the sea, are grazed by cattle. Horses munch away along the edges of the right of way.

Here and there in the golden fields are sprawling old adobe ranch houses with tile roofs, their plaster chinked, graceful porches providing shelter from the sun, doorways leading into the privacy of courtyards. And right on the road tread oxen pulling carts laden with sweet, freshly harvested cane. It is mostly a placid, archaic scene, redolent of lazily gathered fruits of the earth. But there are also agglomerations of plank houses on stilts, and huddled structures of exposed concrete block or adobe in dirt yards on the edge of cattle pastures. There is no way to gloss over the hard life of many of the residents.

RIVAS

- *111 kilometers from Managua*

Rivas is neat, clean, cheery and bustling, a farming center, as the nickname, *Ciudad de los Mangos*—city of mangos—implies. It's the first town of any size on the road from Costa Rica, and a pit stop on the way to the coast at San Juan del Sur. At its very center is the most marvelous bad-taste public square, with a fountain of concrete logs enclosing water-spouting flamingos. A hand-cranked mini ferris wheel is available to any young citizen.

Little Rivas looms large in the annals of Central America. It was here in 1856 that Juan Santamaría, the Costa Rican drummer boy, set afire the headquarters of William Walker, the American who had taken control of Nicaragua. Though the campaign against Walker faltered thereafter, the Central American allies eventually prevailed, and the anniversary of the battle is celebrated every April 11 in Costa Rica.

GETTING THERE

Buses for Rivas leave about every half-hour from the Roberto Huembes Market in Managua, and there is also frequent bus service from Granada.

Buses for the Costa Rican border leave Rivas about every two hours. Local buses run as well to San Jorge, the port for Ometepe Island on Lake Nicaragua; and for San Juan del Sur on the Pacific.

WHERE TO STAY AND EAT

The choice, basically, is the **Hotel Nicarao** or the Hotel Nicarao, tel. (046)33234, 1½ blocks west from the Bank of Nicaragua on the main square. There are 20 white-painted brick rooms behind the blue-and-white aluminum fascia, going for $13 single/$19 double. The folks are friendly and helpful. Rooms have fans, except for one with air-conditioning, at a higher rate.

If the Nicarao is full, El Coco, near the bus stop for the Costa Rican border, will do.

Meals are available at the Hotel Nicarao, and there are a few eateries near and even right in the square with inelegant but edible snack food.

Or, for a *real* change of pace, continue back to the Pan American Highway. At kilometer 119 (seven kilometers from Rivas) is **Restaurante La Lucha**. Feast your eyes on the stuffed deer, squirrels, owls and armadillos, or the caiman fashioned into an ashtray, or the sisal heads, all of which bear a top price of under $100. Or, you can fill your stomach with more conventional home-cooked food for a lot less, and pay with Master Card or Visa.

RIVAS SIGHTS

The Rivas **church**, dating from around 1800, is notable for its graceful interior wooden arches, and the allegorical frescoes of sea battles in its dome, which are partly restored.

REGIONAL MUSEUM AND HACIENDA

The **Museum** of Rivas (*Museo*) lies behind the market. From the square, walk three blocks west past the Bank of Nicaragua, one block north, then take the diagonal road behind the market. To the right, atop a hillock, past the cannon on the lawn, you'll see a tile-roofed, hacienda-style house with tile roof and gracious front porch: that's the museum.

Inside are several attics' worth of collectibles: stuffed armadillos, alligators, turtles, foxes, ocelots, pumas, and many more; exhibits regarding the tectonic movements of the region, the origin of Lake Nicaragua, and the ancient peoples who inhabited its shores; pottery from the several cultures that preceded today's Nicaragua, in a variety of forms, including an incised jar in the shape of a bird, tripod vases, double pots, and the cream, brick-red and black pottery of the Nicarao, who were masters of much of the region when the Spaniards arrived.

The museum building, also known as the house of Máximo Espinosa, was the great house (*casona*) of a cacao plantation in the eighteenth century, and was used by William Walker's forces. Later, it was the residence of José Dolores Gámez, who edited a local paper. It passed into the hands of the Somoza family (who also owned estates across the border in Costa Rica), and was confiscated by the state after the triumph of the insurrection in 1979.

Elsewhere in Rivas, a **plaque** commemorates Juan Santamaría's heroism in setting afire the headquarters of William Walker. To find it, walk one block past the Bank of Nicaragua from the square, turn left, and look along the left side of the street. The plaque is set into the wall of a nondescript contemporary building.

Between Rivas and San Jorge, the **Cruz de España (Cross of Spain)** marks the spot where the Spanish conqueror Gil González Dávila first negotiated with the native chieftain Nicarao.

CELEBRATIONS

A **pilgrimage** and **fair** take place every year, starting almost two weeks before Easter, lasting from Tuesday until Friday. Townspeople from Masaya, Granada and the White Towns of central Nicaragua travel by oxcart to honor Jesus of Salvation (Jesús del Rescate), an image and deity incorporating the redeeming attributes of the Lord. This age-old tradition no doubt goes back to pre-Columbian times, and was incorporated into the religion brought by the Spaniards. Whatever its origin, the pilgrimage remains a deeply revered practice.

SAN JORGE

San Jorge is Rivas' port on Lake Nicaragua, neater than other little towns in the area, with an old adobe church. It's located about a kilometer from the Pan American Highway, with a view toward Concepción volcano on Ometepe Island right across the water.

Boats for Ometepe depart from the dock in San Jorge. For recent schedules, look just ahead (page 236). **Meals** are available at a couple of stands on the beach nearby, as are basic **rooms**, but the beds are better in Rivas.

A **bus** for Rivas meets boats from Ometepe, or, if you're stuck, it's a short taxi ride.

Ometepe Tours tel. 34779 and 33805, has a kiosk at the lakefront with information about the limited accommodations on the island.

Southeast

OMETEPE

Ometepe means, literally, "two mountains," and that's exactly what the island consists of: extinct Maderas (1394 meters), draped in a furry carpet of vegetation, and perfectly shaped, steaming Concepción (1610 meters), the volcano of one's imagination, shooting up from the innards of the earth, descending on steep and then gradually more gentle slopes to the lake waters. Concepción last ejected boulders in 1956.

About 30,000 people live on Ometepe, which, with an area of 276 square kilometers, is the largest island in Nicaragua. Access is by lake boat from San Jorge, 15 kilometers across the water, and about four kilometers from the city of Rivas, on the Pan American Highway.

SEEING OMETEPE

From top to bottom on the outer crust of the volcanoes, within the reduced confines of the island, is much of the variety of the tropics: fields of volcanic ejecta too tough and broken to grow anything; sloping mountainside beaches of black sand; dense cloud forest tangled with vines, home to lizards and macaws and peccaries; moist coffee land, and tobacco farms; rolling pasture holding ancient ceramics of the Niquiranos who flourished on the island in succession to the original Nahuas.

You came to Nicaragua to see a continent in miniature. You came to Ometepe to see it in a couple of hours.

That's all it takes to drive the Ring of Ometepe in a taxi and see a good part of the above—make sure you negotiate your fare before starting; $10 should be enough. The route circumnavigates Concepción volcano, from the port village of Moyogalpa along the water's edge to Altagracia, and back across the sash of land that connects to Maderas volcano. With some time to spare, ask for a stop at the **Hervideros de San José del Sur**, sulphur springs located alongside the highway.

With even more time, and good legs, get an early start to climb **Concepción volcano**, before the clouds close in on the peak. With an ascent at a steady pace, you'll make it in five hours, and see all of Lake Nicaragua and a band of the Pacific; out the other way, over the great lowlands, you will imagine that you can spy the Caribbean. **Maderas**, culminating in a crater lake surrounded by cloud forest, is a somewhat—somewhat—less arduous climb. Several hot springs sprinkle the route to the summit.

Before you start out on any climb, inquire about the best route and current conditions along the slopes. The town halls of Moyogalpa and Altagracia are good places in which to consult.

BOAT SERVICES

Boats for Moyogalpa on Ometepe depart San Jorge at 10 and 11 a.m., noon, 2:30, 4:30 and 6 p.m. Return boats from Ometepe are at 6, 7, 7:30, and 8 a.m., and 1:30 and 5 p.m. Fare is between $1 and $2, depending on the boat. Alternatively, boats from Granada for San Carlos usually stop at Altagracia on Monday and Thursday afternoons, and on Tuesday and Friday on the way back to Granada (see page 192). Service is slated to improve with the introduction of hydrofoils.

Buses run regularly between Moyogalpa and Altagracia. Service is available several times a day past Altagracia to Balque, at the base of the northern skirt of Maderas volcano.

WHERE TO STAY

Hospedaje Aly, in Moyogalpa by the gasoline station, has rooms for about $10, and is pleasant enough, if you don't require hot water or a private shower. Meals are served. **Hospedaje Moyogalpa** is nearby, facing the dock, with similarly priced basic rooms, and simple meals. **El Pirata**, newer than other lodging places, charges about $10 for its rooms, some of which have private baths.

Basic and generally less attractive lodgings are available in Altagracia. The owner of the **Hospedaje Castillo** can chat away about the nooks and crannies of the island.

IN TOUCH WITH OMETEPE

There's no automatic phone service to Ometepe, but you can attempt to leave a message for any hotel or other service at telephone (046)33360 or 33213.

AUTOMOBILE RENTAL

Toyota Rent a Car has an agency in Hotel El Pirata, tel. (046)33204.

HORSE RENTAL, GUIDES AND MORE

Inquire at the guide service in Moyogalpa, 1½ blocks south of the Shell gasoline station, about guides for walks, volcano climbing, and horse hire.

Or telephone (046)33360 and leave a callback message for Guías Ecoturísticos de Ometepe.

ARCHAEOLOGICAL REMAINS

Ometepe is the provenance of some of the most notable pre-Columbian statuary of Nicaragua; though the archeological sites are not prepared for visitors. Some of the figures, carved in volcanic rock, are on exhibit in the town square of Altagracia.

ON THE MAINLAND AGAIN

La Virgen is a ramshackle village alongside the Pan American Highway and Lake Nicaragua, of sandy lanes lined with huddled cacti serving as fences. Who would guess that this was once an important port on Commodore Vanderbilt's Gold Route route across Central America? More than 130 years ago, passengers headed for California disembarked from lake steamers at La Virgen, to take horse-drawn coaches down to San Juan del Sur on the Pacific. Not a sign remains of those inglorious days, not even a dock for local use.

From La Virgen, a good branch road runs the 30 kilometers down to the sea through rolling pasture land, ascending and descending over several unchallenging ridges.

SAN JUAN DEL SUR

- *141 kilometers from Managua; 30 kilometers from Rivas*

Saint John of the South (the other San Juan, del Norte, is the onetime Greytown, on the Caribbean) is a small fishing village in a bay, picturesque and huddled at the base of hills. With only a few sleeping places and eateries, a languid pace, and a life that depends on the water, San Juan del Sur fits your fantasy of a seaside hideaway that *you* discovered.

The village nestles in a cove, one of dozens between low promontories that march into the Pacific. Offshore are coral spots, and schools of grouper, morays and porgies. With its guaranteed-dry climate and full-day sun for much of the year, seclusion available at the price of a boat ride, and sere hills and remote air, San Juan del Sur suggests what Huatulco must have been before it was Huatulco.

San Juan del Sur is the principal rival of Montelimar in attracting visitors for a few days, a few weeks, or indefinitely. Montelimar has *notoriety* as the ex-vacation spot of Anastasio Somoza. San Juan del Sur has *history*, as the quondam terminus of Commodore Vanderbilt's trans-isthmian, inter-oceanic steamship service. This is where thousands of passengers alighted from stage coaches to continue to San Francisco, at the conclusion of their journey across Nicaragua. But you'd never guess.

Montelimar is a planned resort without thought of a town and the prosaic rhythms of daily life. San Juan del Sur is a living village, with shops and fishermen, and boats in the bay, and sand-side eateries serving the catch of the day, be it snapper or marlin or sea bass.

Right along the seafront, a few private clapboard houses with intricately worked trim suggest that grandees of an earlier era once took the sea air in this spot, and the shell of a two-story edifice, suitably fallen in, confirms that glory is fleeting. The block-paved streets are clean and fresh with a sea breeze, houses are set back on dirt lots bordered with cheery bougainvillea. A couple of yachts reveal that adventurous souls make it in and out of port from afar, and a few outsiders, obviously persons of good sense, have been known to settle in for the long term.

WHERE TO STAY AND EAT

Hotel Barlovento, tel. (046)82374, 82298. 21 rooms. $25 single/$33 double.
Beautifully situated on a hill looking down to huddled San Juan del Sur and its bay, the Barlovento has recently been returned to its former owners, after a period in government hands. The two-story concrete structure is in the process of being upgraded. For now, you can get a bed in a bare but clean room, with a terrace. By the time you visit, the restaurant and bar will probably have been reactivated.

Elsewhere . . . San Juan del Sur is just a few square blocks on the bay. Head to what looks like the center, along the water, and all of the available accommodations will be in full view.
Two hotels face each other at the seafront in the center of town. The **Buengusto** is a two-story affair which offers cubicles, at $10 per person per night sharing bath, breakfast included. They plan to add on some better digs. The restaurant, open to the street and the beach across the street, is pleasant enough, with breakfast available à la carte for under $4, grilled meats for $6 and up.

Opposite is the **Hotel Estrella**, older, massive, with high ceilings in its central public rooms, and rockers on which to get off your weary feet, but otherwise, cubicles similar to those of the competition, also at $10 with breakfast.

More to the taste of many a traveller is **Casa Internacional Joxi** ("HOxi"), tel. (046)82348, a half-block inland from the beach. Eight air-conditioned rooms are available at $18 single/$27 double (credit cards accepted). Accommodations, small and clean, some with cooking facilities, are on two levels opening from an extemporaneously designed patio, with gazebo and concrete terrace. The accommodations are small, but they're quite clean, and include a stovetop.

Meal offerings at the Joxi are a break from Nicaraguan country fare: pancakes and fruit plates at breakfast, and sandwiches for under $2, a chicken platter available for $5.

They'll also take you in their own vehicle to where you need to go: The border of Costa Rica ($27), or all the way to Managua ($85).

Lesser lodgings are available along the streets that run back from the water.

ACTIVITIES

The area off San Juan del Sur, and continuing south into offshore Costa Rica, is famous for **billfish**. Marlin, sailfish and swordfish are the most sought-after species in deeper water. Closer in are barracuda, yellowfin tuna, bonito, dorado (mahi-mahi), roosterfish, and jacks, among others.

Sailing trips are available, either by looking for a boat to charter, or booking passage on a scheduled excursion. One such regular outing can be arranged by calling Chris Berry in San Juan del Sur (046-82110) or John Wyss in Managua (02-667302, fax 663907). The boat sets sail at 9 a.m. for secluded bays down the coast, and stops for fishing. The cost is about $40.

Another **yacht rental** can be arranged through Toyota Rent a Car in Managua, tel. (02)663620.

Casa Internacional Joxi offers rentals of **bicycles**, **windsurfers** and **boogie boards**.

NEARBY

Punta La Flor, about 20 kilometers down the coast, is one of the dozens of coves that line the water; but its distinction is that it is also a nesting area for sea turtles.

Nicaragua Guide

Access to the inlets down from San Juan del Sur is by boat (of course), and by the poor road that runs just inland from the hills that border the sea. This track runs from a turnoff inland from the Barlovento Hotel, and continues down to the Costa Rican border, though to cross legally, you have to return to the Pan American Highway. Two buses run daily to Ostional, a hamlet 20 kilometers from San Juan del Sur; to reach El Coco, one of the more beautiful of the coves, you have to get off the bus and walk to the sea.

PEÑAS BLANCAS AND COSTA RICA

Peñas Blancas, the village on the border with Costa Rica, is 147 kilometers from Managua. Buses leave Rivas several times a day for this point. The Nicaraguan checkpoint is at Sapoá, a few kilometers inside the border.

INTO COSTA RICA

A van shuttle, taxi, or through bus service from Managua will take you to the Costa Rican border post, after you check out on the Nicaraguan side.

Official border hours are 8 a.m. to noon and 1 p.m. to 6 p.m. on the Costa Rican side, while the Nicaraguan officials take a break from 12:30 to 1:30 p.m. Get to the border early, if you can, especially if travelling by bus.

If you're picking up buses as you go, you'll find local shuttles to La Cruz, about ten kilometers into Costa Rica, where there is lodging, as well as access to some little-visited beaches. At least two buses leave daily for San José. Otherwise, the Costa Rican capital can be reached in stages by more frequent bus service to Liberia, then onward. For bus service into Costa Rica from Managua, see page 159.

Visas: Canadian and U.S. citizens currently do not require visas to enter Costa Rica, but check requirements shortly before your visit if you plan to enter by the land route. If you need a visa for Costa Rica, you must obtain it before you reach the border, either at a consulate in your home country, or at the Costa Rican embassy in Managua.

12
HIGHLAND NICARAGUA

SPRINGTIME ALL YEAR

What counts as cool in Nicaragua would be mid-range coffee altitudes elsewhere in Central America, the thousand-meter-high rolling ridges exposed to seasonal rains from the Pacific and more consistent year-round storms that blow over from the Caribbean, unhindered by lofty mountain stops. The great peaks of the central highlands, Musún, Peñas Blancas and Kilambé, are only about 1500 to 1700 meters (5000 to 5700 feet) above sea level.

That makes the terrain low enough to be sheltered from the frost that occasionally afflicts the highland tropics; and high enough to avoid the sweating temperatures and humidity of the plains in the rainy season; in other words, Nicaragua's highlands enjoy permanent springtime.

Add cloud forests alive with abundant wildlife and even the elusive quetzal, stands of oak and pine on drier western slopes, rivers encased in mountain flanks descending through rapids, and you have the tranquility, and wonderland of surroundings, of the sort widely desired in retirement destinations.

All that was missing in the formula was tranquility. Hardly settled at all until the last few decades, the highland's coffee plantations and tobacco farms became crucial to Nicaragua's economy. Here in the central north, the war against the Sandinistas of the 1980s simmered and exploded in fits and starts, disrupting agriculture, destroying families as U.S.-supported Contras attacked from havens in Honduras. The central highlands are now in the process of healing from their recent history.

THE HIGHLAND ROAD

From the junction for Boaco, the main trunk of the Pan American Highway runs northwestward through lightly populated cattle country.

HACIENDA SAN JACINTO

At kilometer 39 is the Hacienda San Jacinto, scene in 1856 of a battle between the forces of William Walker and his Nicaraguan allies, on one side, and another force of patriotic Nicaraguans. In one notable incident in the encounter, Andrés Castro, finding his musket useless, managed to heave a stone in a Samson-like manner, so squarely that he killed one of Walker's soldiers.

The hacienda is open for visits, and provides insight into a way of rural life that still lingers in much of Nicaragua.

MOYUA

About 100 kilometers out of Managua, in lightly inhabited country at the foot of table lands, is Lake Moyuá (moy-yu-A"), rich in guapote ("guaPO-teh," tropical bass) and tilapia, and legendary haunt of Ciguacoatl, the Serpent Goddess whose ruinous temple lies on an islet amidst the waters.

Moyuá and the lesser lakes Tecomapa and Las Playitas are frequented by ducks and herons, and are excellent locales for observing wildlife, especially in the dry season. Irrigated rice fields also attract feeding birds farther north, around Sébaco and La Trinidad.

BIRTHPLACE OF THE POET

The main road continues to climb gradually, reaching a plateau and running by **Ciudad Darío**, formerly called Metapa, or Chocoyos. Though poet-hero Rubén Darío is associated with the city of León, where he was

Highlands

raised, his birthplace was here, on January 18, 1867, and his modest first home is open to visitors.

Sébaco, farther on, is a market garden center.

COUNTRY OF COUNTRIES

From here, the main highway and branch roads ascend ridges, descend into valleys, run past towns and villages and farms and forests, and ascend again. Each valley is a republic to itself, with a single major town that consolidates produce from the area and services the farms and acts as seat of government. Each valley has its traditions, its attitudes, and even, to some extent, its way of speaking.

MATAGALPA

- *130 kilometers from Managua; altitude 700 meters*

Matagalpa is a city in the midst of the lushness of the cool tropics, rolling hills and mountains carpeted with evergreen forests and evergreen pastures, where the homesteads of smallholders as well as the villas of the well-off are decorated with flowers, where the earth is rich from the moisture that rains down or blows through in clouds. Streets follow the terrain, up and down, winding around hills, revealing unexpected vistas with every turn.

While Matagalpa has a venerable cathedral, the climate and lush vegetation are the main attraction, to be appreciated casually by stopping in town, or more intensively with a visit to a rain forest lodge. There is also artisanry, especially the black pottery made nowhere else in Nicaragua. Look for it in the market near the highway. As for coffee . . . for some tested tasters, Matagalpa roast is the cup of choice.

THE TOWN

Matagalpa lies just to the east of the Pan American Highway. Major orientation points are the Cathedral and its large plaza on the north end of the central area; and the church of San José and the Parque Rubén Darío, the square at the south end.

WHERE TO STAY

Hotel Ideal, two blocks north, one block west from Cathedral, tel. (061)22483. 30 rooms. $15 to $20. Visa and Master Card.
Fairly good rooms and facilities: t.v., restaurant, bar, protected parking, private bath.

Estancia de Don Diego, km 134, road to Jinotega, tel. (061)2219. About $20 per room. Convenient if you have a car.

Cheaper lodging is available facing Parque Rubén Darío in the Hospedaje Plaza and Hospedaje San Martín, both about $5 per person sharing bath.

SELVA NEGRA

Selva Negra ("Schwarzwald," or "Black Forest"), km 139½, Matagalpa-Jinotega highway (10 kilometers from Matagalpa). 22 units. $45 to $140 per cabin, from $23 single/$33 to $55 double in hotel rooms, discount for youth hostel members. Tel. (061)23883, (2)658342 in Managua, fax (061)22554. Visa, Master Card.

U.S. reservations: 58 Glendale Dr., Miami Springs, FL 33166, tel. 305-883-1021.

"Black Jungle" is as near as one comes to translating *Schwarzwald*, or Black Forest, into Spanish, and Selva Negra is somewhere in between, and a bit of both, a private 200-hectare reserve of cloud forest: dense cedar and pine trees and occasional mahogany, bedecked with ferns and moss and orchids, intertwined with vines and avian flight paths.

Almost 200 species of bird have been spotted at Selva Negra, including many kinds of parrots, and, reputedly, the quetzal. Plant life includes dozens of orchids. Howler monkeys, coatis, sloths and scurrying armadillos can usually be spotted, and sometimes larger cats will come out of hiding.

Did you need an escape from computers and freeways? Here it is.

The Selva Negra property has for a century been in the hands of the Kuhls, a family with German origins (of course), and Black Forest touches are everywhere, from the design of the chalets to the sauerkraut on the menu. Yet there is also a jarring reminder of the real world close by: a tank remains from the fighting that went on in the area during the insurrection against Somoza.

Services available include horse hire, 14 hiking trails, and rowboats for use on a pond.

Highlands

Take along your binoculars and lightweight hiking boots, or at least some gee whiz, for a stay at the cabins of Selva Negra. Rain gear will also help; if you don't experience a shower, chances are a misty cloud will blow through.

If you don't plan to stay the night, Selva Negra can be enjoyed on a daily basis for about $5. But call first to check that you'll be allowed onto the property. The proprietors have a conservationist ethic, and control entry.

COFFEE LORE

Aside from its award-winning conservation efforts, Selva Negra contains a fair amount of off-the-beaten-track coffee history and lore.

The area was settled by German coffee planters toward the end of the last century, and the Selva Negra property includes the remains of the "terrocarril," a miniature locomotive that once transported coffee-laden carts to port without benefit of tracks. Sluices, water wheels and other once-advanced agricultural technology also dates from that period.

The Hammonia coffee plantation is known for the quality and ecological integrity of its product. According to the Kuhl family,

> Hammonia is producing the registered brand Selva Negra Coffee, which is totally ecological. This means that in processing, rivers and forests are protected. This is done by using special machines and complete processes to use the pulp as fertilizer. The mucilages are processed through biodigestors in order to produce methane gas, which is used in the workers' kitchen. A hydraulic turbine is also used to operate the coffee-processing facility.

Of course, a **coffee tour** is one of the options at Selva Negra.

. . . AND WHERE TO EAT

Aside from restaurants in the hotels, roast chicken is available at La Casona, 1½ blocks south of the Perla theater, and La Posada, a half-block west of Darío park. Several snack places are near the square, and there is a Chinese restaurant a block north and a block east from the northeast corner of Parque Darío.

TOWN FAIR

Matagalpa celebrates its fiesta on September 24, in honor of La Virgen de La Merced (Our Lady of Mercy), with horseback processions and bullfights.

GETTING THERE

Buses run about every half hour to Matagalpa from the Roberto Huembes market in Managua. The trip takes about three-and-a-half hours. The **market** and **bus terminal** are about eight blocks west of the Parque Rubén Darío.

Buses for Estelí leave about every 30 minutes to one hour, buses to Jinotega about every hour. For León, take the Estelí bus as far as San Isidro, where you can pick up an onward bus.

REMOTE POSSIBILITIES

For the adventurous, and those with time to spare (who should in all cases be the same persons), Matagalpa offers several choices beside a continuing journey in the highlands or a return to Managua. The wet highlands directly to the east, traversed by a road that eventually descends to Matiguás, are cattle country. Matiguás is on the Río Grande de Matagalpa, which winds through sparsely inhabited rain forest to the Caribbean. Board a canoe or a shallow-draft river boat, if you can find one, and make the journey seaward.

Or, inquire about passenger-and-goods vehicles that ply Nicaragua's single transcontinental "highway," the track that runs northeast from Matagalpa, along valley slopes above jungle floors, finally descending to the remote mining camps of Siuna and Bonanza, then continuing to the Caribbean at Puerto Cabezas. One way should be enough for most travellers, if you manage to get through. The airstrip at Cabezas offers service back to Managua.

Highlands

JINOTEGA

- *160 kilometers from Managua; altitude 1000 meters.*

Jinotega, the Misty City, rules its own long and narrow valley, carpeted by plantations of coffee, girt by ridges of pine-oak and rain forest. Just thirty kilometers separate Jinotega from Matagalpa, but they are 30 winding ones, reaching peaks and crossing mountainsides covered with dense trees and plants with impossibly large, glistening leaves, broken by rushing clear streams.

Little Jinotega has a small archaeological museum and an unusually large church, well adorned with religious statuary.

WHERE TO STAY AND EAT

Hotel Primavera, 4 blocks north of Esso station, tel. (063)22400. 20 rooms, from $10.

Hotel Sollentuna Hem, 2 blocks east, half-block north of Banco Nacional de Desarrollo, tel. (063)22334. Small businessmen's hotel, from about $20 per room, well-kept and comfortable, surprisingly good for the provinces.

Of several eateries, the most reliable is probably the **Oriental**, a Chinese establishment a block-and-a-half north of the square.

WHERE TO GO

Northeast of Jinotega, the waters of the Tuma River are dammed for a hydroelectric project, to form Lake Apanás. Though not far from the main regional highway, this mountainous area was, until several decades ago, remote and hardly settled, known for a time as the base of operations of the guerrilla army of Gen. Augusto César Sandino.

With a rented four-wheel-drive vehicle, it's possible to continue this way on a little-frequented road through Yalí to rejoin the northern branch of the Pan American Highway at Condega or at Estelí; but public transportation is limited, and the easy way is to take a step backward through Matagalpa.

SAN ISIDRO

Back on the Pan American Highway, San Isidro is the junction point for the road toward the Pacific, through low-lying, irrigated cotton country, and over a low point in the volcanic Los Marabios range. On the way are the hot springs of San Jacinto (see page 228).

Buses ply this road about every two hours.

ESTELI

- *Altitude 800 meters; 148 kilometers from Managua*

Tobacco is the business of Estelí, a town set at the perfect height to cultivate the crop, in a long, moist valley; those vertically distorted doll house sheds are where the leaf is hung to cure before it's rolled into cigars. But much of the uplands in the vicinity are forested with oaks, walnuts, and other species familiar to dwellers of the temperate zones; and the relatively cool, well-drained earth has served to guard ancient secrets more surely than the steaming lowlands.

Fossil bones found at El Bosque, near Pueblo Nuevo to the northwest of Estelí, are thought to be over 30,000 years old. Petroglyphs—carved stones evidencing prehistoric habitation—are exhibited in front of the youth center along the south side of the square. But the town itself is not particularly cozy or old-fashioned, and the Cathedral is strikingly modern.

Estelí was the scene of fighting during the insurrection against Somoza, and again of sabotage against the Sandinista administration. Restaurants run by solidarity organizations and Salvadoran refugees, language schools for volunteers from abroad, and agricultural cooperatives are all a legacy of the activism of recent years.

THE TOWN

Estelí lies just west of the Pan American Highway, oriented along Avenida Bolívar (bo-LEE-var), the north-south strip.

Highlands

WHERE TO STAY

As one of the larger towns in northern Nicaragua, Estelí has fair accommodations for travelling salesmen, people in transit to Honduras, and the occasional tourist.

Hotel Moderno, 2½ blocks south of Cathedral, tel. (071)32378. 11 rooms. $20 and up.
Best in town, with restaurant, private bath, hot water.

In the $10 range are:

El Mesón, 1 block north of the Cathedral, tel. (071)32655, with private bath and meals available.

Barlop, tel. (0171)32486, 14 rooms, private bath, meals available, protected parking. Located toward the north end of Bolívar.

Right on the square, the **Hotel Miraflor**, tel. (071)32312, has rooms for about $6 per person, or less with shared bath. The **Hospedaje Chipito**, about 10 blocks south of the square, has basic rooms for under $5 per person.

. . . and there are other, cheaper lodgings. Try the Hotel Chalet on Bolívar as it winds into town, or the Hotel Mariela near the bus station, or the Hospedaje Chipito. All charge $6 per person or less, but take a good look at the room and bed before you check in.

. . . AND EAT

You'll find a couple of basic cafés and a pizza place along the block west of the square. The Restaurante Nahualí, a block north from the northeast corner of the square, is more formal than other eateries. El Faisán, a block south of the square, is vegetarian. There are additional spots right on the square.

WHAT TO BUY

Leather furniture is the local craft specialty. If you're driving, pack a few pieces in your trunk. What we're talking about here is not a stuffed sofa, but tooled leather stretched over a frame, which in some cases can be disassembled and carried off.

TRANSPORTATION

The **bus terminal** and **market** are off the south end of Bolívar. Buses run southward to Matagalpa and Managua about every 30 minutes to one hour; and northward to Somoto and Ocotal about every hour.

NEAR ESTELÍ

About 20 kilometers northeast of Estelí is the **Mesa de Moropotente Reserve**, a plateau of pine and oak forest reached by a Jeep road.

About seven kilometers south of town, also reached by jeep trail, are the **Estanzuela Falls**, dropping 30 meters from a rocky cliff into a canyon carved in mineral-rich walls. The approach is by jeep, or by hiking from town, taking a turnoff about a kilometer south of Estelí. Ask directions continually as you go.

UP AND UP

North from Estelí is the **highest part of Nicaragua**, the piney Dipilto-Jalapa ridge that runs along the border of Honduras, peaking at Mogotón, 2107 meters above sea level. The Coco River (known variously as the Segovia, Wanks and Wanghi) drains these ridges toward the Caribbean. The remote banks and the lands to the north were once hotly contested by Nicaragua and Honduras, in part because of the gold washed down by the river and its tributaries through these granitic masses.

That dispute was settled to the benefit of Honduras, and the Coco now marks the border. Gold is still panned in tributary streams, as it has been since before the Spanish conquest; and the mineral riches of the mountains include as well opals and marble and jasper and assorted other stones and minerals.

Highlands

WEST TO HONDURAS

The main route of the Pan American Highway runs westward from Yalagüina, in the tobacco country, through **Somoto** (700 meters), with its old colonial church in an area of brushy vegetation, to El Espino on the border of Honduras, 230 kilometers from Managua.

Border Formalities: The land border with Honduras is officially open from 8 a.m. to noon and 1 p.m. to about 4:30 p.m. Get there well before closing!

Transport Notes: Shuttle buses serve the border from Somoto, while several buses a day run between Somoto and Estelí. There is also direct service between Managua and Somoto, from the Roberto Huembes market.

From the Honduran side, the highway descends toward Choluteca and the lowlands of Honduras around the Gulf of Fonseca. This route bypasses Tegucigalpa, if you're heading toward El Salvador and northward.

If you're stuck for the night, you can find a basic hotel, the Baghal, off the main square, but for better lodging, try to get to Estelí.

NORTH TO HONDURAS

A less-transited road continues north from Yalagüina, through Ocotal at the River Coco, winding and ascending the Dipilto y Jalapa ridge, cut by rushing streams and waterfalls. The town of Dipilto, amidst pines north of Ocotal, is an old mining center. The border of Honduras is reached at Las Manos, 240 kilometers from Managua.

Ocotal is a picturesque town of white houses, quintessentially highland Central American.

Transport and Border Notes: The border at Las Manos is about 20 kilometers onward from Ocotal. Hours are the same as at El Espino: 8 a.m. to noon and 1 p.m. to 4:30 p.m.

The road on the Honduran side leads to Danlí, and onward to Tegucigalpa, through picturesque mining towns.

Small shuttle **buses** operate between Ocotal and Las Manos. Ocotal can be reached by bus from Estelí, either directly, or by getting off a Somoto-bound bus at Yalagüina and waiting for onward transport on the branch road.

For overnight basic **lodging** in Ocotal, try the Hospedaje Centroamericano or Hotel Frontera, otherwise continue to Estelí.

EAST TO THE GOLD MINES

Another, less-transited road leads eastward from Ocotal into the heart of the department of Nueva Segovia, where Gen. Sandino campaigned against the coalition government backed by the United States in the 1930s. **San Fernando** and **Telpaneca**, among other towns, have venerable churches and tile-roofed houses that recall colonial days when Spain quickly established its authority in areas that yielded silver and gold.

SOUTH TO THE BONES

South of Yalagüina, in relatively dry country, evidence has been found of some of the first human inhabitants of Nicaragua. The **Cueva del Duende** ("Spirit Cave") is thought to have been a refuge for hunters. At **El Bosque**, 20 kilometers south of Pueblo Nuevo on the way to San Juan de Limay, fossilized animal bones, dated at 30,000 years, have been found, along with primitive stone tools, and carvings in white stone.

San Juan de Limay is known for carvings in white marble mined in the hills all around.

A branch road from the Pan American Highway runs this way over mountain ridges toward León, while an unpaved road leads northward toward Somoto on the way to Honduras.

13
THE ROAD TOWARD THE CARIBBEAN

NORTH FROM MANAGUA

Managua dissipates quickly to the north. After the duty-free zone by the airport, the wide sash of land between the two great lakes is turned over to cattle ranches and loading ramps. Along the way are the public pools and restaurants of **Centro Turístico El Trapiche**, and the **Warm Springs of Tipitapa** (see page 151).

COW COUNTRY

A turn to the right at the junction on the Pan American Highway takes the traveller onto the Rama highway, which leads around the far side of Lake Nicaragua, through rich lowlands drained by rivers descending from lumpy, higher plateaus covered with scrub vegetation, backed by humid hills, and mountains as high as a thousand meters that separate the lake from the Caribbean jungles.

This zone shares its climate with the coastal belt: dry half of the year, and rainy the rest of the time. But winds are stronger when the rain is absent, and the certain flow of rivers throughout the year makes the valleys ever green. At higher altitudes, clouds blowing from the Caribbean moisten the foliage and disperse their rain throughout the year.

While cattle-grazing is a mainstay of much of Nicaragua, the lakeside regions of Boaco and Chontales are the Wild East, the area that takes its cultural cues and identity from cowboy customs. Grazing, herding, and roundups are part of the daily round of activities for many residents of the area. But the East is more settled than the U. S. West: the dairy industry is also big-time, and Chontales is known for its cheeses.

BOACO

"*La ciudad de dos pisos*" ("the city on two floors") is just that, set on two adjacent plateaus, in the midst of the cattle zone, inland from the lake and reached by a branch road from the Rama highway. A relatively young settlement in ancient Mesoamerica, Boaco celebrated its 100th anniversary in 1995.

Boaco holds its town fair on July 25, in honor of St. James the Apostle (Santiago).

Accommodations are available at the Hotel Boaco, tel. (054)434, and at the Hotel Loma Linda, opposite the stadium.

Camoapa, another foothills town off the Rama road, is known for its locally manufactured hats ("manufacturing" used here in the literal sense of "hand-made"), fashioned from straw and the fibers of the hemp plant, known in Nicaragua as *cabuya*. Hemp is also cultivated in the pocket-valley around **Santa Lucía**, just to the northwest of Boaco. Much of the product is shipped to the artisans of Masaya for conversion into hammocks.

JUIGALPA AND CHONTALES

Inland from the eastern shore of Lake Nicaragua, Juigalpa sits on a low-lying plateau overlooked by the nearby hills of the Amerrisque range. Juigalpa and its region (or *departamento*), Chontales, had a settled population well before the arrival of the Spaniards. Their descendants have largely been acculturated, but signs of the old ways remain in the stelae and small stepped pyramids that have been unearthed in the region, as well as burial sites, known locally as *calpules*.

A **museum** (the Museo Gregorio Aguilar) exhibits some of their artifacts, including stelae and rounded altars carved with swirling glyphs, which bear more than a passing family resemblance to the stone monuments of Copán, in Honduras. There's also a small **zoo** with regional animals.

ACCOMMODATIONS

Rooms are available at the **Hotel El Bosque**, tel. (081)205, next to the Esso gas station, for about $10; **Hotel Imperial**, tel. (081)2294; and **Hotel La Quinta**, with disco attached, opposite the hospital, tel. (081)2485.

For quick eats, try Rostichería El Pollito, a roast chicken shop, four blocks south of the square, then one block east.

Northeast of Juigalpa, gold is mined at La Libertad and Santo Domingo, in the lush, steaming sierra that separates Chontales from the Caribbean lowlands.

Acoyapa is near the junction for a branch road that continues southeasterly through the cattle country along the lake, toward its outlet at the San Juan River.

Farther on, the Rama road, paved in its entirety, roughly follows the course of the Mico River, overlooked by cliffs that bear ancient indigenous inscriptions. Unusually, a stepped pyramid was found in the area, indicating what might be the southmost penetration of the influence of Mayan culture in the Classic period.

EL RAMA

At the end of the road, 300 kilometers from Managua, El Rama lies at the point where the Siquia, Mico and Rama rivers converge to form the Escondido River, one of the widest through the lowlands, and hence the de facto highway to the coastal town of Bluefields, five hours away (see page 268). El Rama is a cluster of houses and service facilities, nothing more, nothing less, with a few hundred residents.

If you miss the boat at El Rama, **lodging** is available at the basic Hotel Amy, a block south of the Esso station, and at the "Ramada Inn," four blocks east of the dock and a block north of the River Escondido, no cousin at all to other Ramadas, but still the best in the village.

Buses run about every hour to El Rama from the Iván Montenegro market in Managua. Count on all day for the trip. If you are planning to continue immediately to Bluefields, inquire—before you leave Managua—about connections at the Ministry of Tourism (a block west of the Inter-Continental Hotel). Currently, there are midnight buses on Monday, Wednesday, Friday and Saturday, which connect with the boat for Bluefields early the next afternoon (see page 268).

SAN CARLOS

- *260 kilometers from Managua*

San Carlos lies strategically at the far end of Lake Nicaragua, at the head of the San Juan River. Before William Walker arrived on the scene in 1855, passengers transferred here between riverboats and larger lake steamers of Commodore Vanderbilt's Transit Company; but nowadays, there's little movement of people or goods through the sleepy town.

GETTING THERE / STAYING / MOVING ON

By road, San Carlos is anything but easy to reach. It's a long trip down a road that follows the shore of the lake but stays well back from the water. The final stretch is a four-wheel-drive track that forks from the El Rama road at Acoyapa. With the appropriate vehicle, travel time is about six hours from Managua.

Buses ply this route from the Iván Montenegro Market in eastern Managua.

From Granada, **boats** leave on Mondays and Thursdays at 2 p.m. and 4 p.m., and arrive at the docks of San Carlos twelve hours later. A faster, three-hour service is expected to be functioning by the time your read this. Inquire at the Ministry of Tourism in Managua, or at the pier in Granada, tel. (055)4313.

Nica Airlines (tel. 663136 in Managua) has daily service to San Carlos in small **planes**, departing the capital at 7:30 a.m., via Nueva Guinea, leaving at 9 a.m. for the return trip. An additional flight goes on Mondays, Wednesdays and Fridays at 2 p.m. Fare is about $40.

Basic **lodging** is available at Hotel Azul, tel. (083)102, on the lakefront.

Small boats for **El Castillo** downriver (see page 264) are *scheduled* to depart daily except Sunday at 2 p.m., arriving at 6 p.m., at a fare of about $3. A charter trip in a small boat can cost as much as $200, but it's also sometimes possible to buy your way for less onto a boat already going your way.

Inquire at the immigration office in San Carlos about occasional boats for **Los Chiles** in **Costa Rica**. There's also a Jeep road that heads that way from across the river. Los Chiles is only about 15 kilometers from San Carlos, and if the border is open, you can easily proceed onward to San José.

SOLENTINAME ISLANDS

At the remote southeast corner of Lake Cocibolca (Nicaragua) is another group of islands, the Solentiname Archipelago, less disturbed by settlement and farming than Ometepe, Zapatera, and the Isletas of Granada. The archipelago numbers 36 volcanic outcroppings, covering a total of 189 square kilometers.

Strangely—to those unaware of Nicaragua's distinguished artistic tradition—they are the home of a colony of fishermen-artists, who carve figures in wood and create untutored paintings of local subjects. Ernesto Cardenal, priest, activist, and minister in the Sandinista government, founded a commune of worker-artisans on Mancarrón Island in the 1970s, along an idealist model of combining manual labors with artistic expression. But long before Cardenal, pre-Columbian artisans shaped ceramics and stones into figures of animals and humans, and many pieces still lie just under the soil of the islands.

Birding is one of the pleasures of a visit to the archipelago. Commonly sighted species include anhingas, herons, hawks, oropendulas, flycatchers, ospreys, and numerous hummingbirds.

Access to the islands is generally from San Carlos, at the mouth of the San Juan River.

STAYING

Several lodges are available on the islands.

The **Hotel Isla Solentiname** on San Fernando Island charges about $30 double.

Albergue Mancarrón, Isla Mancarrón (Mancarrón island), Río San Juan, tel. (055)2059, fax (02)603345. 15 rooms. $40 double. U.S. reservations: El Centro de la Raza, 2425 16 Ave. So., Seattle, WA 98144, tel. 206-329-2974. Mailing address: P. O. Box 1545, Correo Central, Managua.

The albergue, or lodge, is a set of tile-roofed ranch structures on rolling, grassy, somewhat austere terrain. Rooms are either double, triple, or family-size, the latter sleeping up to five persons.

This is a getaway spot for families and groups, and they have a play area and meeting rooms, as well as boats for rent. Electricity is turned on in the evening only. Activities include horseback rides, lake fishing, hiking, and visits to Los Guatusos reserve on the south shore of the lake, and to settlements on nearby islands, including the primitive painters' colony.

Access to the lodge is by boat from San Carlos. In a small motorboat, the trip takes under one hour; in a larger and slower lake vessel, it's a two-hour run.

LOS GUATUZOS WILDLIFE REFUGE

Los Guatuzos wildlife refuge takes in the sash of land between the southern shore of Lake Nicaragua and the border of Costa Rica. The name derives from the pre-Columbian tribe that inhabited the area. While the Solentiname Islands have been farmed since pre-Columbian times, the reserve of Los Guatusos represents a virtually untouched yet accessible stretch of forest. Common species include Spanish cedar, balsa, bay, and the rubber tree, along with orchids and bromeliads. Among unusual creatures are fisher bats, and assorted insects that masquerade as twigs and leaves.

14
THE *OTHER* NICARAGUA
THE VAST CARIBBEAN LOWLANDS

SAME COUNTRY, SEPARATE NATION

To most Nicaraguans, the eastern half of their country is a mysterious region that might as well exist on another continent. The *other* Nicaragua is the country that includes vast stands of virtually untouched rain forest, swamps, and piney savannas. It is decidedly waterlogged: precipitation reaches several hundred inches per year in some locales, and keeps the numerous rivers full almost to overflowing.

This "Atlantic Coast," in fact, includes most of the surface of Nicaragua, but only a small fraction of its population.

And it is a population apart, Sumus and Ramas and Miskitos, descended from the Indians who first inhabited these lands, and in part from escaped slaves of the British.

The Spanish conquerors had little contact with the natives in the eastern lowlands, and what they had, they didn't like. Migrant tribes who hunted game, and slashed and burned temporary corn plots, easily escaped the grasp of Spanish authorities. Fevers and diseases and insects and snakes

INDEPENDENCE OF A SORT

Caribbean Nicaragua was never a Spanish dominion, except in theory. The British held sway over the Mosquito Shore informally for much of the colonial period, finally formalizing their domination through a protectorate and a puppet Mosquito king. English traders plundered the forest and provided gunpowder and tools to the Miskito and Sumu and Rama inhabitants, and set up trading posts and plantations along lagoons and rivers. Escaped slaves, rebels expelled from the Antilles, and laborers and adventurers from England's Caribbean colonies established themselves on the coast, joining and sometimes intermarrying with the natives, as is evident from the mixed cast of today's Miskito population.

The British protectorate ended in 1862, but remoteness was a fact of life and geography, even after Nicaragua formally extended its administration in 1895. Managua was as distant and different as any foreign capital. English remained the principal language, a heritage of the old contacts, and of Protestant missionaries who schooled children and provided spiritual sustenance over the years.

During the Contra rebellion under the Sandinista administration, the gulf turned into open hostility, as Miskito inhabitants were sometimes forcibly relocated to strategic, defensible villages.

Eventually, in 1987, the central government granted legal autonomy to the non-Hispanic peoples of the Caribbean, who now run their communal affairs, and attend schools in their own languages.

RICHES

Today, no road reaches the coast, but for a long track that meanders to Puerto Cabezas from Matagalpa. Rivers, estuaries and lagoons weave together clusters of people. Here and there, hardwoods are cut and exported, while gold mines have operated at Siuna and Bonanza in the far northeast, and coconut plantations along the coast. Bananas were once cultivated around Puerto Cabezas, but disease and storms brought down the plantations.

The natural treasures of the area remain, fortunately, little known. The soils are poor, their nutrients leached by downpours; but that scarcity of resources engenders a surface lushness, through the endless recycling of the nutrients in decaying plant matter, and the capture of moisture by competing species.

Tarpon crowd the rivers and coastal lagoons. More green turtles nest on the beaches of Nicaragua than anywhere else in the region, and are a staple of the Miskito diet. Even the threatened manatee is easily spotted, while the rain forest, except for cleared patches along the rivers, is largely intact.

TRAVEL TO THE "ATLANTIC"

A few riverboats, coastal freighters, a limited service in small planes to Bluefields and Puerto Cabezas, a track through the forest to Puerto Cabezas . . . that's all that ties Caribbean Nicaragua with the rest of the country. But the remoteness of the untouched forest, and the off-beat mélange of cultures, are the area's principal asset for visitors.

Allow time for late boats, high water, delayed departures; have some tolerance for different food and limited supplies; and you'll be rewarded with sights and sounds and flavors incomparable, from sharks navigating the San Juan River to an Island carnival in the heart of Central America to the roar of howler monkeys resounding in the wake of your river steamer.

THE SAN JUAN RIVER

The San Juan River flows out of Lake Nicaragua and runs 200 kilometers through virtually uninhabited lands and obscure but hugely significant chapters of history to the Caribbean.

The War of the American Revolution, fought in part on a worldwide scale, had its Nicaraguan interlude. In 1780, Captain Horatio Nelson attempted to divide the dominions of Spain (then allied with the American rebels) by driving across Nicaragua. He was forced to surrender at El Castillo on the San Juan to Spanish forces, but eventually made it home, and sailored on toward a glorious death at Trafalgar.

Never settled by farmers or plantation owners, this remote part of the isthmus again saw intrigue in the 1850s. American entrepreneurs focussed their attention on low-lying Nicaragua as the route of least resistance between Atlantic and Pacific, and thus between the two coasts of the United States. Commodore Cornelius Vanderbilt of railroad fame opened the Accessory Transit Company, a steamer service on the San Juan and across Lake Nicaragua to a stagecoach terminal at La Virgen. The San Juan River became a highway of dreams for many headed to the gold fields of California.

William Walker, once he had commandeered Nicaragua, proceeded to confiscate the Transit company to secure his line of reinforcement. Eventually, it was a force of Costa Ricans and Nicaraguan exiles, backed by Vanderbilt and the British, who cut the Transit route near El Castillo. Walker's fate was sealed.

After the Walker conflicts, victorious Costa Rica moved its border up to the south bank of the San Juan for most of its course, and claimed rights to navigate the waterway, the better to keep an eye on an area of possible unfriendly intervention. Rapids at the entry to the river and shifting water levels discouraged deeper-draft, more modern vessels from entering service.

But there were later booms, busts and outbursts. Rubber was bled from plantations along the river for almost a century after the Walker adventures, and lumbering and banana plantations had their brief periods of glory.

During during the Sandinista-Contra battles of the 1980s, Contras occasionally crossed the San Juan from bases in Costa Rica, sometimes with the tacit aid of the Costa Rican government

And the dream of an interoceanic route across Nicaragua never died; feasibility studies of an alternative to the Panama Canal remain a not insignificant industry.

In today's less troubled times, attention focuses once again on the natural treasure house along the banks of the San Juan. Undisturbed rain forest, odd insects and plants, and remote projects that tap botanicals for medicines are some of the attractions of the region.

Chief among the curiosities, and a notable hazard to recreational swimming, are the sharks of the San Juan. Once thought to reside exclusively in Lake Nicaragua, they have been uncovered as commuters to the open sea, feeding along the way on the abundant smaller denizens.

ON THE SAN JUAN

In its upper stretches, the river flows fast and wide out of Lake Nicaragua; from bank to bank, it averages 300 meters along its entire course. But a shallow course it is, said to have decreased in depth over the years as the uneasy earth has shifted fitfully in quakes, raising the river bottom.

Twisting, turning, widening, narrowing, the river splits to enclose finger islands, and appears to stop altogether in level stretches through bottomlands subject to flooding, then suddenly shoots rapids known as El Toro, Santa Cruz, Las Balas ("the bullets"), San Pablo, and others. Novice captains have no place in this country; only seasoned pilots can gauge the depths, calculate conditions, and head for the precise spot in the waters that will allow a safe passage.

In its lower reaches, fed by the tributary San Carlos and Sucio rivers, the San Juan flows faster and deeper between rocky banks, then spreads fingers of water reaching through its swampy delta toward the sea.

EL CASTILLO

Of the hamlets along the river from San Carlos to the Caribbean, El Castillo, 60 kilometers downriver from San Carlos, is the most important, and has the most history. El Castillo de la Concepción—the Castle of the Conception—is where the Spaniards in the eighteenth century built a fortress to protect the settled part of Nicaragua from pirate depredations, and to keep the British navy from cutting Central America in two. That protection was sometimes questionable.

Today, the stone fortress, known as **El Morro**, still stands on a rise dominating the wooden buildings huddled at the river's edge. It has been partially restored, and holds historical exhibits.

BIOSPHERE RESERVE

Three kilometers downriver from El Castillo, where the Río Bartola joins the San Juan, is an entry point to the **Indio Maíz Biological Reserve** (Reserva Biológica Indio-Maíz), classified a world biosphere reserve, covering 22,500 square kilometers of practically untouched lowland tropical rain forest. Among the riches of Indio Maíz are medicinal plants, orchids, countless insects, and wildlife that includes 25 species of snakes, monkeys, deer, peccaries, tapirs, coatis, and many, many others.

WHAT TO BRING FOR THE JUNGLE

Recommendations from Albergue El Castillo
- Waterproof boots
- Raincoat or poncho
- Plastic bags for gear and papers
- Mosquito netting, if camping
- Insect repellent
- Sunscreen
- Sun hat
- Minimal clothing, but include one long-sleeved, full-length pants outfit
- Sun glasses
- Flashlight
- Pocket knife with opener.
- Film
- Binoculars
- Canteen and day pack
- swimsuit and towel

GETTING THERE

Small boats for El Castillo depart daily except Sunday at 2 p.m. from San Carlos, arriving at 6 p.m. The fare is about $3.

Other boats ply the river on an irregular basis. Speedy motorboats can make the trip from San Carlos to El Castillo in about two hours. Longer and slower riverboats (*planas*), which are something like collective taxis of the river, take about six hours.

Caribbean Nicaragua

ECOLOGICAL LODGES ON THE RIVER

Albergue El Castillo (El Castillo Lodge)
El Castillo, San Juan River. Tel. (055)4635, ext. 3. In Managua, fax (2)678267. Mailing address: Distribuidora Vicky 2 c. al sur, 1 arriba, 1 al sur, Managua. 9 rooms, with two queen or three single beds. Lodging, $15 per person, plus $15 for meals. Call the Managua office first to arrange your stay.

Albergue El Castillo is a two-story polished hardwood lodge with wrap-around porches, a club in the jungle, situated just 100 meters from the old Spanish fortress. The atmosphere is something like that of a Caribbean fishing camp, where the dining room, open to the squawks and roars of the jungle and the soothing flow of the river, serves as staging area and gathering spot. There are no extraneous frills, but present are all the necessities at a base from which to explore the San Juan River, including nighttime electricity, plenteous food, laundry service, and available guides. Adventures available: boat trips up the San Juan River and its tributaries; hikes and horseback trips; tarpon fishing; swimming in the Bartola river; rafting; kayaking; stargazing from the ramparts of the fortress; visits to cattle ranches and tropical farms; and rain forest treks to spot birds, animals and plants. If you choose the lodge as your base in Nicaragua, they'll also arrange trips as far as Granada, San Juan del Sur on the Pacific, and San Juan del Norte on the Caribbean. Cuisine includes river fish, shrimp, and steak. And the daily rate is a jungle bargain.

Refugio Bartola, P. O. Box 2715, Managua, tel. and fax (2)897924, tel. (055)4635 in El Castillo.
Downriver from El Castillo, on the edge of the huge Indio-Maíz reserve, Bartola "Refuge" is a set of cottages with a total of eight rooms, each with two beds. Despite the remote location—would you believe it?—meals served under the great conical thatched roof are prepared by a French chef. Solar and diesel generators power the electrical system.

The Refuge is part of Güises Montaña Experimental, a center for research into local flora and fauna. Activities include boat rides, swimming, hikes and walks for birding and wildlife spotting, and fishing for snook and tarpon. Boat trips are also offered to El Castillo and San Juan del Norte, and at night for river shrimping.

You can also look in on some of the more fascinating and unique aspects of life in the rain forest. Join in field research, or visit the Raicilleras de Buenavista Cooperatives, where medicinal plants are produced, or visit an African palm oil plantation in the reserve's buffer zone.

Transport to Refugio Bartola should be arranged when booking space. The same boats that reach El Castillo can take you onward to the refuge. The room rate is about $15 per person, and meals cost another $22 per day.

SAN JUAN DEL NORTE

San Juan del Norte, the village at the mouth of the San Juan, is a settlement of mostly fragile wooden houses. For most of its history it was known as (and even today is occasionally called) Greytown, the name given by pirates and English sailors to the settlement of Caribbean blacks.

Remote, ramshackle Greytown has had its place on the world stage. Pirates, privateers and sailors officially in the service of the Crown in London sailed through on their way to attack Granada on Lake Nicaragua, or to cut the Spanish realms in two. Commodore Vanderbilt's transcontinental service in the 1850s debarked passengers here for the riverboat trip to Lake Nicaragua. And a dredge from a failed attempt to build a canal can still be seen in the harbor. The ruins of the original filibuster base-pirate camp-interoceanic terminal have not yet completely rotted away; the newer town site of San Juan del Norte, though clapboard and hardly permanent, is just up the coast, where the Río Indio estuary finally empties out into the Caribbean

Boats operate irregularly between El Castillo and San Juan del Norte, and between San Juan del Norte and Bluefields, up the coast. Which means that maybe you can find a boat going your way, or maybe not.

BLUEFIELDS

Bluefields lies on the shore of a long coastal lagoon formed by the estuary of the Escondido River, sheltered from Caribbean storm tides and wind by the expanse of shock-absorbing water and the sandy barrier island directly windward.

Such natural protection has drawn seafaring villains and adventurers over the years: though the name rings of English, and even suggests Bluebeard, it is actually a corruption of Blaauveld, the name of a Dutch pirate, by the English-speakers who built the town in the days of the British protectorate.

Alas, Bluefields lived in understandable complacency beside its lagoon; in 1989, a great hurricane bore down and smashed Bluefields to splinters.

Rebuilt, Bluefields is once again a town of clapboard houses, already-rusting tin roofs, roof overhangs and porches providing shade and shelter from the inevitable rains, and gently swaying palms ruling over all. It is the de facto English capital of Nicaragua, a Caribbean island stranded on the Central American coast. While Spanish-speaking Central American countries were establishing themselves after independence, British planters and merchants, and their slaves and servants, were settling and farming largely without interference. Their descendants recognize the lawful government in Managua; but keeping their ways is another matter. The music is reggae, the boats are dories. Other signs of the English touch are the names Corn Island, Monkey Point, Seal Cay, and many others.

Across the estuary, or bay, from Bluefields is **El Bluff**, a port that handles a small part of Nicaragua's overseas trade, and where a shrimping fleet is based. The islands in the bay itself are to some extent planted with coconut palms, from which copra is harvested. And on Rama Cay live the remnants of the Rama, a people who once populated the shores of many of the rivers in the region.

FESTIVAL

Every night is party night in Bluefields in May. The Maypole festival includes costumed dancers, steel drums, loudspeakers, and all the energy of Carnival in the Islands.

WHERE TO STAY

"Basic" is the word to describe most accommodation in Bluefields—in plain clapboard or cement-block buildings, with cement floor, cold water only, little if any furnishings other than a bed and chair, and just a hook or two on which to hang your clothing. Some hotels rely on an hourly trade.

But not to worry. Not only because that is the way of Bluefields, but because "cold" water is lukewarm in this climate, which is warm enough; buildings are all fairly new, following the hurricane destruction of a few years ago, (not to worry, once again), Bluefields is open and usually breezy, and a window and sea view are better decoration than a calendar on the wall.

Hotel South Atlantic, opposite town hall (palacio), tel. (082)242. 20 rooms. $30 and up single or double.
The South Atlantic is a cut above all others in Bluefields, with air conditioning, cable t.v., private baths, restaurant, and bar.

All *other* hotels charge $10 or less for a room:

Hollywood, Barrio Punta Fría, tel. (082)282, 12 rooms, shared bath, meals available.

Costa Sur, central area, tel. (082)452, 12 rooms, shared bath, fans, meals available.

Mini Hotel, next to Joyería (jewelry store) La Filigrana, tel. (082)362, 8 rooms with fans.

Marda Maus, below market, tel. (082)429, 11 rooms, private baths, best of the cheap hotels.

For **food**, aside from the restaurant of the Hotel South Atlantic, none of the eateries in town is either notable or recommendable, though none should do you any harm.

GETTING TO BLUEFIELDS

EL RAMA TO BLUEFIELDS BY BOAT

Where roads are nonexistent, the Escondido River flows wide and reliably, filled by runoff in the rainiest part of Nicaragua, through untouched jungle, and fields hacked from dense growth in the red earth. Some clearings were originally timber cuts, others were banana plantations. What's now left, after exhaustion of valuable tree species and intermittent bouts of banana disease, is cattle pasture.

Boat departures from El Rama are at noon on Tuesdays, Thursdays, Saturday and Sunday, arriving in the early evening at Bluefields. To meet the boat, take the *midnight* bus for El Rama (at the end of the highway from Managua) from the Iván Montenegro market in eastern Managua; but check, check, and re-check the schedule at the terminal itself, or at the tourist office near the Hotel Inter-Continental, at least the day before you intend to travel.

If you miss the scheduled boat, look for a cargo vessel headed your way, or hire a boat for an *expreso* (charter) trip. In fact, anything you charter is likely to be a lot more expreso than the lumbering African Queen-style scheduled steamer. Long and flat-bottomed, it offers superb birding, and occasional views of monkeys where the high vegetation has not been cut back too far.

AIR SERVICE

Nica airlines has flights from Managua to Bluefields, leaving Monday, Wednesday, Friday and Sunday at 6:30 a.m. and 2:30 p.m., returning at 10:40 a.m. and 6:10 p.m. These flights continue to Corn Island. On Tuesday, Thursday and Saturday, the single flight goes at 9:50 a.m., returns at 2:10 p.m. W+G Aero Servicios has flights to Bluefields at 7 a.m. on Tuesday, Thursday and Saturday; at 1:30 p.m. on Monday and Friday. La Costeña (tel. 632142 in Managua, 242 in Bluefields) has flights from Managua at 7 a.m., 10 a.m. and 2 p.m. Monday through Saturday, and at 7 a.m. on Sunday, continuing to Corn Island.

Round-trip fare from Managua to Bluefields is just under $100; and if you're curious about the "Atlantic" side of Nicaragua, you can easily make a **day trip** out of your visit, provided you reserve several days in advance, through a travel agency, or directly at the ticket counters in the domestic terminal at the west end of the airport.

COASTAL TRADE

Lagoon-estuaries, separated from open water by sandy barrier islands, occupy much of the coast of Nicaragua. The Bay (or Bahía) of Bluefields is one of these, connected by shallow passages to the more extensive Laguna de Perlas to the north. These waterways provide safe passage from place to place for shallow-draft motorboats and Miskito *pipantas*.

Here, away from tourist traffic and centers of population, tarpon abound in the coastal estuaries, and coral lies submerged offshore, virtually unviewed.

Scheduled service is come-and-go. A boat is said to leave at dawn for Laguna de Perlas, but even if it doesn't depart, somebody going that way can take you on for a reasonable fee. What will you see? Mangroves supported on eerie fingers probing the water, solid at high tide, and improbably marooned above the surface when the waters recede; silvery tarpon breaking the surface, and perhaps a manatee peacefully chomping leaves, unaware that it is an endangered species; banana plots hacked into the banks, and scattered houses on stilts in untidy clearings; boats drawn up onto mud banks adjacent to paths that lead out of view; and long cargo boats loaded with cases of bottled soft drinks that find a market wherever they can penetrate.

At Pearl Lagoon village, at the south end of the inlet, a room can be found for the night. Ask for Miss Ingrid.

South of Bluefields is more of the clay and alluvial terrain that makes up the entire coast, with an edging of perfect and isolated beaches all the way; with the single exception of Monkey Point, a lonely rock outcropping orphaned from the spine of the Chontal range inland to the west.

THE CORN ISLANDS

Foreigners call them the Corn Islands, or Islas del Maíz, but Nicaraguans call them, in Spanish Nicaraguan, simply Corn Island, thus encompassing in the singular both Great Corn Island and Little Corn Island.

If the grammar and syntax are out of place, so are the Corn Islands, a bit of the Anglo ex-colonial Caribbean marooned within the jurisdiction of Nicaragua, 75 kilometers off the eastern shore. The denizens speak English, as well as Spanish, the music is reggae, and the clapboard houses on stilts look as if they were offloaded for a movie about Jamaica. Miles of white beaches, clear water, swaying coconut palms, sun . . . all that's needed is some development of facilities. Or maybe not.

Spaniards originally called Great Corn "*La Isla de los Mangles*," "the Mangrove Isle"; early English types called them the Pearls. Eventually, the Caribs, who settled these shores toward the end of the eighteenth century, named them for the prevalent plant.

The Corn Islands were once a haven for pirates who preyed on ships carrying the riches of the Spanish colonies, and at least one wrecked galleon has been located in 72 feet of water. To look for others, you'll have to cart along your own gear.

About 2500 persons live on Creat Corn, which measures about five hilly kilometers from north to south; and another 250 or so dwell on Little Corn, about 15 kilometers to the northeast and just over two square kilometers in extent. Many of them are Caribs, or Garifuna, a people who trace their heritage both to escaped African slaves and to an Amerindian people with which the slaves intermarried on the island of St. Vincent. After a rebellion against the British in 1795, they were dispersed to islands off the coast of Central America. Nicaragua exerted its dominion over the islands only in 1894.

At one point, slaves were brought from Jamaica to work cotton plantations, and the abolition of slavery on August 27, 1841, is celebrated every year.

For some years, the Corn Islands were a little United States outpost, leased to the good neighbors of the north. A 1988 hurricane destroyed most houses, but easy go, easy come. Most homes have been re-erected, on stilts, just as they were before.

Bananas and coconuts were once cultivated on the islands for the U.S. market. Today, lobster fishing is the main business of the inhabitants.

YOU CAN GET TO THE CORN ISLANDS

And don't believe anyone who says you can't. Flights operate every day from Managua and Bluefields.

La Costeña (tel. 632142 in Managua) has regular service in small **planes** from the capital, currently departing at 6:30 a.m. and 2 p.m. on Monday through Saturday, at 7 a.m. on Sunday (via Bluefields), and taking off soon after they arrive. W+G Aero Servicios has service on Monday and Friday via Bluefields. Nica has departures at 6:30 a.m. and 2:30 p.m. on Monday, Wednesday, Friday and Sunday via Bluefields, on Tuesday, Thursday and Saturday at 9:50 a.m. Buy your tickets several days in advance. One-way fare is about $60.

To go in style, you can **cruise** to both Great Corn and Little Corn. In addition to regular visits by coastal vessels, the 80-passenger M/V Polaris calls at the islands several times each winter, for a half-day, on its cruise between Belize and Panama. Passengers go ashore and snorkel at nearby reefs. For information, contact Special Expeditions, 720 Fifth Avenue,

New York, NY 10019, tel. 800-762-0003 or 212-765-7740, fax 212-265-3770.

From El Bluff, the port of Bluefields, there is occasional service to the Corn Islands by **boat**. Inquire in Bluefields; a departure was scheduled recently on Wednesdays, with return on Thursdays.

The **Pearl Cays** are still another offshore part of Nicaragua, about 28 kilometers out to sea from Great Corn Island.

WHERE TO STAY ON GREAT CORN ISLAND

Bay Side Hotel, 20 rooms. $60 double.
The new Bay Side is *the* tourist hotel on the island, in the absence of competition, and has a vehicle that will pick you up at the airstrip. Rooms are air conditioned, and if meals are taken (and there's no reason otherwise—they have lots of lobster to offer), the inclusive price is about $50 per person. The bar is out on a wooden pier, and affords plenty of opportunity for observing fish without getting wet.

For $10 or less, rooms are available at the **Beach View**, **Morgan** and **Playa Coco** hotels.

WHAT TO DO?

If you have to ask, maybe you shouldn't go. Corn is where you just hang loose and snorkel. If you have a destination, there are cabs that will take you anywhere on a circular road around the island for a dollar or so. For drinking or dominoes, head to Morgan's, the reggae disco.

PUERTO CABEZAS

Talk about remote—Puerto Cabezas (Bilwi to the local Miskito inhabitants) is near the northeast tip of Nicaragua, reached by an arduous journey over a Jeep road, or by a flight over the largest nearly uninhabited stretch of Central America. Unlike most of the lowlands, the hinterland of Cabezas is pine savanna, and lumbering was once a major business in the area, though marketable supplies have been reduced. Banana plantations existed as well in the glory days of United Fruit, but were brought down by hurricanes and Panama disease.

To go where few outsiders have gone before, continue from Cabezas on the inland track that leads to Waspán, one of the Miskito villages on the Coco River bordering Honduras.

GETTING TO CABEZAS

With a lot of time and a four-wheel-drive vehicle, you can get into Puerto Cabezas by road from Matagalpa, through the remote mining camp of Siuna; but travel is usually by **air**. Nica airlines (tel. 663136 in Managua) flies four days a week from Managua at 11 a.m., from Puerto Cabezas at 2:10 p.m. for Managua. W+G Aero Servicios provides service the other three days, leaving at 7 a.m. for the coast, while La Costeña (tel. 632142 in Managua) has a daily 9 a.m. flight to Puerto Cabezas. For latest schedules and tickets, inquire at the domestic terminal at the airport.

There is also irregular boat service from Bluefields.

Basic **lodging** is available at Hotel Cayos, tel. (068)201; and Hotel El Viajante, tel. (068)263. Call if you're thinking about going to Cabezas, and ask about what they might currently have available. At the moment, it's not much.

15
SPEAKING *NICA*
SPANISH IN NICARAGUA

Spanish is the official language of Nicaragua, and it's what most people, in fact, speak. But it has its own *Nica* characteristics.

To start with, spoken Spanish is somewhat slurred in Nicaragua, in the Caribbean fashion. The s sound is often elided. *Tostado* may come out sounding like "to-ta-do."

Grammar and usage follow Central American forms, which at times are not exactly what the Royal Spanish Academy preaches. **Vos** replaces **tu** to indicate the friendly "you" (as opposed to the more formal **usted**). **Vos** has its own grammar: *vos sab*és, for example, instead of *tu sabes*.

Then there are indigenous influences. Chorotega and other Indian languages, while they have not survived into the present age intact, have lent some of their vocabulary, and many of their place-names, to Nicaragua at large. Lake Cocibolca (Nicaragua) and Lake Xolotlán (Managua) are prime examples. The "*x*," when it turns up in an indigenous word, is pronounced like the English "*h*," though in ancient days it was a "*sh*." When you read *Xolotlán*, say "ho-lot-LAN."

Many of the ancient Nahuatl words that have come into the modern language of Nicaragua are more faithfully rendered than in neighboring countries. A filled corn dumpling steamed in a banana leaf (to put it succinctly) is a *nacatamal*, rather than a Mexican or Guatemalan *tamal*; a wild fig tree is an *amatl*, rather than an *amate* or *higuerón*.

Spanish is by no means the only language spoken in Nicaragua.

Out on the Caribbean coast, where pirates once roamed, the language of communication and smuggling is English, legacy of pirates, slaves, and British masters, as well as continuing links with English-speaking domains elsewhere in Central America (Belize, coastal Honduras and the Bay Islands), the Caribbean islands, missionaries, and expatriate settlements in the United States.

In addition, the Miskito, Rama and Sumu peoples of the Caribbean lowlands have their own languages, while the Black Carib, or Garifuna language, spoken in a few enclaves, is an amalgam of an Arawak language, African vocabulary, and later English additions.

If you don't speak Spanish already, don't even think about an intensive course in preparation for your trip. Nicaraguans are friendly and outgoing, and they speak the language of hospitality, which, even if exact words are missing, will smooth your way.

But a few words, especially a few *local* words, will get you far.

When using Spanish words, pronounce each syllable slowly and clearly, even if it's not what the locals do. Remember that the **z** is pronounced like an **s** in English. Follow written accents, otherwise the last syllable is accented (or next-to-last, if a word ends in a vowel, **n** or **s**).

Here are some terms and expressions that might come in handy.

Nica	Nicaraguan, short for *nicaragüense*.
Panga	motorboat
Peso	Córdoba (the Nicaraguan currency)
Plana	flat-floored, extended riverboat
Pulpería	Corner Store
¡Pura Vida!	Great! *¡Lo máximo!*
Típico	Native-style. *Comida típica*, "typical meal," is local cuisine.
ü	indicates **w** sound retained in variations of a word: *nicaragüense* ("ni-ka-ra-GWEN-seh"), Nicaraguan, derived from *Nicaragua* ("ni-ka-RA-gwah"). This diacritical mark just happens to turn up a lot in Nicaragua.

Spanish

CATACLYSMIC SHORTHAND

Even if your Spanish is limited, after a few days in Nicaragua, you'll recognize some key words and phrases that summarize recent earth-shaking events:

El Desastre	The earthquake that wrecked Managua, 1972. Also called, occasionally, **La Tragedia**
El Cambio	The change of government, from Sandinista to Center-right coalition, in 1990.
La Insurrección	The struggle against the Somoza regime, leading to open warfare in 1978-79.
El Triunfo	The victory of the Sandinista revolution, 1979.

A LA MESA / AT THE TABLE
COMIDA TÍPICA (NICARAGUAN FOOD)

Charraca	pork skin.
Chiles rellenos	stuffed peppers.
Fritangas	strips of fried vegetables
Gallo pinto	rice and beans with herbs and spices
Maduros	fried plantains
Mondongo	tripe soup.
Nacatamal	filled corn dumplings, steamed in banana leaves, similar to Mexican *tamales*.
Patacones	mashed plantain fritters
Pipas	young juice coconuts
Tajadas	deep-fried plantain chips
Tiste	beverage made from ground tortillas and cacao
Tortillas	classic corn flat-cakes; fold 'em, fill 'em, fry 'em, enjoy 'em.
Vigorón	*yuca* (a root vegetable) with pork rind and greens, served in a banana leaf.

MEAL TIMES

Desayuno	breakfast
Almuerzo	lunch
Cena	dinner

STAPLES

arroz	rice	langosta	lobster
atún	tuna	leche	milk
avena	oatmeal	lomito	sirloin
bistec	beef	mantequilla	butter
café	coffee	mermelada	marmalade
calamar	squid	milanesa	breaded (veal or beef)
camarón	shrimp		
carne	meat	naranja	orange
cerveza	beer	omelete	omelet
ceviche	marinated fish cocktail	pan	bread
		papa	potato
chorizo	sausage	(frita, al horno, puré)	(French-fried, baked, mashed)
chuleta (de cerdo)	(pork) chop		
churrasco	charcoal-broiled meat	pastel	cake
coco	coconut	pescado	fish
corvina	sea bass	piña	pineapple
dorado	dolphinfish (mahi-mahi)	plátanos	plantains
		pollo	chicken
ensalada	salad	pozol	corn soup
filete	filet	queso	cheese
frijol	bean	refresco	beverage
frito	fried	ron	rum
fruta	fruit	salsa picante	hot sauce
helado	ice cream	sopa	soup
huevos	eggs	té	tea
jamón	ham	tostadas	toast
jugo (de naranja)	juice (orange)	vino	wine

GEOGRAPHICAL

norte, al lago	north
sur, a la montaña	south
abajo, poniente, oeste	west
arriba, este, oriente	east
derecha	right
izquierda	left
derecho, adelante	straight, ahead

bahía	bay
cerro	hill, peak
ciudad	city
finca	farm
golfo	gulf
hacienda	ranch
isla	island
lago, laguna	lake
parque nacional	national park
playa	beach
punto	point
refugio	refuge
reserva	reserve
río	river
villa	town
volcán	volcano

SHOPPING

barato	cheap
caro	expensive
¿cuánto?	how much?
mercado	market
precio	price

Nicaragua Guide

tienda	store, shop
más grande	bigger
más pequeño	smaller

TRAVEL, GETTING AROUND

¿a qué hora sale?	what time does it leave?
abanico	fan
aire acondicionado	air conditioning
alto	stop!
automóvil	car
avión	airplane
baño	bathroom, toilet
bus	bus
cama	bed
camino	road
carretera	highway
estacionamiento	parking
hora de salida	checkout time
hotel	hotel
parada	bus stop
piscina	pool
taxi	taxi
velocidad máxima	speed limit
¿dónde queda . . . ?	where is . . . ?
¿habla inglés?	do you speak English?

PHARMACY

anticonceptivo	contraceptive
aspirina	aspirin
comprimido	pill
condón, preservativo	condom, prophylactic
dolor de cabeza	headache
estómago	stomach
enfermo	ill

NUMBERS AND MONEY

banco	bank
casa de cambio	exchange house
cheque de viajero	travellers check
córdoba	(local currency)
cuenta	bill
efectivo	cash
tarjeta de crédito	credit card
tasa de cambio	exchange rate

uno	1	dieciocho	18
dos	2	diecinueve	19
tres	3	veinte	20
cuatro	4	treinta	30
cinco	5	cuarenta	40
seis	6	cincuenta	50
siete	7	sesenta	60
ocho	8	setenta	70
nueve	9	ochenta	80
diez	10	noventa	90
once	11	cien	100
doce	12	doscientos	200
trece	13	trescientos	300
catorce	14	cuatrocientos	400
quince	15	quinientos	500
dieciséis	16	mil	1000
diecisiete	17		

INDEX

Acahualinca, Footprints (Huellas) of, 31, 109, 110, 146-47
Accessory Transit Company: see Transit Company
Agriculture, 42
Air travel, 75-77, 80, 112-13, 165
Airlines, 165
Altagracia, 235, 236, 237
Apanás lake, 247
Apoyeque, lake, 151
Apoyo lake, 203, 204
Area of Nicaragua, 15
Arts, 48-51, 153
Asese, 193
Asososca, lake, 150
Astillero, 212
"Atlantic coast," 259
Atlantic-North Autonomous Zone, 20
Atlantic-South Autonomous Zone, 20
Automobile rental, 83, 85, 167
Automobile travel, 77-79, 81-83, 160

Banks, 62, 154
Baseball, 89-90, 144
Bay Islands, Honduras, 37
Beaches, in general, 204-205
Belize, 35
Bilwi, 272-73
Blacks in Nicaragua, 51-52, 19
Bluefields, 23, 26-68
Boaco, 254
Bonanza, 246
British influence, 12, 260, 267
Bryan-Chamorro treaty, 38
Bus travel, 79, 80-81, 155-56, 159-60
Business hours, 96

Camoapa, 254
Captaincy-General of Guatemala, 34
Car rental: see Automobile Rental

Car travel: see Automobile Travel
Caribs, indigenous group, 53
Carter, Jimmy, 41
Casares, 212
Castillo de la Concepción: see El Castillo
Catarina, 202-203
Cathedral of Managua, 142, 146
Catholic church, 46-47
Celebrations, 72-74
Centro Cultural, Managua, 110
Ceramics, 31, 50
Cerro Negro volcano, 27, 213
Chacocente, 212
Chamorro, Pedro Joaquín, 40, 43
Chamorro, Violeta Barrios de, 40, 43
Charter flights, 77
Chichigalpa, 229
Chinandega, 229
Chontal mountain range, 270
Chontales, 254
Chontales, indigenous group, 31
Chorotega, 32
Ciudad Darío, 242-43
Class structure, 47
Climate, 56, 57-60
Clothing for visitors, 66-68, 264
Cloud forest, 22, 241
Cocibolca: see Lake Nicaragua
Coco river, 23, 250, 273
Cocoa beans as money, 32
Coffee agriculture, 38, 245
Columbus, Christopher, 32
Concepción volcano, 235
Condega, 247
Conservative party, 36, 37, 110, 183
Consulates of Nicaragua, 69-71
"Contra" movement and war, 41, 43, 241, 260, 260

Index

Corinto, 230
Corn Islands, 20, 38, 270-72
Cosigüina volcano, 26, 229-30
Costa Rica, 37, 159, 240, 262
Costs of travel, 96-97
Cotton agriculture, 219
Couriers, 104
Coyolito island, 194
Credit cards, 63
Cross of Spain, 234
Cruises, 90-91
Cruz de España, 234
Cuba, 41, 157
Cuisine, 9, 98-103
Currency and exchange, 62, 61-64, 154
Customs regulations, 68, 86-87

Dance, 11, 49
Darío, Rubén, 11, 50-51, 142-43, 224, 242-43
Díaz, Adolfo, 8
Dipilto-Jalapa mountain ridge, 250, 251
Diriá, 204
Diriamba, 199-200
Dirianes, indigenous group, 32
Diriangén, 33
Diriomo, 204
Driving, 77-79, 81-83, 160
Duende cave, 252

Earthenware, 31, 50
Earthquake of 1931, 110
Earthquake of 1973, 110
Economy, 42
Education, 43
Educational programs, 92-93
El Bosque, 30, 248, 252
El Castillo, 35, 257, 261
El Coco, 240
El Espino, 251
El Hoyo volcano, 27
El Morro: see El Castillo
El Muerto island, 195

El Rama, 23, 31, 253, 255-56, 259, 268
El Realejo, 230
El Toro Huaco, dance, 49
El Trapiche, 151, 253
Electricity, 97
Embassies in Managua, 160
Embassies of Nicaragua, 69-70
English language, 12, 260, 267
Entry formalities, 65-66
Escondido river, 23
Espino Negro, Pact of, 39
Estanzuela waterfall, 250
Estelí, 30, 247, 248-50
Estero Real, 230

Family life, 46, 48
Fauna, 20-25, 28, 176, 190, 192, 198, 257, 262, 263
Festivals, 72-74, 152
Fiestas, 72-74, 152
Fish, 28
Fishing, 13, 91-92, 207, 209, 239, 261, 270
Flora, 20-25, 176, 198, 258, 263
Folklore, 45
Fonseca Amador, Carlos, 43, 156
Fonseca, Gulf of, 229
Food, 9, 98-103, 130-31
Frente Sandinista de Liberación Nacional, 39-43

Galleries, 153
Gambling, 94, 141
Gámez, José Dolores, 233
Garífunas, 53, 271
Geography of Nicaragua, 15-28
Gold mining, 250
Gold rush, California, 29, 36
González Dávila, Gil, 33
Governmental system, 40
Gracias a Dios, cape, 33
Granada, 11, 35, 37, 48, 182-93
Grande de Matagalpa river, 246
Great Corn Island, 271
Greytown, 36, 266

283

Guasaule, 230
Guatemala, 33
Güegüense dance-theater, 50
Guerrilla warfare, 39

Handicrafts, 147-50, 179-80
Health conditions, 103
Hernández de Córdoba, Francisco, 33, 182
Hertylandia, 198-99
Highlands, 12, 241-252
History of Nicaragua, 29-44
Hitchhiking, 85
Holidays, 56, 72-74
Honduras, 34, 159, 251
Hot springs, 12, 235, 253
Hunting, 92

Imabite museum, 216
Immigration department, 66, 163
Independence of Nicaragua, 35-36
Indigenous groups, 51-54
Indio river, 266
Indio-Maíz biological reserve, 263
Information sources, 69-71
Inter-Continental Hotel, 124-25, 145
Islas del Maíz, 270-72

Jérez, Máximo, 224
Jinotega, 246
Jinotepe, 196-98
Juigalpa, 254

Kilambé mountain, 241

La Boquita, 211
La Gigantona, dance, 49
La Paz Centro, 219
La Virgen, 237, 261
Laguna de Perlas, 270
Lake Managua, 33, 111, 143
Lake Nicaragua, 33, 34-35, 190, 191-95, 257
Lakes, 17, 22
Las Isletas, 194
Las Manos, 251
Las Nubes, 206
Las Vegas Jr., 199

Lenca, 32
León, 33, 36, 48, 182, 213, 220-27
Liberal party, 36, 37, 110, 183
Lima, Peru, 223
Limay, 31
Literature, 50
Little Corn Island, 271
López Pérez, Rigoberto, 51
Los Guatuzos wildlife reserve, 258

Maderas volcano, 27, 235
Managua, 109-78
Managua, 220
Managua, 36; airport, 112; , 165; bars, 139-41; bus travel, 114, 155-56, 159-60; gambling, 141; hotels, 119-30; map, 116; orientation, 114-18; restaurants, 130-39; sights, 142-53
Managua, lake: see Lake Managua
Mangles Altos, 230
Mangroves, 25
Maps, 71
Maribios, indigenous group, 32
Markets, 147-50, 180
Masate island, 194
Masatepe, 201
Masaya volcano and national park, 27, 173-78
Masaya, town, 179-82
Matagalpa, 243-46
Matagalpa, indigenous group, 31
Matiguás, 246
Maya, 32
Maypole, 267
Mesa de Moropotente reserve, 250
Mexico, 33
Minority groups, 51-54
Miskito Coast, 20, 53, 260
Miskitos, indigenous group, 51-52, 259, 269
Mombacho volcano, 27, 193
Momotombito island, 219
Momotombo volcano, 27, 111, 213, 218
Moncada, José María, 38

Index

Money in Nicaragua, 61-64
Money, 154
Monkey Point, 270
Monte Galán lakes, 218
Montelimar, 207-11
Morgan, Henry, 35
Mosquito: see Miskito
Movies, 162
Moyogalpa, 235, 236
Moyuá, 242
Munguía Alvarez, Edgardo, 224
Museums: Gregorio Aguilar, 255; Imabite, 216; Masaya volcano, 176; of the Revolution, 156; of Rivas, 233
Musún mountain, 241

Nagarote, 214
Nagrandanos, 32
Nandaime, 231
Nandasmo, 202
National Autonomous University, 224
National character, 45-54
National Museum, 145
National parks, 95
Nelson, Horatio, 35, 261
Nicaragua Pacific Railway, 217
Nicaragua, agriculture, 42; economy, 42; flora, 21-25, 28; general, 9-13; geography, 15-28; governmental system, 40; history, 29-44; national character, 45-54
Nicaragua, lake: see Lake Nicaragua
Nicaragua, indigenous nation, 30
Nicarao, 30
Nicaraos, 32
Nindirí volcano, 173, 177
Niquinohomo, 202
Niquirano, 30
Nueva Segovia, 33

Ocotal, 251
Old León, 214-17
Olmec, 32

Olof Palme Convention Center, 145, 156
Oluma, 31
Ometepe, 191; Ometepe, 234-37
Ortega, Daniel, 43
Ostional, 240

Packing suggestions, 66-68, 264
Palo Volador, 49
Pearl Lagoon, 270
Pedrarias, 216
Peñas Blancas mountain, 241
Peñas Blancas, 240
Personalismo, 38, 43, 47-48
Piracy, 20, 35
Pochomil, 206-207
Poneloya, 227-28
Postal service, 104, 163
Precipitation, 60
Pueblo Nuevo, 248
Pueblos Blancos, 196-204
Puerto Cabezas, 246, 260, 272-73
Puerto Momotombo, 214-17
Punta La Flor, 239

Railroad, defunct, 86
Rain forest, 11, 20, 24, 259-64
Rama: see El Rama
Ramas, indigenous group, 52, 53
Reagan, Ronald, 41
Religion, 11
Rivas, 232-41
Rivers, 22-23
Roosevelt, Franklin Delano, 39

Sacasa, Juan Bautista, 39
Sailing, 209, 239
San Carlos, 191, 256-57, 264
San Carlos river, 263
San Cristóbal volcano, 27, 228
San Fernando crater, 178
San Fernando, 252
San Isidro, 222, 248
San Jacinto hot springs, 228
San Jacinto, hacienda, 242
San Jorge, 234
San José del Sur hot springs, 235

285

San Juan de Limay, 252
San Juan de Oriente, 203-204
San Juan del Norte, 266
San Juan del Sur, 237-40
San Juan river, 23, 34-35, 37, 182, 261-66
San Juan crater, 178
San Marcos, 200-201
San Pablo fortress, 194
San Pedro crater, 177
San Rafael del Sur, 206
Sandinista government and party, 39-43, 242, 262
Sandino, Augusto César, 29, 39, 43, 157, 202, 252
Santamaría, Juan, 232, 234
Santiago crater, 177
Santos Zelaya, José, 38
Sapoá, 240
Sculpture, 48
"Sea Season," 8
Seasonally dry tropical forest, 25
Seasons, 58
Sébaco, 243
Selva Negra, 244-45
Sesame agriculture, 219
Sharks, 190, 192, 262
Shopping, 13, 93-94, 147-50, 179-80, 189-90
Siuna, 246
Solentiname islands, 257
Somoto, 31, 251
Somoza Debayle, Anastasio, 39, 40, 41, 44, 220, 226, 233
Somoza Debayle, Luis, 39
Somoza García, Anastasio, 39
Soviet Union, 41
Spain, as colonial power, 32-35, 46
Spain, as cultural determinant, 46
Spanish language in Nicaragua, 46, 118, 275-81
Spanish occupation, 259
Sports, 89-90, 209, 239
Stratification, 47
Study programs, 92-93

Subtiava, 226
Subtiava, indigenous group, 32
Sucio river, 263
Sumus, indigenous group, 31, 51-52, 259

Taxes, 104-105
Taxis, 85, 158
Telephone service, 105-107, 120, 163
Telica river, 227
Telica volcano, 27, 228
Telpaneca, 252
Theater, 163
Time of Day, 107
Tipitapa, 110, 151, 253
Tipping, 107-108
Tourism in Nicaragua, 9-13
Tourism, Ministry of, 69, 119
Tourist cards, 65
Trafalgar, 35
Train network, defunct, 86
Transit company, 37, 238, 261
Transportation, means of, 10
Travel agencies, 168
Travel to Nicaragua, 75-79
Travel in Nicaragua, general, 55-108
Trujillo, Honduras, 37
Tuma river, 247
Turismo, Ministerio de, 69, 119
Turtles, 25, 28, 212

United Provinces of Central America, 35-36
United States, intervention in Nicaragua, 38, 39
University of Mobile, 92

Vanderbilt, Cornelius, 36, 37, 238, 261, 262
Veracruz, 212
Viejo León, 214-17
Visas, 65
Volcanoes, general, 26-27

Walker, William, 37, 183, 188, 262
Waspan, 273
Water, drinking, 164

Index

Weather, 56, 57-60, 164
Weights and measures, 108
"White towns," 12, 196-204
Whites, as ethnic group, 54
Windsurfing, 209, 239

Xiloá, lake, 151, 213
Xolotlán, lake, 33, 112

Yalagüina, 251, 252
Yalí, 247

Zapatera Archipelago national park, 195
Zapatera island, 187-88, 195
Zoo, Hertylandia, 198; Juigalpa, 255; national (Managua), 152

NICARAGUA GUIDE

Did you enjoy your visit?
Send a copy of *Nicaragua Guide* to a friend!

To **TRAVEL LINE PRESS**, Box 1346, Champlain, NY 12919

Please send ___ copies of *Nicaragua Guide* to the persons listed below. I enclose $14.95 for each copy. Total ___ copies.

My name_____

Address_____

___ Check Enclosed   ___ Charge to my American Express Card

Number _ _ _ _ _ _ _ _ _ _ _ _ _ _ _ Expires_____

Signature (credit card order only)_____

Send books to:

_____
_____
_____

_____
_____
_____

_____
_____

Or call **1-800-417-0109** to charge to your American Express card. (U.S. Only)